THE COMPLETE **IDIOT'S** GUIDE® TO

iPad and iPhone App Development

Troy Brant

ALPHA

A member of Penguin Group (USA) Inc.

ALPHA BOOKS

Published by the Penguin Group

Penguin Group (USA) Inc., 375 Hudson Street, New York, New York 10014, USA

Penguin Group (Canada), 90 Eglinton Avenue East, Suite 700, Toronto, Ontario M4P 2Y3, Canada (a division of Pearson Penguin Canada Inc.)

Penguin Books Ltd., 80 Strand, London WC2R 0RL, England

Penguin Ireland, 25 St. Stephen's Green, Dublin 2, Ireland (a division of Penguin Books Ltd.)

Penguin Group (Australia), 250 Camberwell Road, Camberwell, Victoria 3124, Australia (a division of Pearson Australia Group Pty. Ltd.)

Penguin Books India Pvt. Ltd., 11 Community Centre, Panchsheel Park, New Delhi—110 017, India

Penguin Group (NZ), 67 Apollo Drive, Rosedale, North Shore, Auckland 1311, New Zealand (a division of Pearson New Zealand Ltd.)

Penguin Books (South Africa) (Pty.) Ltd., 24 Sturdee Avenue, Rosebank, Johannesburg 2196, South Africa

Penguin Books Ltd., Registered Offices: 80 Strand, London WC2R 0RL, England

International Standard Book Number: 978-1-61564-010-2
Library of Congress Catalog Card Number: 2009943484

12 11 10   8 7 6 5 4 3 2

Interpretation of the printing code: The rightmost number of the first series of numbers is the year of the book's printing; the rightmost number of the second series of numbers is the number of the book's printing. For example, a printing code of 10-1 shows that the first printing occurred in 2010.

Printed in the United States of America

Note: This publication contains the opinions and ideas of its author. It is intended to provide helpful and informative material on the subject matter covered. It is sold with the understanding that the author and publisher are not engaged in rendering professional services in the book. If the reader requires personal assistance or advice, a competent professional should be consulted.

The author and publisher specifically disclaim any responsibility for any liability, loss, or risk, personal or otherwise, which is incurred as a consequence, directly or indirectly, of the use and application of any of the contents of this book. Most Alpha books are available at special quantity discounts for bulk purchases for sales promotions, premiums, fundraising, or educational use. Special books, or book excerpts, can also be created to fit specific needs.

For details, write: Special Markets, Alpha Books, 375 Hudson Street, New York, NY 10014.

Publisher: *Marie Butler-Knight*
Associate Publisher: *Mike Sanders*
Senior Managing Editor: *Billy Fields*
Acquisitions Editor: *Tom Stevens*
Development Editor: *Ginny Bess Munroe*
Senior Production Editor: *Megan Douglass*

Copy Editor: *Emily Garner*
Cover Designer: *Kurt Owens*
Book Designer: *William Thomas, Rebecca Batchelor*
Indexer: *Tonya Heard*
Layout: *Ayanna Lacey*
Proofreader: *John Etchison*

Contents

Introduction

One of the principles to keep in mind when developing iPad and iPhone apps is designing for short bursts of activity. Think about how you use your own mobile device. Likely, you open an app, use it for a spell, and close it. This book is written using the same philosophy. Each chapter is bite-size, and exercises never span more than one chapter. Sample code is short. Descriptions are succinct. I know you're busy and don't have time to waste.

I have found the only way to learn iPhone programming is to actually write iPhone apps. As such, this book is designed assuming that you are at your computer and writing the sample applications in each chapter as we go through them. You can read about programming all day, but it won't stick nearly as well as sitting down and working through the projects yourself. This book is not written to *tell* you how to program for the iPad or iPhone, but rather to *guide* you through the process.

Building applications for the iPad and iPhone is full of learning opportunities you won't find anywhere else. If you're coming from Windows-world as I did, then you're in for some amazing technical challenges. A new operating system, a new programming environment, a new programming language, designing mobile applications instead of desktop applications, distributing your app using the App Store ... there is a veritable truckload of fun topics to learn.

Conventions Used in This Book

Writing apps for the iPad or iPhone doesn't always require writing code, but when it does, you find code examples in the book to assist you in learning the material. For the sake of consistency, you will find all code examples in this book formatted as follows:

```
- (IBAction)buttonTouchDown:(id)sender

{
   NSLog(@"Welcome to iPhone programming!");
}
```

Any time you see text in **bold**, on the other hand, it represents an action, such as a key combination or a menu item you need to select. For instance:

> To create a new project in Xcode you can either press **⌘-N** or select **File > New...** from the top menu bar when Xcode is running.

How This Book Is Organized

This book is broken into five parts. In the early chapters, you learn the basics of iPad and iPhone programming using Xcode and Interface Builder. After building your first few apps, learn how to add controls to your interface, like sliders, text fields, and pickers. Multi-view topics such as view controllers, navigation controllers, and tab bar controllers are next. Then, learn some of the remaining core topics, including data management, networking, and animation. At that point, dive into multi-touch, Core Location, and other unique iPad and iPhone APIs. Finally, see how the pros optimize their apps, and follow the step-by-step guide to submit your app to the App Store.

Part 1, Getting Started—Download the SDK and you're on your way to becoming an iPad and iPhone developer. Get to know the tools you use day-in and day-out as a developer: Xcode, Interface Builder, and the iPhone Simulator. You write your first lines of code and learn what Objective-C is all about.

Part 2, Building Your User Interface—Start digging deeper into building your app's interface. Learn all the built-in controls in Interface Builder, including sliders, pickers, and text fields. At the same time, figure out how to control the behavior of these elements in Xcode. The core iPad and iPhone programming concepts of delegation, protocols, and collections are also covered in this part.

Part 3, Multi-View Applications—How do you manage an application that has multiple screens? What the heck is a controller? What the heck is MVC? What is a table view, and why is it a big deal? All these questions are answered in full detail in Part 3.

Part 4, The APIs You Can't Wait to Use—This is the moment you've been waiting for. You know all those cool things you love most about your iPad or iPhone: multi-touch, camera, and maps? This part is all about tapping into the APIs for these excellent features. Once you learn the general blueprint for using the APIs in this part, you can apply it to the plethora of other APIs the phone has to offer.

Part 5, Make Your Millions—So, you want to put your app on the App Store? If you want to maximize your chance of success, there are some steps you should take before making the leap. In this part, learn how to test your app on your own iPhone or iPod Touch. Learn how to use the debugger to fix memory issues and other bugs in your application. Find memory leaks and optimize your code using Instruments, Clang, and Shark. Finally, when you are ready to cross the finish line, we will walk you through the entire process of submitting your app to the App Store.

Extras

Here are explanations of the sidebars that have been provided to elaborate on terms, ideas, and concepts presented throughout the book.

> **DEFINITION**
>
> Key terms in iPhone programming.

> **CRASH AND LEARN**
>
> We point out error-prone development issues here.

> **THERE'S A TIP FOR THAT**
>
> Advice that will make life easier for you.

> **ONE MORE THING**
>
> Interesting factoids to supplement your development know-how.

Acknowledgments

I'd like to thank my parents and my family for supporting me in this crazy book-writing endeavor.

I'd also like to thank Paul Marcos and Evan Doll for choosing me from among much more qualified candidates as teaching assistant for the iPhone programming class at Stanford.

Finally, thank you Steve, Laurie, Amal, and Astra for the wonderful coffee breaks and endless harassment throughout the writing process. I couldn't have done this without you.

Special Thanks to the Technical Reviewer

The Complete Idiot's Guide to iPad and iPhone App Development was reviewed by an expert who double-checked the accuracy of what you'll learn here, to help us ensure that this book gives you everything you need to know about developing iPhone apps. Special thanks are extended to Evan Doll, instructor of the CS193P iPhone programming course at Stanford.

Trademarks

All terms mentioned in this book that are known to be or are suspected of being trademarks or service marks have been appropriately capitalized. Alpha Books and Penguin Group (USA) Inc. cannot attest to the accuracy of this information. Use of a term in this book should not be regarded as affecting the validity of any trademark or service mark.

Getting Started

How do you get started writing iPhone and iPad applications? Do you need special hardware? What is Objective-C, and how do you manage memory on the iPhone? This part eases you into the world of iPhone programming and answers these questions along the way. Get acquainted with Xcode and Interface Builder, the two tools you will use to do all your iPhone and iPad development.

Welcome to the Party!

In This Chapter

- What you need to get started
- New to Mac?
- iPhone features and constraints
- Getting the iPhone SDK

During my first year at Stanford, I met with my buddy Steve after class one day to toss around an idea for an iPhone app. We brainstormed for hours and latched on to the idea of a running application, one that utilizes the phone's GPS unit to track workouts. The next day, I was in an Apple store buying my first Mac.

Since then, I've immersed myself in every aspect of iPhone — and now iPad — development. If you're excited about the idea of developing apps for the iPhone, believe me, I'm right there with you. I'll do my best to guide you through the app development process and try to help you avoid some of the costly mistakes I made along the way. Before you jump into the meat of the material, though, there are a few things you need to know to get started.

Before You Begin

You are likely chomping at the bit, ready to start building your first app, but there are a few things you should be aware of before forging ahead.

Hardware

To develop for iPhone and iPad, you must have an Intel-based Mac with OS X version 10.6 or later installed. If you have a Windows or Linux machine, you'll need to take the plunge and buy a Mac if you want to do iPhone development. If you have a Mac, you can check the version you have by selecting **Apple icon on the top bar > About This Mac**.

The good news is that you do not need a physical device to get started developing for iPhone and iPad. The *iPhone SDK* comes with a software simulator you can use in lieu of running your app on a real device. The simulator can't do everything a real device can, however, so you will need to test your app on a real device if you intend to do serious development.

> **DEFINITION**
>
> The **iPhone SDK** is a suite of tools and applications you will use to build iPhone, iPod Touch, and iPad applications. Since all three devices use the iPhone operating system, the iPhone SDK can be used to build apps for all three devices.

Knowledge

It is impossible to predict exactly how much you know before reading this book. So it is assumed you have the following knowledge:

- **Some programming experience.** You don't have to be a genius software architect, but if you come across terms like "arrays," "variables," "pointers," "constants," and "functions," you should know what they mean.

- **Some familiarity with OOP (object-oriented programming).** The terms "class," "subclass," "object," and "method" should all be familiar to you. Chapter 5 reviews some of the basics of object-oriented programming if you are a bit rusty.

- **Some experience with C.** If you haven't programmed in C before, you may want to brush up on pointers and C syntax. Objective-C, the language used to develop iPhone apps, is a derivative of C.

> **THERE'S A TIP FOR THAT**
>
> You can flip to the appendix for some great sites that can supplement your iPhone programming knowledge.

If any of these assumptions about your experience are wrong, you are still encouraged to forge ahead. Resources that help with particularly challenging topics will be identified along the way.

New to Mac?

One of Apple's more brilliant business strategies in providing an iPhone SDK was requiring development to be done on a Mac. While a large number of developers migrated over rather seamlessly, a massive influx of developers had never touched a Mac in their life. At Stanford, around 75 percent of the CS193P iPhone programming class landed in this category. They bought a Mac specifically for the course and wanted to start coding right away. But they could have avoided much of the pain they experienced early on in the course if they had spent some time getting comfortable navigating Mac OS X. So if you're new to Mac, you can avoid the problems they ran into by going through this mini–Complete Idiot's Guide to Mac OS X.

Quick Overview of Mac OS X for Windows Users

If you just purchased your first Mac, you have to admit, it is a gorgeous piece of hardware. The interface is sleek and beautiful, and the animations are captivating. However, after you are finished gawking at the interface, you probably want to *do stuff*, like creating documents or launching programs. Well, that is when you can quickly go from enamored to frustrated with OS X. There is no Start menu for launching applications, no Control Panel for customizing your setup, and even the cut, copy, and paste commands aren't mapped to Ctrl-X, Ctrl-C and Ctrl-V. Mac OS X has an equivalent action for everything you want to do on Windows, but the key is figuring out the mapping between the two.

Here is a quick rundown of some of the more important Mac OS X applications:

- Dock

The Dock is at the bottom of your screen and makes launching common applications quick and painless.

- Finder

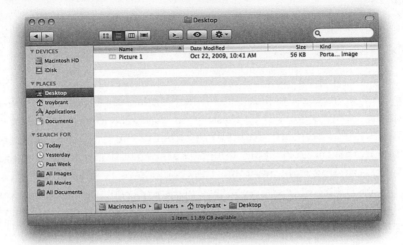

Finder is the interface you use to navigate your file system.

- Spotlight

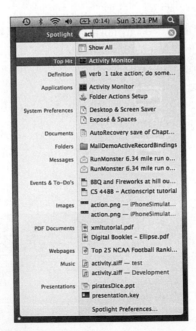

*Spotlight is an all-everything search tool that you can use to search your computer
for applications, documents, images, and anything else that lives on your hard drive.*

- System Preferences

When you need to configure and customize your Mac, use the System Preferences application.

- Activity Monitor

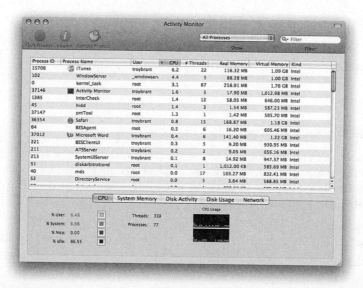

Activity Monitor shows your running applications, and you can use it to force quit unresponsive apps.

Your Mac keyboard may also appear strange if you have previously used Windows machines. Throughout the book, the following symbols will represent the corresponding keys on your Mac keyboard:

- ⌘ is the symbol for the command key.
- ∧ is the symbol for the control key.
- Ctrl also refers to the control key.
- ⇧ is the symbol for the shift key.
- ⌥ is the symbol for the option key.

Now that you know some Mac terminology, you can use the following table to translate the interface elements you're accustomed to on Windows to the equivalent on Mac.

Translating Windows to Mac

Windows	Mac
Explorer	Finder
Taskbar	Dock
Start menu	Apple Menu
Programs folder	Applications folder
Right click	Ctrl-click
Search	Spotlight
Ctrl-C/X/V/tab	⌘-C/X/V/tab
Control Panel	System Preferences
Task Manager	Activity Monitor

THERE'S A TIP FOR THAT

If you own a MacBook, I highly recommend enabling two-finger tap to right click on your trackpad. To set this up, open the **System Preferences** application and check the box next to **Trackpad > Secondary Tap**. **Tap to Click** is an extremely useful setting to enable as well.

To summarize, the Applications folder is where all your applications live. To open a particular application, you can open it in Finder, or, even better, you can use Spotlight to launch the application. Most of the key combinations that you're used to that require holding down the Ctrl key on Windows are the same on Mac except they use the command (⌘) key instead.

THERE'S A TIP FOR THAT

One of the more unknown features of Spotlight is that you can actually use it as a simple calculator. Try adding, dividing, and even taking the log of a number!

Keyboard Shortcuts

To get around the Mac interface quickly, keyboard shortcuts are a must. The following table lists some of the more common shortcuts that will make your life much easier:

Mac OS X Keyboard Shortcuts

Keys	Action
⌘-Space Bar	Spotlight
⌘-X	Cut
⌘-C	Copy
⌘-V	Paste
⌘-W	Close current window
⌘-Q	Close current application
⌘-~	Switch windows within an application
⌘-Delete	Send file straight to trash
⌘-Shift-3	Take a screenshot of the entire screen
⌘-Shift-4	Take a screenshot of part of the screen

Although far from complete, these tips should give you the tools you need to make getting around OS X a little easier. If you still can't make left from right, Kate Binder's *The Complete Idiot's Guide to Mac OS X* (Alpha Books, 2001) is a fantastic resource you should check out.

Device Features

So what exactly can the iPhone do anyway? How about the iPad? These devices look pretty, but what can they do under the hood? As a developer, you have access to a host of features, such as:

- Internet
- Multi-touch screen
- Accelerometer
- Address Book
- iPod Music Library
- 3D Graphics

- Location detection
- Compass
- Camera

- Video
- Bluetooth

CRASH AND LEARN

Not every device has all of these features. For instance, the iPad does not have a camera or video capabilities. 3GS iPhones have a compass while 3G iPhones do not. You can check for the existence of these features in code, but you should be aware that the features you choose to implement may limit the number of users your app can reach.

Just imagine the apps you can build using these features. What can you do with an Internet connection? You get Twitter apps, RSS readers, and fantasy football apps. What can you do when you combine 3D graphics with the accelerometer? You get novel game play controls in games like Labyrinth, Dizzy Bee, and Rolando. What can you do with GPS, video, and the compass? Augmented reality apps like Layar and Yelp's "Monocle" feature continue to amaze users. Your imagination is the limit in deciding what kind of app to build for your iPhone or iPad.

Device Limitations

iPhone programming is different from developing a PHP web application or a Java desktop application. Instead of having nearly limitless visual real estate at your disposal, you have a relatively small 320×480 pixel screen on the iPhone or a 1024×768 pixel display on the iPad. Instead of letting the garbage collector take care of all your memory issues for you, you are now responsible for making sure every allocated byte is accounted for.

You are about to develop on a platform that is a fraction as powerful, a fraction as fast, with a fraction as much space as today's beefy desktops. And that is precisely why developing for mobile devices is so *exciting*. These constraints drive innovation. You have to think more creatively to solve problems that have an obvious solution on the desktop.

Now, what exactly are these limitations? For various good reasons, Apple restricts how your application interacts with the rest of the operating system. These are some of the constraints you are under as an iPhone developer:

- **Only one app at a time**: Your app can run only in the foreground. After the user closes your app, it is dead and gone and does not run until the user manually starts it again.

- **Sandbox**: When your app launches, you are given a "sandbox" to play in by the iPhone OS as a protective mechanism. This means that you cannot reach out and corrupt another application's data, or worse, the core iPhone OS. This also means that you cannot communicate directly with other apps on the phone.

- **No garbage collection**: Most modern programming languages have some form of garbage collection that handles the nitty-gritty details of memory management for you. However, the iPhone does not have any garbage collection, and instead you alone are responsible for making sure memory is handled correctly.

- **Limited memory**: You have a limited amount of memory to use at your discretion. If the iPhone OS begins to run low on available memory, it may ask your application to reduce your usage. It may even forcibly quit your app entirely if memory is at critical levels. We'll go over how to handle these low memory situations in Chapter 5.

- **Limited screen size**: The iPhone's screen is only 320×480 pixels. The iPad display is only 1024×768 pixels. Most desktop monitors are considerably larger than either of these devices. Designing your interface for a small form factor is one of the main challenges you will face as a developer.

- **Your app can (and will) exit unexpectedly**: If you have used an iPhone or an iPad before, you know that users do not politely ask for an application to close. When you are done, you instantly hit the home button with no regard to what the app is doing. The best apps are the ones designed with this interaction in mind—apps that facilitate short, quick bursts of activity.

- **Limited access to system services**: You do not have direct access to certain data on the device. In particular, you cannot access the user's calendar data, SMS database of text messages, or the user's call history or voicemails.

Whether you love them or hate them, these constraints are realities of iPhone and iPad development. Instead of railing against Apple for enforcing these limitations, take a look at other apps to see how they creatively worked within these constraints.

Getting the SDK

Enough with the pleasantries; on to development! The first thing you need to do is pull up a browser like Safari or Firefox and navigate to http://developer.apple.com/iphone/. This site is the single most important resource you can have as an iPhone developer (besides this book, of course). It has documentation, sample code, and video guides, not to mention the iPhone SDK. Bookmark it, memorize it, or write it down; this is a site you will come to time and time again when developing iPhone and iPad apps.

The proverbial gold mine of online resources for iPhone developers.

Get a Registered iPhone Developer Apple ID

Our current goal in coming to the site is to download the iPhone SDK. But before you can start the download, you must first register for a free iPhone Developer Account. To register, just follow these steps:

1. Click **Register** in the top right-hand corner on http://developer.apple.com/iphone/, as seen in the figure above.

2. On the next screen, click **Continue.**

3. Now, you need to either create an Apple ID if you do not have one or sign in with one. You can find your Apple ID by opening iTunes on your computer and selecting **Store > View My Account…** If there is no account information in iTunes, then you will need to create an Apple ID. Select the option that applies to you, and click **Continue.**

4. If you selected **Use an existing Apple ID,** sign in with your Apple ID and click **Continue.**

If you have made purchases from the iTunes Store or the App Store, then you already have an Apple ID.

5. If you selected **Create an Apple ID,** fill out all the fields because they are all required. Use your email address as your Apple ID because it's easy to remember. After you are done, click **Continue.**

6. At this point, whether you had to create an Apple ID or not, you will need to fill out a short survey on how you plan to use the iPhone SDK.

The survey is short and relatively painless.

7. Check the box to agree to the license, and click **I Agree.**

8. At this point, an email is sent to the address you specified for your Apple ID. The email contains a verification code you need to finish the registration. Copy and paste the verification code from the email into the text box on the "Email Verification" web page, and click **Continue**.

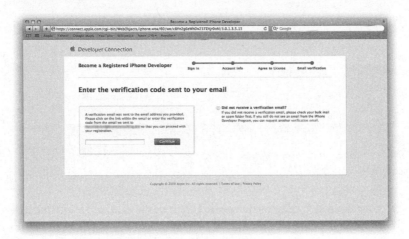

Check your email for the verification code.

9. And that's it! You will be logged into http://developer.apple.com/iphone/ where you can download the iPhone SDK.

After successful registration, you'll see the Registered iPhone Developer view of the site.

After successful registration, scroll down http://developer.apple.com/iphone/ to find the iPhone SDK link in the Downloads section. At this point, you have to determine if you are running Mac OS X Leopard or Snow Leopard. You can easily figure out which you are running by going to the top left-hand corner of your screen and clicking **Apple icon > About This Mac**. If your version is instead prefixed with 10.6, you are running Snow Leopard. If your version is prefixed with 10.5, then you need to upgrade your operating system to Snow Leopard before you can continue.

THERE'S A TIP FOR THAT

You can order a Snow Leopard DVD from http://store.apple.com or by visiting your local Apple Store.

Back in your web browser, click the first link in the Downloads section to start the SDK download.

iPhone Developer Program

The SDK download is rather large — a few gigabytes in size — so you should be prepared to wait a while for the download to finish. In the meantime, now is a great chance to learn about the iPhone Developer Program. You might be thinking: *Didn't I just sign up for the iPhone Developer Program?* It turns out Apple makes a distinction between a "Registered iPhone Developer" and a developer in the "iPhone Developer Program." At this point, you are a Registered iPhone Developer, which gives you access to the SDK, the website, and all the online resources Apple has to share. You are free to run your apps in the iPhone Simulator, a program that comes packaged with the SDK and allows you test your apps on your Mac.

As a Registered iPhone Developer, however, you *can't* run your application on your iPhone or iPod Touch. You also can't distribute your app in any way — including on the App Store. If you want the ability to run your app on a real device and eventually release your app to the public, you need to register for the iPhone Developer Program. And this program, sad to say, is not free. There are two ways to join the iPhone Developer Program: Standard and Enterprise.

The Standard program currently costs $99 and lasts for one year. With this program, you can run your apps on your phone. After signing up, you can also release your app on the App Store. If you want to beta test your app, you can put your app on a limited number of devices (currently 100).

If $99 is breaking the bank or seems like way too much money right now, you can hold off on registering and still test your app in the iPhone Simulator, which comes free with the SDK. In fact, you can make it through the first four parts of this book before you even need a real device to test with, so you will be fine if you don't sign up for the program right away.

The Enterprise program costs $299 and gives you the ability to write and release apps within your company and outside of the App Store. You can also set up a team of developers if you are planning on having multiple people work on your apps. More than likely, the Standard program is the right program for you, and only if you have a company or a group of developers working on the same app should you consider the Enterprise option.

If you decide you do want to register for the iPhone Developer Program, you can do so at any time when you are logged in to http://developer.apple.com/iphone/.

Installing the SDK

After the download completes, the iPhone SDK .dmg file will be on your desktop or in your Downloads folder. Installation of the SDK is similar to installing other Macintosh software. Double-click the .dmg file to mount the installation drive.

Double-click the iPhone SDK bundle to launch the installer.

To begin the installation, double-click the iPhone SDK icon.

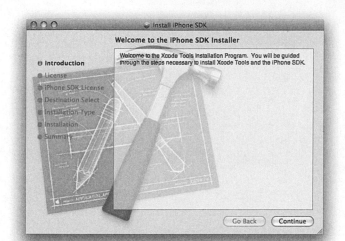

The default settings for each screen in the installation assistant are just fine for the iPhone SDK install.

The installation assistant shown in the previous figure will guide you through the install. You can use the default options for each screen; the install will take about 15 minutes to complete.

ONE MORE THING

After you finish installing a .dmg file, you need to manually eject the install drive. Find the drive in the same folder your .dmg file is located, Ctrl+click on the drive, and select **Eject**.

After the installation completes, as shown in the previous figure, you can get started with some real iPhone development. In the next chapter, you'll put together your first iPhone app and learn all about Xcode and how to run your application in the iPhone Simulator.

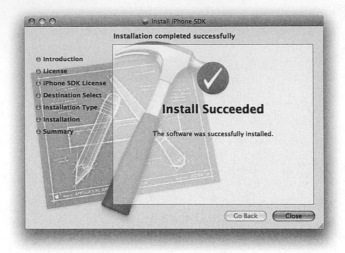

The installation is complete, and now the fun begins.

The Least You Need to Know

- You must have a Mac running OS X 10.6 or later to develop for iPhone and iPad.
- You can use Spotlight as a shortcut for starting apps, finding files, and even for doing arithmetic.
- iPhone apps don't have garbage collection, can't run in the background, and operate in a sandbox to simplify the user experience.
- There is one website above all others you should know very well, and that is http://developer.apple.com/iphone/.
- Downloading the iPhone SDK is free.
- You pay $99 for the Standard iPhone Developer Program if you want to put an app on a device or release the app to the App Store.

Your First App in a Flash

In This Chapter

- Getting acquainted with Xcode
- Creating projects in Xcode
- Running apps in the iPhone Simulator
- Write your first app

Back in the summer of 2008, the iPhone App Store had yet to launch, and there was incredible excitement about how apps would transform the iPhone. All of a sudden, your phone became much more than a phone. It was now a light saber, a guitar tuner, or an ocarina. The phone was imagined as a gaming platform, a social media hub, or even a tool that could listen to the radio and tell you exactly which songs were being played. Unbelievable technology was on the horizon, and the possibilities were endless.

Would you then expect that one of the most successful apps in those heady first days was Flashlight, an app that simply displayed a pure white screen? The metaphor was so easy to understand and the app was so easy to use that sales for the app went through the roof. In this chapter, you learn how to write your own Flashlight app and also learn how to test it in the iPhone Simulator.

Creating Your First Project

The first step in writing an iPhone app—a step you will perform time and time again as an iPhone developer—is creating a new project in *Xcode*. If you are familiar with Visual Studio, Eclipse, or any other development environment, you will be right at home with Xcode.

> **DEFINITION**
>
> **Xcode** is the Integrated Development Environment (IDE) used to develop iPhone and iPad applications.

To get started, go ahead and launch Xcode either from the Applications folder or via Spotlight. You can also add it to the Dock for easier access.

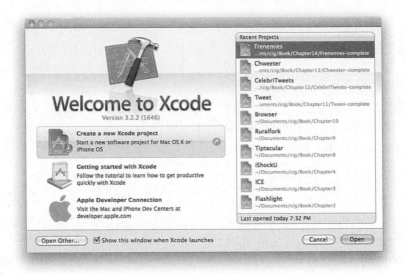

Xcode brings up a series of shortcuts and hints when first launched.

When Xcode launches, you will see the welcome screen as shown in the previous figure. The resources it links to are useful, but they are also easily reachable on the web. If you would rather not see the welcome screen in the future, be sure to uncheck the **Show at launch** checkbox.

Create a New Window-Based Application

To create the project, select **File > New Project...** from the menu bar at the top of the screen.

At this point, you will see the New Project assistant window in the following figure. From here, you can choose a template for your project that will automatically generate files and code common to that type of project. Under the iPhone OS category, select Application, and choose the Window-based Application template. From the Product drop-down menu, you can select iPhone, iPad, or Universal. A *universal application* is a single project that can be run on iPhone *and* iPad. To follow along in this chapter, select iPhone as a product, though I encourage you to experiment with the different product types. After selecting a product, click **Choose....**

The Window-based Application template creates a very simple project.

 DEFINITION

A **universal application** is a combined iPhone and iPad app. When a user downloads a universal app from the App Store, the app will work on all their devices—iPad, iPhone, and iPod Touch.

When prompted for a name for the project, enter "Flashlight." Navigate and save the project to a location of your choosing. I would suggest creating a directory for doing exercises from this book and saving it there.

Tour of the Xcode Interface

After choosing the project name and saving it, you will see the project window for the Flashlight application. For those accustomed to using IDEs like Eclipse and Visual

Studio, you will notice some similarities in the interface, but there are enough new elements to make it feel like a different animal.

The project window is broken down into several components, listed below:

- **Groups & Files Section:** This is where you can navigate between files in your project. The folders that you see (Classes, Other Sources, Resources, Frameworks, and Products) are called groups in Xcode-speak. You can add and remove groups as you see fit to keep your project organized.

CRASH AND LEARN

Even though they may look like folders, groups in the Groups & Files Section do not necessarily correspond to folders on disk. For instance, if you select **Other Sources > main.m**, Ctrl-click, and select **Reveal in Finder**, you will find that main.m is not in a folder named Other Sources. Groups are just a way to keep your files organized inside Xcode without affecting how files are organized on your hard drive.

- **Detail Section:** The Detail Section shows a list of elements in each item in the Groups & Files Section. If you select a group, for instance, you will see all the files inside that group.

- **Editor Section:** This is where the magic happens. After selecting a file, you can modify the code in the editor section.

- **Editor Toolbar:** This small bar sits on top of the Editor Section and packs a big feature punch. The arrows at the far left can be used to move back and forth in your file history, similar to a web browser. Next to the arrows is a popup button that can also be used to visually navigate within your project by selecting the file you want to jump to from a list. The next button to the right allows you to jump to a specific section or method within the current file. To the right of this button are several smaller buttons whose functions you can see by hovering your mouse over them. These buttons won't be discussed in this book, but feel free to try them out for your own benefit.

- **Status Bar:** When *building* your project, the Status Bar shows you whether your application completed the build successfully.

DEFINITION

Building your project is the combined process of compiling your files, linking your files with libraries, running custom scripts, and packaging your application into a single binary.

- **Toolbar:** The toolbar lives on top of the window and is most often used as a shortcut for building and running your project. From the Overview section at the far left, you can choose whether you are building for the iPhone Simulator or a real device.

Next to the Overview section is the Action button. It allows you to perform various actions depending on what you've selected on screen. For instance, FlashlightAppDelegate.h is selected in the Groups & Files Section, so if you right-click (which is another name for Ctrl-click) on the FlashlightAppDelegate.h file itself, you will see exactly the same menu as if you clicked the Action button.

To the right of the Action button are shortcut buttons. These buttons make it easy to perform common tasks, like toggling breakpoints, running your application, and cleaning your project. You can customize the buttons in this bar by right-clicking the bar and selecting **Customize Toolbar...**

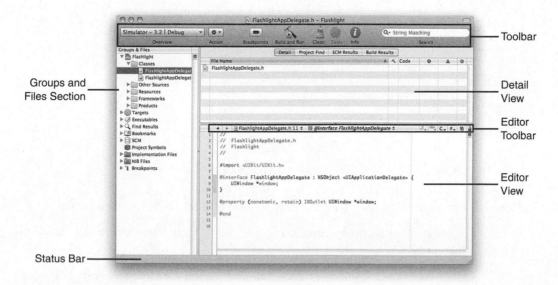

The Xcode project interface: where iPhone apps are born.

Don't worry. It can take a while to get completely comfortable with the interface, but after going through the programming exercises in this book, Xcode will feel like home in no time.

Tour of Your Project

As explained in the previous section, the Groups & Files Section is where you can find all your project files. That's all well and good, but what do these files actually do? Why are there so many? Which ones are important? All the files are required to build your project, but some you will leave alone while you will edit others frequently.

You can use the Groups & Files Section to navigate through your project.

Here is a description of the groups in the previous figure from top to bottom:

- **Classes:** Most of your source code goes here. Your files can be organized into subgroups.

- **Other Sources:** A group of files that are needed for the project to build but aren't necessarily source code.

- **Resources:** Your images, sound clips, videos, and other media go in this group. Also, your nib files (files that define your interface) go in this group. Next chapter, nib files are covered in full.

- **Frameworks:** A framework is another name for a library. The project comes prepackaged with the three frameworks in the previous image, and these frameworks give you everything you need to get started developing most iPhone applications. Later, when you want to add audio, location-detection, or iPod access, other frameworks need to be added to your project to allow access to those features.

- **Products:** The products group contains the application binary. This is the binary that actually runs on your iPhone when you launch an application. The only time you need to do anything in this group is when you want to put your application on the App Store or send it out to beta testers.

ONE MORE THING

In the Groups & Files Section, if you see a file name in red text, it means the file does not exist on disk. In the previous image, Flashlight.app is in red, which means it cannot be found. In this case, it's perfectly fine because you haven't built the project yet, which will generate the Flashlight.app file. However, if one of your source code files is displayed in red, its absence may keep your application from building.

In short, you spend most of your time editing or adding files to the Classes and Resources groups and occasionally adding new libraries to the Frameworks group. Keep your files organized. In the CS193P iPhone programming class at Stanford, students often turned in assignments with source files and frameworks scattered haphazardly throughout the project. In the long-term, it is important to keep your files organized as your project grows more and more complex. So go ahead and get in the habit of putting your code files in the Classes group, images in the Resources group, and so on.

Recommended Xcode Preferences

You haven't started writing code at this point, but you can save yourself some future pain and suffering by setting a few Xcode preferences now. It is not strictly necessary to use these settings, but they will greatly help with both coding and debugging.

These Xcode settings can save you a lot of time and trouble once you get to writing and debugging code.

To access your Xcode preferences, on the top menu, select **Xcode > Preferences.** From here, set the following:

- Choose the **Debugging** category, and next to "On Start:" select **Show Console**. The console displays all log output generated by your application. You will almost always need to see the console when debugging, so this setting will bring it to the foreground when your app launches.

- Under the **Debugging** category again, check **Auto Clear Debug Console**. By default, the console will retain the output from every run of your application, which can get very hard to navigate if you have a lot of output. Auto-clearing the console will make it much easier to see new output, which is likely what you care about most anyway.

- Choose the **Text Editing** category, and check **Show line numbers**. Almost every IDE has this off by default, but it's actually a very useful feature. When the debugger says you have an error on line 236, if you don't have line numbers displayed, you're stuck either manually counting lines or guessing which line the error was on. Displaying line numbers is a must for debugging effectively.

- Under the **Text Editing** category again, check **Show page guide**. This setting is more of a personal preference than a strict necessity. The page guide is a vertical line usually displayed at the 80-character mark in the editor view. This visual cue helps to keep the length of each line of code in check since very long lines of code are stylistically frowned upon and also hard to read.

These settings will help you avoid much of the frustration developers experience when they get started programming for iPhone and iPad. There are a plethora of other preferences you can set to customize Xcode to your liking. Take a few minutes to check those out.

Get Up and Running

Okay, so you've created the project, poked around Xcode, and set some preferences. So, now what? Well, the next thing you need to do is build your project. Building your project consists of compiling your source files, linking the output files to the included frameworks, then combining all the project resources with the output files into a single application bundle. For the Flashlight project, this is the Flashlight.app file in the Products group.

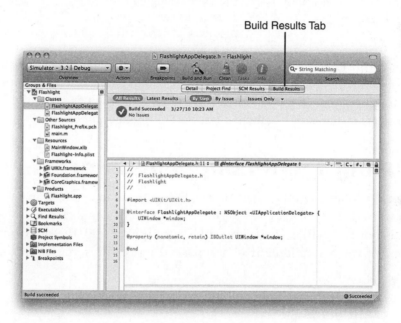

The "Build Results" tab will list any warnings or errors generated when building your project.

Once you successfully build your project, you can finally run the app in the iPhone Simulator. Before you do that, though, there is a bit of terminology to clarify. When you want to launch your newly built application, you have three ways to "run" the application, which are described in the following table:

Options for launching your application

Action	Description	Keyboard Shortcut
Debug – Breakpoints On	Launch your application with the full debugger	⌘-Y
Run – Breakpoints Off	Launch your application with limited debug output	⌘-R
Debug	Launch your application using the same debugger settings as the previous launch.	⌘-Enter

The easiest way to launch your application is to simply click the **Build and Debug** button in the Toolbar at the top of your Xcode window. When the build is successful, you will see the application launch at last in the iPhone Simulator.

Introducing the iPhone Simulator

Shown in the following image, the iPhone Simulator is an application packaged with the iPhone SDK that enables you to run, test, and debug applications on your Mac. The simulator is versatile. If you are building an iPhone app, the simulator displays as an iPhone. If you are building iPad or universal applications, the simulator displays as an iPad.

CRASH AND LEARN

The name is a bit misleading, but the "iPhone Simulator" Mac application simulates both iPhone *and* iPad apps. So any time you read "iPhone Simulator," think "iPhone and iPad Simulator."

The simulator is the single fastest way to test if your application works. You will quickly discover it to be indispensable for app development.

On the left, Flashlight running in a simulated iPhone. On the right, the iPad version is displayed instead.

The simulator does a good job of recreating some of the physical properties and behavior of a real device. You can find all the options under the iPhone Simulator menu item **Hardware**. These include:

- **Rotate Left/Right:** This option rotates the iPhone Simulator by 90 degrees and can be used to see your interface in landscape mode.

- **Shake Gesture:** If your application responds to shake events, you can easily test it using this option.

- **Home:** This will close your application and jump to the home screen as if you pressed the home button on a real device.

- **Lock:** This simulates pressing the button on the top right of the phone that suspends your application and displays the lock screen.

- **Simulate Memory Warning:** This option sends a low-memory warning to your application. Memory management is covered in great detail in Chapter 5, but the short story is it is important to handle low-memory situations in your app.

- **Toggle In-Call Status Bar:** Next time you make a phone call, check out the status bar at the top of the screen. Notice how it's larger? It's double the normal size, in fact. This option simulates the larger bar size, which you need to properly take into account when developing your app.

In addition to simulating hardware, the iPhone Simulator also recreates taps, swipes, and pinch gestures using the mouse.

Sending gestures to the simulator is pretty natural. Think of the mouse cursor as your finger, and you know how it works. Reference the following table to figure out how to perform each gesture on the simulator.

Gestures in the iPhone Simulator

Gesture	iPhone Simulator Equivalent
Tap	Click
Swipe	Click, then drag, then release
Centered two-finger pinch	Hold ⌥ (option key), then click-and-drag
Free two-finger pinch	Hold ⌥ and Shift, then click-and-drag

The centered two-finger pinch in the previous table always keeps the two fingers centered on the middle of the iPhone. This gesture is great for testing a zoom feature in your app. The free two-finger pinch lets you move the two fingers around the screen with a constant distance between them. This gesture, on the other hand, is good to use for testing a two-finger swipe.

The problem with both two-finger gestures, though, is that you can't properly simulate every gesture a user can do using a single mouse or trackpad. To truly test multiple fingers on your interface, you need to run the app on a real device. The lack of two-finger gestures is one of the limitations to consider when testing your apps on the iPhone Simulator. This brings us to our next topic: the limitations of the iPhone Simulator.

Simulator Limitations

In a perfect world, you don't need to run your application on a real device because the Simulator can recreate the exact same experience as running on a device. In a perfect world, you wouldn't need to pay $99 so you can put your app on your device, because you can just test it in the iPhone Simulator. In a perfect world, rivers would flow with chocolate and money would grow on trees.

Unfortunately, to the chagrin of both my stomach and wallet, the world is not perfect. The iPhone Simulator is flawed both in *how* it simulates and *what* it simulates. The limitations and inaccuracies of the iPhone Simulator are laid out in the following:

- **Computing resources:** The simulator does not try to simulate the memory usage restrictions of a physical device. You are free to use as much memory as any other desktop application. Additionally, simulated applications run on your speedy desktop, which is many times faster than an iPhone or iPad. These differences mean your app will run a bit more slowly on a real device.

- **Only one simulator instance allowed:** If you're building an application that networks two devices together, it would be helpful to launch two simulators and test out the network code. Sadly, your only option is to test the app on multiple physical devices.

- **No GPS:** The iPhone Simulator reports a single, fixed location when using the Core Foundation framework: Apple headquarters in Cupertino, California.

- **No Camera:** The simulator doesn't try to recreate the camera at all.

- **No Accelerometer:** Don't try waving your Mac in the air expecting to get accelerometer readings, because it just won't work. The one caveat is that you can simulate a shake event in the simulator by selecting the menu item **Hardware > Shake Gesture**.

- **No iPod:** You can use the Media Player framework to play music from the user's iPod application on a device, but not in the iPhone Simulator.

- **No Bluetooth:** If you want to develop a game that uses the Game Kit framework to add sweet multiplayer Bluetooth support, you will need at least two physical devices for testing.

- **No In-App Purchases:** Want to test out purchasing that +5 dexterity vest in your game? You need to use the Store Kit framework to get in-app purchases to work, and like the long list of features before this one, you can only test it out on a real device.

THERE'S A TIP FOR THAT

The iPhone Simulator does not simulate most aspects of iPhone and iPad hardware. Many of the limitations above fall into this category.

The simulator is not a perfect replacement for a physical device. How can you accurately test your apps, then? The only foolproof way to test your app is by actually running it on your iPhone or iPad. If you plan to put your application on the App Store, you absolutely need to test it on a real device before even thinking about submitting your app. Unforeseen, wacky problems *will* show up when you first put your app on your device, and the only way to detect and fix those problems is by testing them out in the wild.

So should you still use the iPhone Simulator? Absolutely. There are great reasons for using the simulator, not the least of which is that it's drastically faster to run your app in the simulator than on a device. It takes a while for the app to upload to your iPhone or iPad, while launching on the simulator takes a matter of seconds. It is also more convenient to have your code and app running side by side instead of constantly switching between computer and device.

Just be aware of the limitations mentioned previously, and tuck away the knowledge that even if your app works perfectly in the iPhone Simulator, it may not really work. The only way to know for sure, particularly for performance, is by testing on real, bona-fide physical device.

Xcode Debugger View

If you configured Xcode to display the console when an app is launched, you will notice that the Xcode interface changed when you launched Flashlight. The new layout is known as the debugger view, and you can see what it looks like in the following figure. If the view doesn't appear automatically, you can launch it by selecting **Run > Debugger** from the top menu.

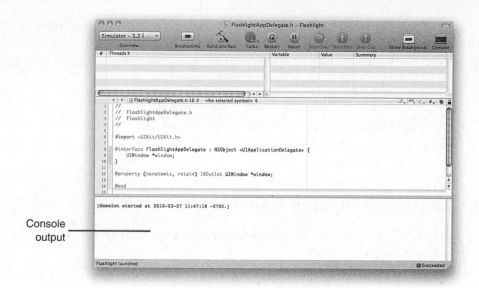

Console
output

You can view console output at the bottom of the debugger view.

Any time your app doesn't work as anticipated, the debugger view is excellent for figuring out what went wrong. In Chapter 24, you will learn how to master the debugger interface in Xcode, but for now, note that the console output is at the bottom of the debugger view.

To dismiss the debugger view and return to the original project view, select **Project > Project**.

THERE'S A TIP FOR THAT

If you want a really simple way to switch between project and debugger views, select **View > Layout > Show Page Control**. This will add a button to your Toolbar you can use to toggle between the two views.

Finding Your Way Through the Dark

Your goal in this chapter was to recreate an application that has had spectacular success on the App Store. After building your project, you launched it on the iPhone Simulator, which you also found out wasn't perfect by any stretch of the imagination.

But still, you were presented with a pure white rectangle that was Flashlight blazing in its entirety. It may not seem like much, but not only did you learn a boatload about Xcode and the iPhone Simulator in this chapter, you also wrote an application that has been downloaded untold thousands of times on the App Store.

Of course, submitting Flashlight nowadays would get you laughed out of the App Store. Flashlight is a good starting point, but follow along to next chapter, where you learn how to build an interface for your app using Interface Builder.

The Least You Need to Know

- Launch Xcode, then select **File > New Project...** to generate the skeleton code for a new app.

- In Xcode, the Groups & Files Section is where you see a hierarchy of your project files. The Editor View is where you will write code.

- Keep your files organized by putting code files in the Classes group and media image, sound and video files in the Resources group.

- To try out your project, you build and launch it by selecting **Build > Build and Run** in Xcode.

- Although the iPhone Simulator does a pretty good job, the only way to see if your application truly works is by running it on a real device.

Interface Building

In This Chapter

- Interface Builder in a nutshell
- How to create an interface for your app
- Adding a label to your interface
- Adding an image to your interface
- Creating an icon for your app

By the end of this chapter, you will know how to create an interface for your iPhone app that contains a text label and an image. Would you believe that using only this knowledge, you can write an app that would sell for $1,000?

Common sense says no, that's ludicrous. But an app called "I am Rich" did indeed go on sale in August 2008 for the low, low price of $999.99. The app simply displays an image of a red crystal that you could show to your friends to prove that yes, in fact, you are rich.

The app sold eight copies before it was quickly taken off the App Store. Since then, Apple has tightened their approval process so that objectionable apps like "I am Rich" don't show up on the App Store. In this chapter, you will honor the spirit of "I am Rich" by building your own app that can display an image and some text.

ICE, ICE, Baby

Although you hope it will never happen, what would you do if you are in an accident and knocked unconscious? It would be great if the first responders had a way to get in touch with your family or loved ones to find out what care they can provide without risk of further injury.

This is precisely the situation that has given rise to the idea of ICE (In Case of Emergency). Originally, the idea behind ICE was that you keep a contact named ICE in your phone's address book so paramedics and first responders know who to get in touch with if you need help. In this chapter, you will build an ICE iPhone app. The app will display a photo of your ICE contact, along with the person's name and relationship to you. Completed, the app will look like this:

The ICE interface consists of an image view and several labels.

As you can see, the app is fairly simple but provides an important service.

Making ICE

To get started writing ICE, you will need to create a new project in Xcode, just like you did in the previous chapter. Instead of a Window-based Application, however, you will create a View-based Application. What's the difference? In a Window-based Application, when you add a text label to the interface, you add it directly to the window itself. In a View-based Application, you add the text label to a view in the window. The View-based template is great for building apps that consist of a single view.

Before creating the project in Xcode, you should understand what exactly a *view* is and where it fits into the grand scheme of things in the iPhone interface.

Views

There are simple *views* that draw text and images, and there are complex views that draw tables and pickers. A view can span a single pixel or it can fill the entire screen. It can be transparent or opaque. You can define your own views to draw polygons, shapes, and paths. Views are the basic building blocks of all user interface elements on the iPhone.

DEFINITION

A **view** is a rectangular portion of the screen that draws content. Everything in an iPhone interface—text, images, buttons—is part of a view.

Views are also hierarchical. Every view has a single superview, or parent view, and every view has zero or more subviews, or child views. At the top of the hierarchy is the window, which is a view itself, and the subviews of the window determine what is rendered to the screen.

To illustrate how views work, consider this screenshot from the built-in Mail application for iPhone:

Here are some e-mails in the Mail app.

If you were to break down the interface, here are the major pieces you would end up with:

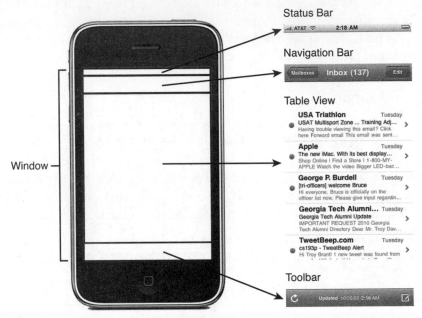

It is easy to mix up the bars, so note the location of each one: status bar, navigation bar, and toolbar.

The screen is composed of five main elements: a window, a status bar, a navigation bar, a table view, and a toolbar. The table view is composed of several subviews, one for each cell. And each cell, in turn, is composed of an image subview to render the blue circle, several label subviews to render the text, and another image subview to render the right arrow. Visually, the hierarchy becomes clear if you break the interface into a tree:

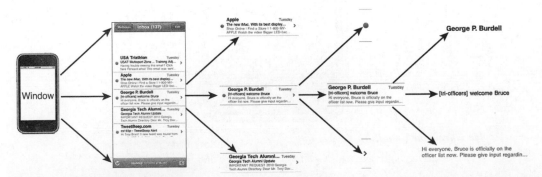

The view hierarchy for the Mail app turned on its side.

The view hierarchy also determines the *order* in which the views are drawn. In the previous image, the views are rendered from left to right and top to bottom. That is, the window is drawn first, then its subviews, starting with the navigation bar. The table view is then rendered, and because it has subviews, the cell views are rendered next. Any time you reach a view that has subviews, those subviews are rendered before moving on to the next view at the current level in the hierarchy.

ONE MORE THING

For tree algorithm fans out there, the view hierarchy is traversed using BFS (Breadth First Search).

However, what does this mean for you, the programmer? The key takeaway is that if you have two views, one on top of the other, the one that is added *last* will appear on *top*. Imagine stacking two photographs. If you put them down on the same spot, one after the other, you see the second photo because it is on top of the first photo. Similarly, the last view you add to the window will be drawn on top of the other views.

Though this may appear obvious, a misunderstanding of the view hierarchy can lead to perplexing bugs. In particular, several Stanford students had problems with views "disappearing," which was almost always because they were *underneath* other views.

In this chapter, you are going to use Interface Builder to build your own view hierarchy for the ICE app, though not nearly as complex as in the previous image.

Create the Project

Now that you know a bit more about views, go ahead and create a View-based Application for iPhone in Xcode. Name it ICE. Expand the Resources group in the Groups & Files section. There, you will find two files that end in .xib: ICEViewController.xib and MainWindow.xib. The purpose of these files will be explained in a moment, but for now, double-click the **ICEViewController.xib** file to launch Interface Builder.

CRASH AND LEARN

If you accidentally start editing the MainWindow.xib file instead of ICEViewController.xib, you won't see any changes you make to your interface. Why not? The changes you made were to the window, not the ICE view. And the ICE view is drawn *on top*, hiding the interface of the window below it.

What the Heck Is a Nib?

While Interface Builder is loading, let's take a moment to go over the term used previously: *nib*. When you construct your interface in Interface Builder, the position and properties of all your text views, image views, and all other views are saved to the nib.

> **DEFINITION**
>
> A **nib** (NeXT Interface Builder) is a file that defines the interface for a single view in your application. Nibs are editable using the Interface Builder application.

The view objects themselves aren't stored in the nib. Instead, the *blueprint* for the view objects is stored in the nib. So when you run your application in the iPhone Simulator, the application engine gets instructions from the nib files and then builds the interface at runtime.

Why the funny name? Nibs were historically binaries that ended with a .nib extension—thus the name *nib*—before they were replaced with XML-based .xib files. Today, the .xib file format is used exclusively in iPhone and iPad development. Regardless of the .nib or .xib extension, these files are collectively known as nibs, and that is the name you will see for them in this book.

Interface Builder

If you see the following image, then welcome to Interface Builder! You will likely spend a substantial amount of your time in this application, so it will be worth your while to become intimately familiar with how it works.

So what exactly is Interface Builder? The name itself is quite descriptive, and yes, in fact, you do build interfaces with Interface Builder. You can use it to visually lay out exactly what your interface will look like, from what fonts to use to how you want your images scaled.

Yet, Interface Builder is much more powerful than a layout tool. Say you add a button to your interface. Using Interface Builder, you can have one of your methods called when the button is tapped. So, not only do you use Interface Builder to define what your button will *look like*, you use it to determine how your interface *behaves* when the user taps the button.

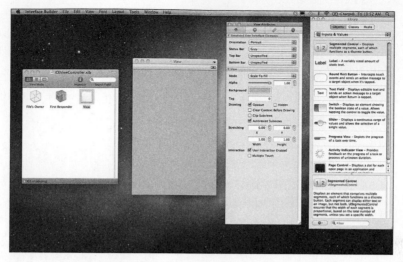

Reader, meet Interface Builder. Interface Builder, reader. The two of you will get to know one another very well over the course of this book.

Another big difference from other interface design tools that you may have used is that you won't ever write code in Interface Builder. You simply connect interface elements to objects and methods that have been defined elsewhere in your project.

For ICE, you will focus solely on the visual side of Interface Builder. Before jumping in, you should take a few minutes to familiarize yourself with the multiple windows of Interface Builder.

The Grand Tour

There are four primary windows you will use when creating an interface in Interface Builder:

- **Document window:** The document window, as shown in the previous image, gives you a bird's-eye view of your interface. You can ignore the File's Owner and First Responder objects for now (they will be covered later). The View object is the root node in the view hierarchy, so it contains all the views in the interface.

THERE'S A TIP FOR THAT

In the top-left corner of the document window, you will find the large icon view selected by default. I highly recommend changing it to list mode, the middle option. In list mode, you can see the entire view hierarchy by expanding the arrow next to the View object.

- **Workspace window:** The workspace window is your canvas, your playground, where you will actually build your interface. In the image that follows, the workspace window is sized for iPhone. If you are building an iPad app, the window will match the size of an iPad instead.

  If you close the workspace window, you can open it again by double-clicking the View object in the document window.

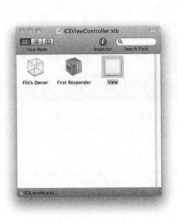 

Document window   Workspace window

The document window is on the left. The workspace window is on the right.

- **Inspector window:** The inspector window is not displayed when Interface Builder is first opened. To view the window, select **Tools > Inspector** from the top menu bar.

  Context-sensitive information about the currently selected object is displayed in the inspector window. The buttons along the top act as tabs. From left to right, the tabs are Attributes, Connections, Size, and Identity. For instance, if you click the workspace, you can use the Attributes tab to specify the view's background color, transparency, and whether it is hidden.

- **Library window:** Buttons, text fields, image views, and many more built-in views can be found in the library window. To add any of the views to your interface, simply click and drag the view you want and release it on the work-space window. Drag-and-drop is king in Interface Builder.

THERE'S A TIP FOR THAT

All four of these windows can be reopened if you accidentally close them. To open the document window, select **Window > Document**. To open the workspace window, double-click the View object in the document window. To open the inspector window, select **Tools > Inspector**. And to open the library window, select **Tools > Library**.

Inspector window

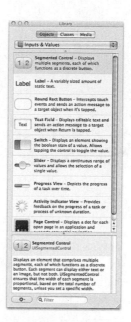

Library window

From left to right: the inspector window and the library window.

It may take some time to feel comfortable with Interface Builder. As you develop applications over the course of this book, however, you will master this extremely useful application.

Interface Building

Now that you know a little more about Interface Builder, you can get started building the interface for ICE.

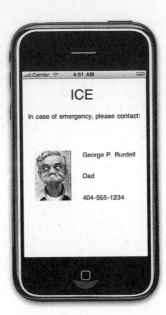

On the left is the interface before you work your magic. On the right is the completed ICE app.

Interface Builder offers an image view for displaying images and a label for displaying text. As you can see in the image above, the interface will consist of several labels, one for each line of text, and an image view. You will build your interface by combining several of these elements together.

Before you add the text and images, you will first change the background color to something other than that boring gray. After that, you will add the labels and the image view.

ONE MORE THING

The text in a label is not editable by the user while an application is being used. However, you, the developer, can programmatically edit the text in the label as you please. If you do want to display text the user can edit, you will need to use either a text field or text view. Text entry will be covered in Chapter 9.

Changing the Background Color

The default view is set to a light gray, but let's change it to white. To edit the background color, perform these steps:

1. In the inspector window, select **Attributes** (on the far left).

2. Click **Background**.

3. You should see the color chooser window. There are several ways to set the color to white, but the most straightforward way is to use the color picker tool. Click the **magnifying glass** on the top-left side of the window, and then click anywhere on your screen that is white. Pretty neat, huh?

Experiment with the color chooser if you have never used it before.

4. Close the color chooser window after setting the color to white.

Now that the background color is a bit more pleasing, you can move on to adding text.

Adding Text

To add text labels, follow these steps:

1. In the library window, select **Library > Cocoa Touch > Inputs & Values**.

2. From the list of views, click and drag **Label** to the workspace.

3. Continue adding labels until you have a total of five labels in your workspace.

4. Double-click the first label to begin editing its text, and type "ICE."

5. With the first label still selected, click the button next to Font in the Attributes tab of the inspector window. The button will read *Helvetica, 17.0* by default. Set the font size to 36.

6. Double-click the second label, and set the text to "In case of emergency, please contact:"

7. Double-click the third label, and set the text to the name of your ICE contact.

8. Double-click the fourth label, and set the text to the relationship your ICE contact has to you, such as "Mom" or "Friend."

9. Double-click the fifth label, and set the text to the phone number of your ICE contact.

10. Drag the labels so that their positions match the previous image.

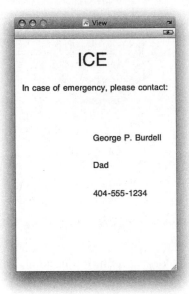

Use the blue guidelines when dragging views around to take the headache out of aligning views.

With all the labels in place, all that remains is adding an image of your ICE contact to the user interface.

Adding Images

Considering how everything else is drag-and-drop in Interface Builder, wouldn't it be great if you could just drag an image into your workspace to add it to the interface? Unfortunately, it's not quite *that* simple, though adding an image is still easy to do.

To add an image to your interface, follow these steps:

1. Download the image located at http://troybrant.net/iphonebook/chapter3/
george.jpg.

2. You must first add the image to the Xcode project, so switch to Xcode.

3. Drag the image to the Resources group and release.

4. A sheet will display with several options. Check **Copy items into destination group's folder** (if needed), and then click **Add**. Make sure your settings match the following image.

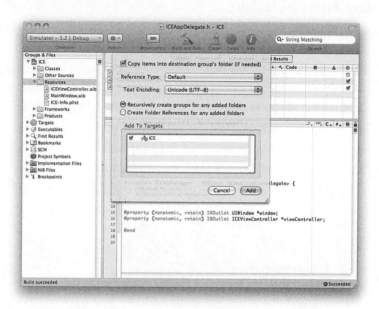

When adding images to your project, always add them to the Resources group to stay organized.

CRASH AND LEARN

If you don't check **Copy items into destination group's folder**, you will run into problems if you try to move your project or share it with someone else. As a rule of thumb, keep this box checked so that added files are always copied into your project folder.

Now that the button image is part of the project, Interface Builder will automatically detect the image. To add the image to your app, follow these steps:

1. Switch back to Interface Builder.

2. In the library window, select **Library > Cocoa Touch > Data Views.**

3. From the list of views, click and drag **Image View** to the workspace.

4. Adjust the size of the view so it fits in the space to the left of the text labels.

5. Click the image view to select it. Then, in the Attributes tab of the inspector window, click the dropdown menu in the Image field.

6. You should see the name of the image file you added. Select it. If you don't see the image name, double-check to make sure you followed all the steps for adding images listed above.

7. You may find that the image is clipped and doesn't look right. By default, Interface Builder just centers the image in the image view and clips the image to the image view size. You can adjust how the image is displayed by changing the Mode property in the inspector window. Two options that usually provide nice results are **Aspect Fit** and **Aspect Fill**. You can experiment with the Mode property until your image looks good.

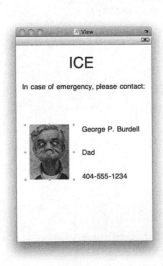

You may need to use Aspect Fit for your image to display properly.

8. Save your interface by clicking **File > Save** or pressing ⌘-S.

Now that the image looks great in your image view, your interface is complete! The last thing to do is to try running your app in the iPhone Simulator.

Taking ICE for a Spin

To see the interface in action, you must again switch over to Xcode so you can launch the iPhone Simulator:

1. Switch back to Xcode.

2. Save the project.

3. Build the project.

4. Run the app.

At this point, you should see the ICE interface you just built running in all its glory in the iPhone Simulator. The following is the completed version of my own ICE app:

You do not want to see my baby pictures.

With your first real app in the bag, you should get up and celebrate with wild abandon. You might even hurt yourself, which is perfectly okay. Just make sure the first person to find you can see the ICE app on your computer screen. The complete

source code for the ICE project is available online at http://troybrant.net/iphonebook/
chapter3/ICE-done.zip.

Looking Ahead

In this chapter, you learned all about Interface Builder and how to use it to define
what your interface will look like. In the next chapter, you learn how to add interactive controls to your interface, like buttons. You will also (finally!) write your first
lines of code.

The Least You Need to Know

- A view is a rectangular area on the screen that draws content and handles touch
  events.
- A nib is a file that contains an interface created using Interface Builder.
- In Interface Builder, the library window is where the view templates live, and the
  inspector window is used to tweak the properties of your views.
- To add an image to your interface, you must first add it to your project in Xcode.
- You may need to set the Mode property of your image view to Aspect Fit for
  the image to look best.
- To test your interface, you must switch back to Xcode and launch the project
  from there.

Buttons, Controllers, and Code

Chapter
4

In This Chapter

- Adding a controller to handle button taps
- Hooking up the controller with the interface
- Writing action methods and updating outlets

For several months in 2009, an app called "Do Not Press the Red Button" was the top-selling iPhone app. The premise of the app is simple: there's a big, red button in the middle of the screen, and you're not supposed to press it. Of course no one can resist that, and so you tap the button. A message is displayed warning you that if you tap the button just *one more time*, the world will come to an end. So, of course, you tap the button again, but instead of the end of the world, you get another warning. After enough taps, *something* dramatic happens, and it's the mystery of what that something is that has led to the app's success.

In the spirit of "Do Not Press the Red Button," you will write iShockU in this chapter. iShockU displays a button on the screen and warns the user not to press it. If users are foolish enough to ignore the warning, then, *zap*—they get blasted with a bolt of electricity. Well, actually they see the text *Zap!* on the screen, which is close enough and won't get you arrested. In this chapter, you also write code for the first time and learn how to integrate Interface Builder with Xcode.

iShockU App

iShockU is a simple app. The interface needs just two elements: a button and a label to output some text. When the app first opens, the label displays the message, "Don't touch this button or else …". When the button is tapped, the message will change to "Zap!" When the user releases the button, the label will revert to the original "Don't touch" text. These two states are displayed in the following figure:

iShockU before the button is pressed (on the left) and after (on the right).

There are two main tasks in building this app: laying out the interface and programming what happens when the button is tapped. The following strategy will be used to build iShockU:

1. Create the project in Xcode.

2. Lay out the interface in Interface Builder.

3. Add a controller object to handle button taps.

4. Generate code for the controller object.

5. Program the button behavior using Xcode.

Interface Building

Just like you did in the previous chapter, you must first create a new project in Xcode:

1. Create a new iPhone project using the View-based Application template.

2. Name the project "iShockU."

3. Open iShockUViewController.xib.

THERE'S A TIP FOR THAT

If you have trouble with any of these steps, review the ICE project that was created in Chapter 3.

Interface Builder should be up and running at this point. You can now get started building the interface:

1. Change the background color of the view to white.

2. Click and drag a label from the library to the workspace.

3. Set the label's text to "Don't touch this button or else …".

4. Click and drag a **Round Rect button** from the library to the workspace. If you don't see the Round Rect button, make sure the library window is using the filter **Library > Cocoa Touch > Inputs & Values**.

5. Use the guidelines to center the label and button, so they match the image that follows:

Your workspace with the button and label added.

Now, it's time to spice things up by adding an image.

Adding an Image to the Button

Throughout this book, whenever you need an image, audio file, or any kind of resource file, you can download them from http://troybrant.net/iphonebook.

For iShockU, the button image can be found online at http://troybrant.net/iphonebook/chapter4/red-button.png. After downloading the image, follow these steps to add the image to the button:

1. To use the image in Interface Builder, you need to add it to your Xcode project like you did in the previous chapter. Go ahead and add the image to your project now.

CRASH AND LEARN

Remember to check **Copy items into destination group's folder** when adding the image.

2. Now that the button image is part of the project, switch back to Interface Builder and select the button.

3. In the inspector window, select the image in the drop-down menu next to the Image field.

4. Notice the image is clipped on the top and bottom. You have two options to fix this problem: either increase the size of the image view or edit the Mode property of the image view like you did in the previous chapter. Try dragging the top edge of the button until the button image is fully visible.

5. To remove the border around the image, change the button's Type field to **Custom** in the Attributes tab of the inspector window.

This completes the button's makeover from a simple rectangle to an imposing trigger button.

Interface Complete

The interface is now complete. Now is a great time to try running the app in the iPhone Simulator. Switch back to Xcode, and run the application.

Your app should look just like you laid it out in Interface Builder. But the button doesn't do anything when you tap it. How do you hook up the button so that it does something interesting, you ask? The answer lies in understanding controllers.

Your workspace interface looks good.

Controllers

When a switch is flipped or a button is tapped in an interface, a controller responds to the interaction. The *controller* is the brain behind your interface. And like a brain, the controller needs to be properly wired to work correctly.

For the controller to do its job, it needs to know about both the button and label you've added to the interface. Right now, the controller is a blank slate, so you need to tell it about the button and label, or *outlets*. In addition, you need to define the methods, or *actions*, that will be called when the button is pressed and released.

DEFINITION

A **controller** connects your interface with the rest of your application. When a button is tapped in your interface, code in your controller is invoked.

An **outlet** is just an instance variable, and an **action** is a method in an object. They are specially labeled so Interface Builder knows they can be connected to the interface.

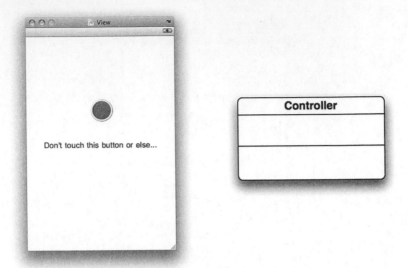

The controller for iShockU is currently empty and needs to be linked to the interface.

You need to explicitly set these outlets and actions in your controller object. In order to do so, jump to Xcode and edit the `iShockUController` class according to the following steps:

1. Switch to Xcode.

2. Select iShockUViewController.h.

3. Add the code in bold:

```
// iShockUController.h

#import <UIKit/UIKit.h>

@interface iShockUViewController : UIViewController
{
    UIButton *button;
    UILabel *label;
}

@property (nonatomic, retain) IBOutlet UIButton *button;
@property (nonatomic, retain) IBOutlet UILabel *label;

- (IBAction)buttonTouchDown:(id)sender;
- (IBAction)buttonTouchUp:(id)sender;

@end
```

4. Save your code.

So what exactly did you just do? What is UIKit at the top? What's up with all the UI, NS, and IB prefixes? Why all the punctuation marks? These questions will be answered in full next chapter, but the short story is that you have just defined your controller's outlets and actions. The interaction between your controller and interface now looks like this:

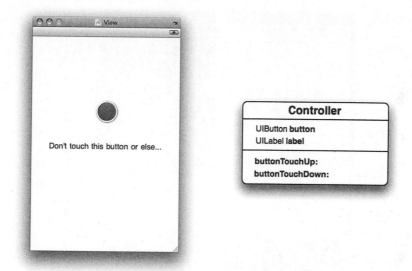

The controller now has outlets and actions defined.

As you can see in the previous image, the outlets and actions on the controller are defined, but they are not hooked up to the interface. Now, you will use Interface Builder to connect the controller with the interface.

Connect the Dots

To hook up the controller to the interface, you need to connect the button outlet in the controller to the red button in the interface:

1. Switch back to Interface Builder.

2. Select **File's Owner** in the document window. File's Owner represents the controller that will be managing the view. In this case, it points to the iShockUController class whose code you just edited.

3. Select **Connections** in the inspector window. Under the Outlets and Received Actions sections, you will see the outlets and actions you added to the controller code.

4. Next, you form connections between the controller code and the interface elements. Click and drag from the circle across from the button outlet, and release it over the button in the interface. See the following image for an example:

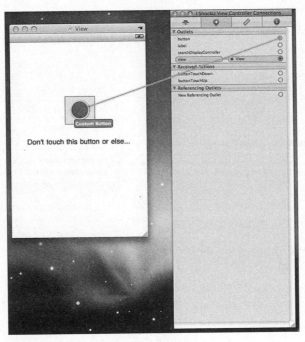

Making a connection is as easy as drag-and-drop.

ONE MORE THING

Try dragging the button connector over the label. Notice how it doesn't highlight? The connector is smart. If you specify the type of the outlet object, such as a UIButton, it will only connect to objects of that type in the interface.

5. Repeat the previous step for the label outlet, but connect it to the label in the interface instead of the button.

6. Click and drag the circle next to the `buttonTouchDown:` action and release over the button in the interface. Interface Builder will display a list of events that may be used to trigger your action method.

```
Did End On Exit
Editing Changed
Editing Did Begin
Editing Did End
Touch Cancel
Touch Down
Touch Down Repeat
Touch Drag Enter
Touch Drag Exit
Touch Drag Inside
Touch Drag Outside
Touch Up Inside
Touch Up Outside
Value Changed
```

You will use the Touch Down and Touch Up Inside events for iShockU.

7. Select **Touch Down** from the event list. Now, any time the button is pressed, the `buttonTouchDown:` action method in your controller will be invoked.

8. Repeat the previous two steps for the `buttonTouchUp:` action, but select **Touch Up Inside** from the event list instead.

You have defined your controller, outlets, and actions, and hooked them up successfully to the interface.

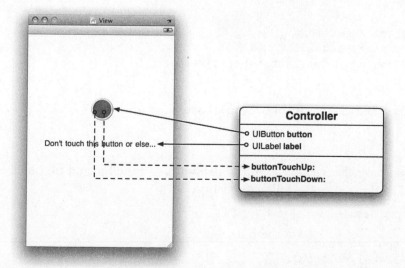

The interface is wired to the controller, as shown in the now-complete diagram.

Now, the only thing left to do is program the button behavior. And for that, you are going to jump back to Xcode.

Make the Button Do Something Interesting

In Objective-C, a single class is split across two files: the interface file and the implementation file. Interface files end in .h and contain the public class definition. You define both the instance variables and the methods you want visible to the entire world in the interface file. Implementation files, on the other hand, are where you write the bodies of those methods. In Chapter 5, interface and implementation files are covered in great detail.

Earlier, you edited iShockUViewController.h, which is the interface file for the `iShockUViewController` class. Now that the interface is defined, you must edit the implementation file. Go ahead and select iShockUViewController.m in the Groups & Files section.

When the file is selected, you will see some commented code and a few methods defined at the bottom of the file. You won't use any of these methods right now, but feel free to read over the text descriptions above each one to see what they do.

The goal in editing this file is to define the action methods that will fire when the button is tapped. Again, even though you may not understand every bit of it, write code to match the following:

```
// iShockUController.m

@synthesize button;
@synthesize label;
- (IBAction)buttonTouchDown:(id)sender
{
}
- (IBAction)buttonTouchUp:(id)sender
{
}
```

After you have that written, scroll to the bottom of the file and fill out the dealloc method so it matches the following definition:

```
- (void)dealloc
{
    [button release];
    [label release];
    [super dealloc];
}
```

Releasing the button and label instance variables is required for proper memory management. If it seems a little strange, don't worry; memory management is covered extensively in Chapter 6.

Try to build and run the project. It should build successfully and launch in the iPhone Simulator. Pressing the red button won't do anything exciting just yet, but you are now ready to add some interaction to the app.

NSLogging

You will now transform the innocuous, innocent-looking button into the iPhone equivalent of an electric socket. To get started, you should test to make sure the button's action methods are actually called when the button is pressed. The fastest way to test is by printing out a line of text to the console. In Objective-C, you achieve this using the NSLog method. All NSLog output will be printed to the console, which can be accessed via **Run > Console** from the top menu bar if it does not appear automatically.

To print messages to the console when the buttons are tapped, edit iShockUViewController.m add the NSLog function calls to your action methods:

```
- (IBAction)buttonTouchDown:(id)sender
{
    NSLog(@"The button is down");
}
- (IBAction)buttonTouchUp:(id)sender
{
    NSLog(@"The button is up");
}
```

Build and run the application. After the app launches, try tapping the red button. You should see the desired log messages in the Xcode console, as shown in the following image. If the messages appear, then you are very close to being finished. The only thing left to do is to change the text of the label.

ONE MORE THING

Note the @ at the beginning of the string in the NSLog statements. Objective-C has its own string class, NSString, that is used almost exclusively in Mac development. The @ prefix indicates the string is an NSString object rather than a regular C string.

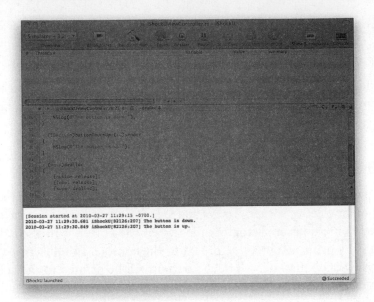

Make sure your debugger console is visible in order to see the NSLog output.

Shocking Finale

To change the label's text, you simply set its `text` *property*. Chapter 6 explains proper-ties in great detail, but for now, all you need to know is how to set the `text` property of the label.

DEFINITION

A **property** is a convenient way to access and set the data for an object in Objective-C.

In Xcode, switch from debugger view to project view by selecting **Project > Project** from the top menu bar. Then, remove the `NSLog` calls, and set the label text proper-ties, like so:

```
- (IBAction)buttonTouchDown:(id)sender
{
    label.text = @"Zap!";
}
- (IBAction)buttonTouchUp:(id)sender
{
    label.text = @"Don't touch this button or else...";
}
```

Save your project, then run it so it launches in the iPhone Simulator. Try clicking on the red button. You should see the label text change to "Zap!" Brilliant! It works! But wait, you'll notice a little problem here. The "Zap!" text isn't centered.

Hey, that's not right. Luckily, fixing the text offset is lightning fast.

The problem is that UILabels assume the text they display is left-aligned. So, all you need to do is tell the label to center its text instead. Conveniently, UILabels have a textAlignment property you can use to coerce the label into centering the text. The code to make this change is short and sweet:

```
- (IBAction)buttonTouchDown:(id)sender
{
    label.text = @"Zap!"
    label.textAlignment = UITextAlignmentCenter;
}
- (IBAction)buttonTouchUp:(id)sender
{
    label.text = @"Don't touch this button or else...";
}
```

Give the app a whirl, and violà! You have a fully functional red button app, created over the course of a single chapter.

Full source code for the finished iShockU application is available online at http://troybrant.net/iphonebook/chapter4/iShockU-done.zip.

Another App in the Books

Congrats! You have completely and successfully written iShockU, your third iPhone application. Although this app was written purely for educational purposes, it is worth noting that some of the most successful apps on the App Store are as simple and easy to use as this one.

If you feel motivated to keep working on the app (and who wouldn't?), then for extra credit, try changing the background color of the label while the red button is pressed. Or try changing the background image of the entire view to a lightning bolt when the red button is pressed. You can use the lightning bolt image provided online at: http://troybrant.net/iphonebook/chapter4/lightning-bolt.png.

Now that you have been exposed to some Objective-C, you are going to learn all about the programming language in the following chapter. You will learn the language syntax, the lingo, and how to write your own custom classes.

The Least You Need to Know

- Controllers are the brains of your app.
- Be sure to hook up the outlets and actions of your controller to the objects in your user interface.
- Update the text property to change a label's text in code.

Objective-C and Cocoa Touch

In This Chapter

- Cocoa Touch
- Object-oriented programming review
- Objective-C basics
- Anatomy of a class in Objective-C

There are many great Objective-C books available. Instead of covering Objective-C as a topic, many introductory texts on iPhone and iPad programming point you to these resources instead of spending time explaining the language. Given how much ground there is to cover, it is completely understandable to refer you to a dedicated book on the topic.

However, you don't want to read an entire book on Objective-C before writing iPhone and iPad apps. This chapter provides a brief introduction to the language so you can start writing interesting apps as soon as possible.

Specifically, this chapter covers object-oriented programming and Objective-C terminology. The goal of this chapter is for you to feel much more comfortable writing Objective-C code for the iPhone OS as you move forward.

What Is Objective-C?

So what exactly is *Objective-C*? Simply put, Objective-C is the main programming language used to develop iPhone and iPad apps. To get a better handle on how to use the language, you first need to know how the iPhone OS works under the hood.

DEFINITION

Objective-C is an object-oriented programming language built on top of C. Objective-C is the primary language used to build both Mac OS X and iPhone OS applications.

Cooking with Cocoa

One of the main reasons iPhone and iPad are such powerful devices is that they share much in common with Mac OS X. Instead of writing a completely new operating system for the phone, Apple started with Mac OS X and trimmed it down until it could fit on a mobile device. Many of the frameworks that power the iPhone OS are nearly identical to the ones you use on a Mac.

There are many frameworks on the Mac, but the ones used most often for application development are collectively known as *Cocoa*. Cocoa provides basic structures—arrays, dictionaries, strings, objects—required for most application development. It also includes the user interface building blocks that make your life as a programmer much easier.

While the Mac has Cocoa, the iPhone has *Cocoa Touch*. Cocoa Touch is a scaled-down version of Cocoa that is designed for the unique properties of a small, portable touch-based device.

DEFINITION

Cocoa is the collection of frameworks, APIs, and standard tools you need to build Mac OS X applications. **Cocoa Touch** is a version of Cocoa used to develop for touch-based, mobile devices like the iPad, iPhone, and iPod Touch.

So where does Objective-C fit into this picture? All the Cocoa Touch classes are written in Objective-C. Although the language has a different syntax, Objective-C is a superset of C. This means that C code will also compile using the Objective-C compiler. In fact, some of the frameworks on the phone—most notably the AddressBook framework—are written entirely in C. However, Objective-C will be used for most of the code in this book except where using C is much more convenient.

ONE MORE THING

You can also combine C++ code with Objective-C. C++ files used in iPhone programming end with a ".mm" extension and are typically referred to Objective-C++ files.

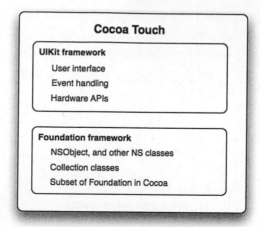

The UIKit and Foundation frameworks provide the basic classes needed for building iPad and iPhone applications.

Object-Oriented Programming Review

To program effectively in Objective-C, you need to have a pretty good idea of how object-oriented programming (OOP) works. Take a few moments to review the topics and terminology introduced below:

- **Class:** Blueprint used to create objects. Also defines the *type* of the object.

- **Object:** Specific allocation of a class. Can also be referred to as an *instance*.

- **Constructor:** Method used to create an instance of a class. In Objective-C, constructors are often referred to as "initializers."

- **Method:** A function that an object knows how to perform. You have seen these referred to as "actions" in Interface Builder.

- **Instance Variable:** A specific piece of data belonging to an instance. You have seen these referred to as "outlets" in Interface Builder.

- **Inheritance:** The practice of one class defining another class as its parent. The child class can access all the instance variables and methods from the parent class.

- **Subclass/Superclass:** A subclass, or child class, inherits instance variables and methods from its superclass, or parent class.

There are other terms associated with object-oriented programming—encapsulation, polymorphism, and dynamic binding, to name a few—but you only need to know the previous terms for the purposes of this book.

The relationship between the object-oriented terms is shown in the following diagram.

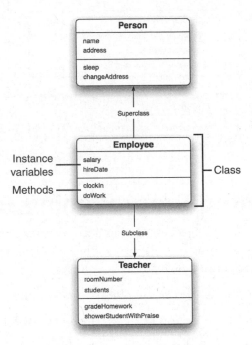

Object-oriented terminology visualized.

One important aspect to note is that Objective-C supports single inheritance only, which means a class can have only one superclass.

The Basics

One of the first things you might notice about Objective-C code is the prolific use of brackets and colons. The syntax of Objective-C is based on Smalltalk, a language developed by Alan Kay at Xerox PARC in the 1970s. Smalltalk is object-oriented programming language taken to the extreme: absolutely everything is an object in Smalltalk. Objective-C, on the other hand, borrows the syntax while supporting C-style primitives, such as ints, floats, and chars.

To get a better handle on Objective-C, the following sections walk you through the syntax and conventions used in the language.

Named Parameters

If you have worked with languages like Java, C, PHP, or almost any other popular programming language, you are likely familiar with code like the following:

```
String xml = xmlParser.parse("data.xml", 4);
```

You can probably figure out the first parameter, but what does that 4 mean? You normally have to hunt down the definition of the parse method or look it up in the documentation (if it exists) to see what that second parameter does.

Objective-C takes a more verbose approach by requiring named parameters in method names. In Objective-C, the parse method would look something like this:

```
NSString *xml =
  [xmlParser parseDocumentNamed:@"data.xml" maxDepth:4];
```

Notice how much more readable the method name is? Every time you call a method, you include the parameter names in the method call itself. This makes Objective-C code much more self-documenting and easy to understand compared to languages that don't use named parameters.

Messages, Selectors, and Methods

When a method is invoked on a particular object, new terminology is used to describe this method call. Here is the breakdown:

- **Message:** Tells an object to invoke a particular method.
- **Receiver:** The object which receives a message.
- **Selector:** The string of characters that represent the *name* of a message.
- **Method:** The code that is invoked when a message is sent to a receiver.

To make this relationship a bit more clear, take the following example:

```
// Assume voter is a valid object and castBallot is defined
Person *voter = ...;
[voter castBallot];
```

In the previous example, the terms are broken down as follows:

- castBallot is the **message**.

- voter is the **receiver**.

- The string castBallot is the **selector**.

- The castBallot function defined in the Person class is the **method**.

Multiple Parameters

One part of Objective-C that can be a little tricky are methods that take in multiple parameters. The names of the parameters are actually part of the method name. Take these method calls, for instance:

```
[object doThing];
[object doThingWithNumber:42];
[object doThingWithNumber:42 andString:@"dolphins"];
```

In the first example, doThing is a method that takes in no parameters. Note that it is defined in a completely different block of code than doThingWithNumber:, which takes in a single argument. The third example is clearer in that it takes in two arguments, but it also is defined in a completely different block of code than the first two. The name of the message in the third example is doThingWithNumber:andString:, which includes both named parameters.

Objects

There are a couple root-level types of objects you should know : NSObject and id.

NSObject

Most objects you encounter in iPhone programming inherit from the same root superclass: NSObject. NSObject is one of the core classes provided by the *Foundation* framework, and among other things it provides the basics of memory management. Memory management is covered in detail in the next chapter, but for now, you should know that NSObject will be the root node of your class hierarchy most of the time.

> **DEFINITION**
>
> **Foundation** is a Cocoa Touch framework that defines the building blocks for your Objective-C classes. The framework includes the root NSObject class as well as classes for managing collections, representing dates, and building strings.

The id Type

In addition to NSObject, Objective-C offers a way to define a loosely typed object: id. Any object in Objective-C can be set as an id variable without the need for casting.

The power of id lies in the fact that you can send *any* message to an object of type id, and it will compile, no questions asked. Even if the method is not actually defined on the object, the application will run just fine until the method is actually called.

```
// Assume someMethod doesn't exist

// Assume these two objects are properly initialized
NSObject *stronglyTypedObject = ...;
id looselyTypedObject = ...;

// This line causes a compile warning
[stronglyTypedObject someMethod];

// This line compiles, but causes a crash if called at runtime
[looselyTypedObject someMethod];
```

The difference between a strongly typed object and a loosely typed object is shown in the preceding code. Note the lack of a * before the id object name. This is intentional. It is a bit confusing, but id objects are still pointers without the * syntax. If you're familiar with C, think of the id keyword as being synonymous with void *.

Objective-C is a dynamic language, meaning you can get away with a lot more at compile time than you can in other languages. For instance, you can even wait until runtime to define entire classes and methods. Using id to define variables is one way to take advantage of these dynamic properties, but most of the time in this book you will use strongly typed objects, such as NSObject, NSString, and UIButton. This way, compile-time warnings can help you catch errors early.

ONE MORE THING

Here's a bit of trivia for you: the NS in NSObject is short for NeXTSTEP, the operating system Steve Jobs built at NeXT Computer before it was acquired by Apple in 1996.

The nil Pointer

In Java, you can set an object to null to point it to the empty memory address. In C, you set a pointer to NULL to produce the same effect. In Objective-C, you set an object to nil.

One of the features of a nil pointer that other languages don't have is the ability to send messages to a nil pointer *without causing an exception* (looking at your NullPointerException, Java). See the code that follows for an example:

```
Person *voter = nil;

 [voter castBallot];
// castBallot does nothing, and doesn't crash!
```

What happens when you send a message to a nil pointer? Absolutely nothing. It's as if the call never happened, meaning you don't have to manually check for nil values all over the place.

This resilient behavior can be very useful as it helps you avoid writing a lot of error-handling code. But it can also cause trouble, since messages to an unexpectedly nil pointer will silently fail.

Classes in Objective-C

All Objective-C classes are split into two files: the interface and the implementation. The interface is where you declare your class and the instance variables it will contain. The interface is also where you declare all the public methods the class will present to the world. You only include the method header, not its body, in the interface.

The implementation, on the other hand, is where you write the methods you declared in the interface. You can also define private methods in the implementation file, simply by not including those method headers in the public interface file.

Interface

Let's look at an example. Here is the Shape.h interface file for a simple `Shape` class:

```
// Shape.h

#import <Foundation/Foundation.h>

@interface Shape : NSObject
{
    int numberOfSides;
}
- (int)numberOfSides;
- (void)setNumberOfSides:(int)inputNumberOfSides;
@end
```

Let's break it down line by line:

```
#import <Foundation/Foundation.h>
```

Here, the `Foundation` framework is imported—the part of Cocoa Touch that gives you access to `NSObject`, `id`, and all the basic utility classes, such as `NSString`, `NSArray`, and `NSDictionary`.

```
@interface Shape : NSObject
```

This is your class declaration. After the `@interface` is your class name, and after the colon is the superclass. Unlike Java, you must *always* declare a superclass in Objective-C.

```
{
    int numberOfSides;
}
```

Inside the braces of the class declaration is where you define your class instance variables. Instance variables may be typed as C primitives, like `int`s and `float`s, or as pointers to Objective-C object types. In this case, there is a single variable declared using the C primitive `int`.

```
- (int)numberOfSides;
```

The section between the end brace and the `@end` statement is where you define the public API for your class. The "–" at the beginning of the method indicates that it is a method you call on an instance of the class. A "+" in that spot indicates a *class method*, one that you call on the class itself—just like a static method in Java.

> **DEFINITION**
>
> A **class method** is a method that you call on a class, not an instance of that class. A class method is prefixed with + while an instance method is prefixed with -.

The return type of the method is shown in the parentheses, in this case an int. The name of the method follows.

```
- (void)setNumberOfSides:(int)inputNumberOfSides;
```

Again, the - indicates this is a method you call on an object that is an instance of the Shape class and not the Shape class itself. The return type is void, which means that it doesn't return anything. The method takes in a single parameter of type int.

```
@end
```

The @end directive indicates the end of the Shape class declaration.

Implementation

That covers the interface file. What about the implementation file? The Shape.m implementation file looks like the following:

```
// Shape.m

#import "Shape.h"

@implementation Shape

- (int)numberOfSides
{
    return numberOfSides;
}
- (void)setNumberOfSides:(int)inputNumberOfSides
{
    numberOfSides = inputNumberOfSides;
}
@end
```

Let's break it apart and look at each piece:

```
#import "Shape.h"
```

The implementation file must always include the corresponding interface file.

```
@implementation Shape
```

The `@implementation` directive is followed by the name of the class. This line signals that every method defined after this point is for the `Shape` class.

```
- (int)numberOfSides
{
    return numberOfSides;
}
```

This is the getter method body for the `numberOfSides` instance variable. Notice the naming scheme. In Java, you would normally define `getNumberOfSides` as the getter name, but in Objective-C, it is convention to simply use the name of the instance variable as the getter name.

```
- (void)setNumberOfSides:(int)inputNumberOfSides
{
    numberOfSides = inputNumberOfSides;
}
```

This is the setter method body for the `numberOfSides` instance variable. As you can see, it simply sets the `numberOfSides` instance variable to the input value.

In the next chapter, you will see how to generate both getter and setter methods for your instance variables so you don't have write the tedious code over and over again.

Up Next

Understanding Objective-C is crucial in moving to the next level of iPhone development. You will find that more of your time will be spent in the trenches, piecing together code bit by bit until your masterpiece is complete. In this chapter, you took the first steps toward getting there. After reviewing OOP and seeing how an example class is structured, code files should start to look a little more comprehensible.

In the next chapter, you will be introduced to memory management in Objective-C. Memory management is the single most aggravating, bug-inducing topic in all of iPhone development, but you will learn the rules that make it quite painless. You will also be introduced to properties and some core utility classes you will use frequently in iPhone development.

The Least You Need to Know

- The iPhone OS is a direct descendant of Mac OS X.
- In Objective-C, a message is a way of invoking a method on an object.
- You can safely send messages to a `nil` pointer.
- Class headers are defined in .h interface files, and method bodies for the class are defined in .m implementation files.

Memory Management

In This Chapter

- Why there is no garbage collector
- Reference counting
- The golden rules of memory management
- Properties

Imagine your app crashes, providing very few details in the console beyond the cryptic string EXC_BAD_ACCESS. Now, multiply the aggravation you feel 100-fold as this EXC_BAD_ACCESS message shows up repeatedly while developing your app. You slowly move code around and hack until the errors go away, but you're left with code you completely don't understand anymore. How did this happen?

You have just roughly approximated the experience of almost every Cocoa developer to come before you. EXC_BAD_ACCESS is a sign of problems with memory management in your app. Memory management is by far the leading cause of pain and misery for new iPhone and iPad developers. However, the rules for memory management are quite simple. Applying them consistently in your application is the hard part. In this chapter, you learn the rules, best practices, and common errors associated with memory management in order to master the topic that has tripped up countless developers, including myself.

Introduction to Memory Management

Now, wait a minute. Haven't we as a species advanced to the point where we don't need to worry about managing memory? Why on Earth should we manage memory when garbage collection algorithms can do just as good a job (or better!)? Look at Java, C#, or any web programming language today. They all use garbage collection and leave you with mental bandwidth so you can solve *real* problems instead of mucking around with allocating and deallocating memory.

In fact, even the desktop Mac programming environment offers garbage collection. So you may be surprised to find out that the iPhone OS does not use garbage collection at all.

Why did Apple make this decision? In a word: performance. A garbage collector is like an unruly teenager. It interrupts you when you're busy, takes forever to do chores, and requires a lot of energy to keep under control. Similarly, garbage collectors interrupt processes, chew up precious computing time, and you never know when they will finish. The iPhone OS does away with the garbage collector and instead relies on you, the programmer, to make sure memory is managed correctly.

However, instead of leaving you at the mercy of the C functions malloc() and free(), Apple provides a rather elegant system for managing memory: reference counting.

Reference Counting

Reference counting is a system for keeping track of the number of pointers that point to the same object in memory. When an object is first initialized, it is created with a reference count of 1. If another object wants to maintain a reference to the first object, then it increments the reference count to 2. When the object is done with the referenced object, it decrements the reference count. When the reference count reaches zero, the object is deallocated, and its memory is ready to be reused.

To initialize a new object with a reference count of 1, use the alloc/init pattern.

alloc/init

To construct a new object, you use the alloc/init methods:

```
Person *voter = [[Person alloc] init];

// voter now has a reference count of 1
```

THERE'S A TIP FOR THAT

A common practice in Objective-C development is chaining message calls together. The init message is sent to the result of the [Person alloc] message.

alloc/init is the equivalent of a default constructor in other object-oriented languages, like Java. The `alloc` message grabs a block of memory sufficient to store a Person object, and the `init` method sets up the object's initial state. It is very common to customize the `init` method to perform more setup. You can even define custom initializer methods that accept additional parameters.

retain/release

To increase the reference count for an object, you send it the `retain` message. When you are finished with the object and don't need it anymore, you decrease the reference count by sending it the `release` message. For instance:

```
Person *voter = [[Person alloc] init];
// voter now has a reference count of 1

[voter retain];
// voter now has a reference count of 2

[voter release];
// voter now has a reference count of 1
```

At its root, there is really only one rule to memory management: if you increase the reference count, you must decrease it. Both alloc/init and retain increase the reference count for an object, and you must make sure there is a corresponding release. If you follow this one rule, you can always have perfect memory management, though it's easier said than done.

dealloc

When the reference count reaches 0, the object is deallocated. Before the memory is handed over to the operating system, however, the object is sent the `dealloc` message. This gives the object a chance to release any instance variables it may have retained. The `dealloc` message is sent to the voter object in the code below:

```
Person *voter = [[Person alloc] init];
// voter now has a reference count of 1

[voter retain];
// voter now has a reference count of 2

[voter release];
// voter now has a reference count of 1
```

continues

```
[voter release];
// voter now has a reference count of 0,
// so voter is sent the dealloc message.
// After [voter dealloc] finishes,
// the voter object is completely freed.
```

CRASH AND LEARN

Never ever call dealloc directly. It is invoked automatically by the reference counting system. If you find that it isn't being called when it should, it means you are likely missing a release call somewhere. You have been warned!

As you can see in the preceding code, when the voter object is released for the second time, its reference count is set to 0. The dealloc message is automatically sent to the voter object as soon as this happens, and then the memory is freed.

Memory-Related Crashes

What happens if you try to send a message to this voter object after it has been freed? You are trying to access memory that doesn't belong to you anymore, and the OS doesn't take kindly to such transgressions. Say you have the following code, again based on the voter example:

```
Person *voter = [[Person alloc] init];
// voter now has a reference count of 1

[voter retain];
// voter now has a reference count of 2

[voter release];
// voter now has a reference count of 1

[voter release];
// voter now has a reference count of 0 and is freed

[voter release];
// Crash!
```

As shown in the previous code, trying to send a message to a freed object results in a crash. This is a very common error. If you find your app crashes inexplicably, make sure you haven't accidentally released one of the objects you wanted to keep around.

Memory Leaks

You may be familiar with the term, but what exactly does *memory leak* mean in the context of reference counting? Let's take a look at the following code:

```
Person *voter = [[Person alloc] init];
// voter now has a reference count of 1

// voter is not released anywhere
```

DEFINITION

In iPhone programming, a **memory leak** is a bug caused when an object is retained more times than it is released. As long as the retain count is greater than zero, the object will remain in memory, thus resulting in a memory leak.

`voter` is allocated and initialized with a reference count of 1. However, assume there is no corresponding release. What happens to the voter object? Because its reference count never goes to 0, it is never deallocated. This means it sticks around ... forever (or at least for the lifetime of your application). This is the definition of a memory leak in iPhone programming.

With the limited amount of memory you have at your disposal in the first place, memory leaks can seriously jeopardize the performance of your application and can even cause the OS to forcibly quit your app for using too much memory. There are tools available that can help you identify memory leaks. However, you can avoid memory leaks altogether simply by practicing sound memory management.

THERE'S A TIP FOR THAT

You do not need to do any memory management for primitive C types, like `int`, `float`, and `char`. The memory management techniques listed here only apply to pointers in your application.

Autorelease

There is one last concept you need to know to properly manage memory: autorelease. Autorelease is best illustrated and explained using an example.

An Example

Imagine you define a method that creates a new object and returns it:

```
- (Person *)makeVoter
{
  Person *voter = [[Person alloc] init];

  return voter;
  // Result: memory leak!
}
```

At first glance, the code might look fine, but there is a problem. The voter object is leaked because there is no corresponding release to balance the alloc/init.

To fix this, let's try adding a release to balance the alloc/init:

```
- (Person *)makeVoter
{
  Person *voter = [[Person alloc] init];
  [voter release];

  return voter;
  // Result: voter is deallocated!
}
```

The code is fixed, right? Let's count the references: when voter is initialized, the reference count is 1. Then, release is immediately called, decreasing the reference count to 0. The voter is now deallocated. Then, you return a pointer to the voter, but the pointer now points to junk memory!

So releasing isn't the correct solution, either. What's the solution? Autorelease is the answer:

```
- (Person *)makeVoter
{
  Person *voter = [[Person alloc] init];
  [voter autorelease];

  return voter;
  // Result: just right!
}
```

Autorelease sends a release message to the voter object, but *not right away*. Instead, voter will stick around long enough for the caller to use the makeVoter method to retain the object if they like. As far as the makeVoter method is concerned, it has completely satisfied its retain/release obligations.

Autorelease is primarily used as shown in the example—to create and return new objects.

CRASH AND LEARN

Although it may seem like magic, autorelease is not a silver bullet you can use to fix all your memory management issues. Balancing your retain/release calls is the only true way to ensure you don't have memory-related bugs.

Golden Rules of Memory Management

So now that you know about alloc/init, retain/release, and autorelease, it's time to go over two of the golden rules of memory management.

1. **If you retain it, you release it.** Use the NARC rule to determine if you have retained an object. The NARC rule states that each time you call the following methods, you must call release or autorelease to match:

   - **+new:** new is a convenience method that combines alloc/init into a single call. alloc/init is used much more heavily in iPhone development, however.

   - **+alloc:** alloc is used in the alloc/init pattern.

   - **–retain:** retain increases the reference count for an object by 1.

   - **–copy:** copy, for objects that support it, creates a new instance of the object that has the same data as the object it was called on.

2. **If you assign an object to the result of a method, and the NARC rule does not apply, you do not need to release it.** This means you can use the objects these methods return without retaining them. For example:

```
// Assume the makeVoter method is defined
Person *evan = [Person makeVoter];

[evan castBallot];

// You are done with evan, but you don't need to release him!
```

In the preceding code, you can apply the golden rules to determine what kind of memory management to use. First, you should ask, "Does NARC apply?" Let's see, you don't call new, alloc, retain, or copy. So no, NARC doesn't apply. Because NARC doesn't apply, then you *do not* need to release the object.

It will take time and practice to fully master memory management on the iPhone and iPad, but you will have plenty of chances to apply what you learned here as you continue to build more and more apps.

Properties

A *property* is an Objective-C convenience that automates the creation of getters and setters for your class. In Chapter 5, you defined a Shape class and manually defined the getters and setters. Here is the Shape class definition without using properties:

```
// Shape.h

#import <Foundation/Foundation.h>

@interface Shape : NSObject
{
    int numberOfSides;
}

- (int)numberOfSides;
- (void)setNumberOfSides:(int)inputNumberOfSides;

@end
```

DEFINITION

A **property** provides a simple way to implement an object's getter and setter methods. @property is used to define a property, and @synthesize is then used to generate the getter and setter for the property.

You can automate the creation of the getter and setter methods for the numberOf-Sides instance variable by declaring a property in the header file.

```
// Shape.h

#import <Foundation/Foundation.h>

@interface Shape : NSObject
{
    int numberOfSides;
}
@property (assign) int numberOfSides;
@end
```

In the previous code, the @property combines both getter and setter for numberOfSides into a single line.

You can see an even more dramatic savings in lines of code in the implementation file. Here is the original Shape implementation file:

```
// Shape.m

#import "Shape.h"

@implementation Shape
- (int)numberOfSides
{
    return numberOfSides;
}
- (void)setNumberOfSides:(int)inputNumberOfSides
{
    numberOfSides = inputNumberOfSides;
}
@end
```

The implementation file using properties simplifies to the following:

```
// Shape.m

#import "Shape.h"

@implementation Shape
@synthesize numberOfSides;
@end
```

The @synthesize directive is used to automatically generate the getter and setter methods for the numberOfSides property. As you can see in the Shape example, you save a lot of code (and tedium) by using properties.

Dot Syntax

Properties not only save code, they also allow you to interact with the Shape object using *dot syntax*. Although you can still use messages to access the getter and setter for a property, you can also use dot syntax to do the same. For an example, see the following code.

DEFINITION

Dot syntax gives you the ability to access and set properties of objects using dots. Properties can also be accessed and set using messages, but dot syntax is often more convenient.

```
Shape *shape = [[Shape alloc] init];

// Use dot-syntax to set the property
shape.numberOfSides = 5;

// Access the property value using dot-syntax
NSLog(@"The shape has %d sides", shape.numberOfSides);

// Remember proper memory management!
[shape release];
```

As shown in the preceding code, you can both assign and retrieve the numberOfSides value using dot-syntax.

Attributes

In the property declaration, assign is one of several *attributes* that modify property behavior. These attributes modify how the property manages memory and whether the property is read-only, among other things. The following table details all possible attributes:

Property Attributes

Attribute	Category*	Explanation
assign	Memory behavior	This is the default setter behavior. Uses simple assignment to set the value. Use this attribute for all C primitives (int, float, char, and so on).
retain	Memory behavior	Releases the previous value, and retains the new value. Use this for object pointers.
copy	Memory behavior	Releases the previous value, and sends the copy message to the new value. You will only really use this for NSStrings.

Attribute	Category*	Explanation
nonatomic	Multi-threading	By default, properties are atomic, which incurs a small overhead but ensures your properties are thread-safe. If you aren't using threads, use this attribute for a small performance boost.
readwrite	Writability	This is the default writability setting. This attribute generates both getter and setter when @synthesize is invoked.
readonly	Writability	Use this attribute to generate only the getter method for your property when @synthesize is invoked.
getter=	Getter name	Specifies the name of the getter method to use for the property.
setter=	Setter name	Specifies the name of the setter method to use for the property.

You can define only one attribute for each category.

As you can see, attributes can drastically change how your property is implemented under the hood.

Instance Variable Not Required

Properties are primarily used to automate the generation of the getter and setter methods for instance variables in a class. However, they don't necessarily need an instance variable. Including the @property directive in your interface file just means that the getter and setter methods must exist in the implementation file. @synthesize automatically generates those methods, but you can also define them yourself.

To illustrate this fact, let's add a property for determining whether the shape is a polygon or not:

```
// Shape.h

#import <Foundation/Foundation.h>

@interface Shape : NSObject
{
   int numberOfSides;
}

@property (assign) int numberOfSides;
@property (readonly) BOOL isPolygon;

@end
```

Notice how isPolygon uses the readonly attribute. This ensures that a setter is not generated for the property.

The updated implementation file for the Shape class is as follows:

```
// Shape.m

#import "Shape.h"

@implementation Shape

@synthesize numberOfSides;

// getter for isPolygon property
- (BOOL)isPolygon
{
   // polygons have 3 or more sides
   return numberOfSides >= 3;
}
@end
```

Notice how the property is not synthesized. A custom getter method is defined instead. Also, it is important that the method signature for isPolygon looks as it does in the preceding code. Unless you use the getter= and setter= attributes, your method header for properties must match the previous format *exactly*.

Objective-C Complete

That concludes your whirlwind tour of the Objective-C language. In this chapter, you learned about two core concepts: memory management and properties. If it all seems a bit overwhelming right now, don't worry; you will have plenty of opportunities during the next several chapters to try out what you learned here.

This chapter also concludes Part 1 of this book. In Part 2, you learn how to use some of the excellent user interface elements offered by the UIKit framework. You will also begin to code in earnest, so get ready to put your Objective-C knowledge to good use!

The Least You Need to Know

- Instead of garbage collection, the iPhone uses reference counting.
- The golden rule of memory management: if you retain it, you release it.
- Each time you call NARC (new, alloc, retain, or copy), you are responsible for calling release or autorelease.
- Autorelease delays sending the release message until a later point in time.
- Properties can be used to automatically generate getters and setters for your instance variables.
- You can use dot-syntax to access or modify properties.

Building Your
User Interface

Arguably the most important part of your entire application is the user interface. Interface Builder makes building your user interface a snap. Many of the controls you see in the built-in applications on your phone—switches, spinners, text fields—are at your disposal in Interface Builder. Learn best practices for adding these elements to your interface and, more importantly, how to make them do what you want in code.

Switches, Sliders, and Controls

In This Chapter

- Built-in user interface controls
- Adding switches, sliders, and segmented controls to your app
- The Fonts app
- Modify labels using `UIFont` and `NSString` classes

When was the last time you entered data into a form on the web? Likely, it wasn't too long ago. Perhaps you had to provide an absurd amount of information, checking checkboxes and clicking radio buttons until you wanted to cry. And this is a scenario you have probably repeated hundreds of times, filling out forms for this and that on the web.

At this point, seeing and using the controls on these forms is second nature for you. However, did you know that you won't find a single checkbox, radio button, or drop-down menu anywhere in the interface of native applications? When Apple built the iPhone, they developed a set of basic controls specially targeted toward a handheld device. In this chapter, you will learn how to use three of these controls: switches, sliders, and segmented controls.

Basic Built-In Controls

Several of the controls on the iPhone and iPad are similar to controls you are accustomed to on the desktop. For instance, the slider control looks very much like sliders you would see in a Java or C# application. However, other controls are unique to the iPhone OS and take advantage of the touch-friendly screen.

Here is a quick overview of the controls covered in this chapter:

- **Switch:** A switch is used to toggle between Boolean values. You normally use switches to turn on or off certain settings or features in your app. In code, a switch is represented using the UISwitch class.

- **Slider:** A slider is used to specify a numeric value within a range of values. In the iPhone and iPad Settings application, you use sliders for controlling volume and brightness. In code, a slider is represented via the UISlider class.

- **Segmented Control:** A segmented control is a multiple-choice control that allows you to select a single value. In essence, it behaves exactly like a radio button. In code, a segmented control is represented via the UISegementedControl class.

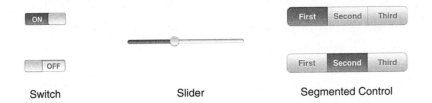

Switch   Slider   Segmented Control

You will experiment with switches, sliders, and segmented controls in this chapter.

You can see what the controls look like in the previous image.

CRASH AND LEARN

Although you might miss it, do not add your own custom checkbox to your app. To stay within the Apple interface guidelines, you should find some other way to get the desired feedback from the user without using checkboxes.

You will master these controls by building a sample app that makes good use of them. And remember all that Objective-C you learned in the previous two chapters? You finally get a chance to try it out.

Fonts App

For the rest of this chapter, you will build the Fonts app, shown in the following image.

You can use the Fonts app to experiment with fonts.

The font controls are used to update the font of the text in the bordered section. You will use the following strategy to build the app:

1. Create the Fonts project in Xcode.

2. Construct the interface.

3. Add outlets and actions to the view controller code file.

4. Hook up the controller and the interface in Interface Builder.

5. Add a few helper methods to the controller that will update the font of the displayed string.

In Chapter 4, you completed steps 1 through 4. If you run into trouble with these steps, refer back to Chapter 4 where these steps were explained in detail.

Build the Interface

Just like ICE and iShockU, you will first create the project, as laid out in the following steps:

1. In Xcode, create a new project using the View-based Application template.

2. Name the project "Fonts."

3. Open FontsViewController.xib.

4. Now that Interface Builder is running, build your interface so that it matches the following image:

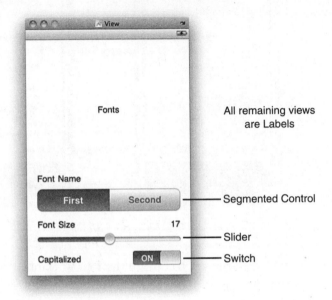

Your interface should match the one shown.

THERE'S A TIP FOR THAT

To find the segmented control, slider, and switch controls, set the **library window** filter to Library > Cocoa Touch > Inputs & Values.

5. Select **segmented control**. Double-click the side labeled "First" and change it to **"Helvetica."** Double-click the side labeled "Second" and change it to **"Marker Felt."**

6. Select the slider. In the Attributes tab of the inspector window, set the following properties:

Minimum: 10

Maximum: 42

Initial: 17

The font size will range from sizes 10 to 42 and start at size 17.

7. Now you are going to add an image of a frame around the "Fonts" label in the top section. Download the following image, and add it to the project: http://troybrant.net/iphonebook/chapter7/frame.png.

CRASH AND LEARN

It has been mentioned a couple times already, but always remember to check **Copy items into destination group's folder** when adding an image (or other resource) to your project.

8. Back in Interface Builder, drag an image view on top of the "Fonts" label. Using the inspector window, set the image of the image view to **frame.png**.

9. That's strange. Where did the text go? And where is the image? There is only white space where text and the image view were a moment before. What happened? Two things happened: first, the image view was added to the view hierarchy after the label, so it is drawn *on top* of the label. Second, the image view might appear empty, but you are just seeing the center of the image, which itself is pure white and too big for the image view to display completely.

To fix the first problem, you need to move the image view behind the label in the view hierarchy. You can achieve this by adjusting the order of the views in the document window. As demonstrated in the following image, drag the image view object from the bottom of the list to the top, so that it is beneath all other views in the interface.

To fix the second problem, you need to adjust the Mode setting of the image view. I recommend setting the Mode to **Scale To Fill** and resizing the image view until it fills the top section.

THERE'S A TIP FOR THAT

Does your document window show a set of icons instead of a list? To see the list (and the view hierarchy), set the **View Mode** in your document window to **list mode** (the middle option). Expand the triangle next to the View object to see the full view hierarchy.

Move the Image View object to the top of the view hierarchy to see the "Fonts" label again.

After the dust settles, you should have built the following interface:

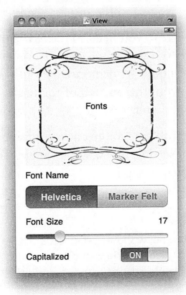

Isn't it beautiful?

If your interface does indeed match, then you have completed step 1. Just as you did in iShockU, your next step is to write the outlets and actions for the controller in Xcode.

Add Outlets and Actions to the Controller

Back in Xcode, add the instance variables, properties, and action methods so that your FontsViewController.h interface file matches the following code:

```
// FontsViewController.h

#import <UIKit/UIKit.h>

@interface FontsViewController : UIViewController
{
  UILabel *resultLabel;
  UISegmentedControl *fontNameControl;
  UILabel *fontSizeNumberLabel;
  UISlider *fontSizeSlider;
  UISwitch *capitalizedSwitch;
}

@property (nonatomic, retain) IBOutlet UILabel *resultLabel;
@property (nonatomic, retain) IBOutlet UISegmentedControl
                                *fontNameControl;
@property (nonatomic, retain) IBOutlet UILabel *fontSizeNumberLabel;
@property (nonatomic, retain) IBOutlet UISlider *fontSizeSlider;
@property (nonatomic, retain) IBOutlet UISwitch *capitalizedSwitch;

- (IBAction)fontNameControlValueChanged:(id)sender;
- (IBAction)fontSizeSliderValueChanged:(id)sender;
- (IBAction)capitalizedSwitchValueChanged:(id)sender;

@end
```

Some important things to note about the preceding code:

- The UIKit framework provides the UISegmentedControl, UISlider, and UISwitch classes.

- Notice you have not defined instance variables for every view in the interface. Instead, you will define instance variables only for the views needed to update the interface. For instance, the label titled "Font Name" does not change, so you do not need a reference to it in code.

- In the property declarations, notice the use of nonatomic and retain. As explained in Chapter 6, nonatomic gives your app a small performance boost while retain ensures proper memory management.

CRASH AND LEARN

The nonatomic attribute should only be used if you intend to access a property from a single thread.

- What is IBOutlet? IBOutlet is just a keyword that Interface Builder looks for when searching your code for outlets and actions. Without IBOutlet, Interface Builder would not be able to see the outlet.

- What is IBAction? Like IBOutlet, IBAction is a keyword that informs Interface Builder the action can be hooked up to the interface.

ONE MORE THING

IBOutlet and IBAction do not affect the behavior of your code in any way. When compiled, IBOutlet maps to empty space and IBAction maps to void.

Now, make the changes necessary so your FontsViewController.m implementation file matches the following:

```
// FontsViewController.m

#import "FontsViewController.h"

@implementation FontsViewController

@synthesize resultLabel;
@synthesize fontNameControl;
@synthesize fontSizeNumberLabel;
@synthesize fontSizeSlider;
@synthesize capitalizedSwitch;

- (IBAction)fontNameControlValueChanged:(id)sender
{
  NSLog(@"font name changed");
}
- (IBAction)fontSizeSliderValueChanged:(id)sender
{
  NSLog(@"font size changed");
}
- (IBAction)capitalizedSwitchValueChanged:(id)sender
{
```

```
    NSLog(@"font capitalized changed");
}

- (void)dealloc
{
    [resultLabel release];
    [fontNameControl release];
    [fontSizeNumberLabel release];
    [fontSizeSlider release];
    [capitalizedSwitch release];
    [super dealloc];
}

@end
```

There are a few things to note in the preceding code:

- Each property is synthesized so the getter and setter for that property are automatically generated.

- Instead of assuming the interface elements are wired to the controller correctly, the code above tests the connection by printing a string to console when each control is changed. You should always start small with tests like these instead of trying to code all the functionality at once.

- Notice how you release all the instance variables in `dealloc`. You always—without exception—need to release your instance variables in the `dealloc` method for a class.

Save your changes, build, and then run the project. After the application launches in the iPhone Simulator, you can try to manipulate the interface. However, you will notice that you don't see the log messages in the console. The output does not appear because you have not hooked up the controller to the interface. Wiring the controller to the interface is the next step.

Hook It Up

Just like in Chapter 4, you are going to switch back to Interface Builder to hook up the controller to the interface elements. To wire the pieces together, follow these steps:

1. Make sure the FontsViewController.xib file is open in Interface Builder.

2. In the document window, select **File's Owner** (which is the FontsViewController class you just modified).

3. Connect the outlets to their corresponding views in the interface, as shown in the following diagram:

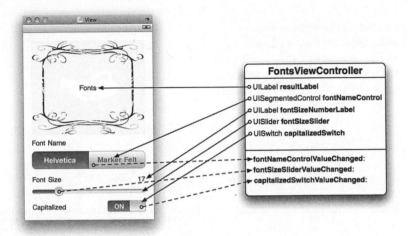

Connect the outlets and actions to the interface.

4. Connect the `capitalizedSwitchValueChanged:` action to the Value Changed event for the switch. As the event name implies, every time the switch value changes, your action method will get called.

5. Similarly, connect the `fontNameControlValueChanged:` action to the Value Changed event for the segmented control.

6. Finally, connect the `fontSizeSliderValueChanged:` action to the Value Changed event for the slider.

Now, switch back to Xcode, save your project, and try running it in the simulator. Try all three of your controls, and if you see the log output in the console, then the controller is wired correctly to the interface! If you do not see the log output, double-check your connections in Interface Builder, and make sure you connect to the action methods to the Value Changed action.

The only step remaining is to update the `resultLabel` in the controller's action methods.

Time to Code

When the user slides the slider, toggles the switch, or taps the segmented control, you need to update the `resultLabel` so it reflects changes the user just made. To edit the font name and font size of the label, you will use the `UIFont` class. Using the `UIFont` class, you can control font properties like the font family, font size, and whether to bold or italicize a particular string. However, to control capitalization, you use built-in methods on the `NSString` class.

The `UILabel` class has two properties for manipulating its appearance. You will use the `text` property to modify the `NSString` object and the `font` property to modify the `UIFont` object.

updateText

To get started, let's write a helper method that updates the text property of the `resultLabel` object. Add the following method under your last `@synthesize` directive:

```
// FontsViewController.m

- (void)updateText
{
    // grab the string
    NSString *text = resultLabel.text;

    // change the string based on the switch setting
    if (capitalizedSwitch.on)
    {
        text = [text capitalizedString];
    }
    else
    {
        text = [text lowercaseString];
    }

    // update the label text property
    resultLabel.text = text;
}
```

ONE MORE THING

BOOL is the Boolean type used in Objective-C. The possible values for BOOL are YES and NO. This may take some getting used to since most every other language uses some variation of true and false.

Checking the state of the switch is simple. The switch has an on property, that returns YES in the on state; otherwise, the property returns NO.

When the switch is on, the string is capitalized using the capitalizedString method on NSString. This method capitalizes the first letter of each word in the string. For instance, the string "new york city" becomes "New York City" after the capitalizedString method is called. As you might guess, the lowercaseString method converts "New York City" back to "new york city."

By updating the text property of resultLabel, the new string is automatically reflected in the interface the next time it renders.

Also note that you did not call any of the NARC methods on the modified string, so you do not have to release it.

updateFont

Now, you need to write a helper method that will update the font property of the resultLabel object. Add the following code to the FontsViewController.m file:

```
// FontsViewController.m

- (void)updateFont
{
    // get the font size
    int fontSize = fontSizeSlider.value;

    // update the displayed font size number
    NSString *fontSizeString = [NSString stringWithFormat:@"%d",
        fontSize];
    fontSizeNumberLabel.text = fontSizeString;

    // get the font name
    int selectedFontIndex = fontNameControl.selectedSegmentIndex;
    NSString *fontName =
        [fontNameControl titleForSegmentAtIndex:selectedFontIndex];

    // create a new font
```

```
UIFont *newFont = [UIFont fontWithName:fontName size:fontSize];

// apply the new font to the name label
resultLabel.font = newFont;
}
```

Let's break this method down into easily-digestible chunks:

- The first line fetches the slider's numeric value. The value is actually a float, but you can assign it to an `int` because you don't need the floating-point precision.

- The second part updates the text of the font size label. You have an `int` ready to use, but the text label requires an `NSString` to display. How do you convert the `int` to a string? As shown, `stringWithFormat:` will make this conversion for you.

    `stringWithFormat:` will become one of your greatest assets. You can use it for log messages, primitive conversion, and string concatenation. For a full discussion on how to use string formatting effectively, flip ahead to Chapter 24.

THERE'S A TIP FOR THAT

NSString's `stringWithFormat:` method uses the exact same syntax as the C `printf` function. You can find the `string` formatting guide here: http://developer.apple.com/mac/library/documentation/cocoa/conceptual/Strings/Articles/formatSpecifiers.html.

- Next, the font name is determined using the value of the segmented control. Determining the name string is a two-step process. First, you need to get the currently selected index, which is conveniently available via the `selectedSegmentIndex` property. Next, you get the name of the selected button by sending the segmented control the `titleForSegmentAtIndex:` message with the selected index. Make sure that you spelled the font names correctly when you titled your segmented control!

- Combine the font size from the slider and the font name from the segmented control to construct a new `UIFont` object. Then, it is a simple matter of assigning the font object to the font property of `resultLabel`.

Glue It Together

Now that you have both helper methods defined, you need to call them when the user slides the slider, toggles the switch, or taps the segmented control. You have already added action methods that respond precisely to these events. All you have to do is invoke these helper methods from the action methods already defined:

```
// FontsViewController.m

- (void)updateInterface
{
  [self updateText];
  [self updateFont];
}
- (IBAction)fontNameControlValueChanged:(id)sender {
  [self updateInterface];
}
- (IBAction)fontSizeSliderValueChanged:(id)sender {
  [self updateInterface];
}
- (IBAction)capitalizedSwitchValueChanged:(id)sender {
  [self updateInterface];
}
```

To make the code even more streamlined, the updateInterface calls the updateText and updateFont methods in sequence. Also, the NSLog function calls in your action methods were replaced with calls to this new updateInterface method. Now, every time the switch, slider, or segmented control changes, the resultLabel will be updated with the latest settings. This type of decomposition makes your code easier to read, debug, and maintain in the future.

Try It Out

So, does it work? Save the project, build it, launch it, and give it a whirl. Try the segmented control. Success! Okay, now try the switch at the bottom. Huzzah! Now try the slider! Wait a minute. The text doesn't increase in size if you slide past size 17. What's going on?

CRASH AND LEARN

Do you get a warning that "FontsViewController may not respond to '-update-Text'"? If so, you can get rid of the warning by moving the –updateText method body *above* the line of code that first calls it. This is due to the fact the Xcode compiler only makes a single pass through each source file, so helper methods must be defined before they are first used.

It turns out that by default, UILabel displays only text that fits inside the label bounds. To fix this issue, you need to head back over to Interface Builder and make some changes:

1. Switch back to Interface Builder.

2. Select the "Fonts" label.

3. To display the larger font sizes, you need to make the bounds of the label itself big enough to display a bigger string. So drag the dots on the edges of the "Fonts" label to resize it until the label is as large as the background image view. Use the blue guidelines to help find the edges of the image view.

4. If the label's text is left aligned, select the **center alignment** button in the Layout section of the inspector window (the middle option above the Alignment label).

After you finish making these changes, your windows in Interface Builder should closely match those in the following image.

Now, switch back to Xcode, save your project, and try to run it again. When you try the slider this time, you should see the text grow and shrink as the font size changes. Provided it all works, nice job! You have successfully completed the Fonts application.

Full source code for the finished Fonts application is available online at http://troybrant.net/iphonebook/chapter7/Fonts-done.zip.

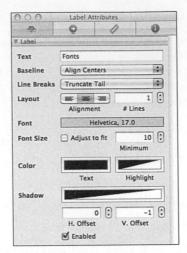

Make sure your settings for the result label match the ones shown here.

Another App in the Books

With the Fonts app complete, you know how to use sliders, switches, and segmented controls in your own apps. In this chapter, you learned how to add these controls to your interface, hook them up to your controller, and access their values in code. Not only that, you built a pretty cool app that lets you play with strings and fonts.

Fonts app: complete.

In the next chapter, you learn about text fields and customization of the software keyboard. More fun lies in the pages ahead.

The Least You Need to Know

- Adding a switch, slider, or segmented control to your interface is as simple as drag-and-drop.
- Use the list view in the document window of Interface Builder if one of your views seems to disappear.
- IBOutlet and IBAction are required in your controller so Interface Builder can detect those outlets and actions.
- Test your controller connections by adding a simple NSLog to your action methods before writing the full methods.
- Connect your action methods to the Value Changed event for all three of the controls you used: switches, sliders, and segmented controls.
- To convert an int to an NSString, use stringWithFormat:.

Text Fields

In This Chapter

- Tip calculator app
- Protocols
- Delegation
- UITextField
- Number formatting

Love it or hate it, the lack of a physical keyboard is one of the defining characteristics of both iPhones and iPads. At first glance, it seems like it would be an awful experience to use the software keyboard, especially if you have big, clumsy fingers. However, with the use of predictive typing techniques and some nifty artificial intelligence, the onscreen keyboard works surprisingly well. Even without tactile feedback, you can quickly type your message, and the phone kindly corrects the big-fingered, clumsy mistakes you happen to make.

Incorporating the keyboard into your application is extraordinarily simple. If you add a text field to your interface, then you get the keyboard for free. In this chapter, you learn how to add these text fields to your interface while building a tip calculator app. You also learn all about protocols, delegation, and keyboard customization along the way.

Tiptacular

Over the course of this chapter, you build one of the essential utility apps—a tip calculator. In the following figure, the app lets the user specify the check amount, tip percentage, and party size using text fields:

The Tiptacular app.

After you enter the check amount and tip percentage, the app displays the tip and the total price of the meal. Also, instead of spending half an hour figuring out how to split the check, you can easily see how much each person owes for the meal.

To build this app, you use the same blueprint that was used for building apps in previous chapters:

1. Build the interface.

2. Define outlets and actions.

3. Hook up the outlets and actions to the interface.

4. Add code to the controller for handling interaction.

Without further ado, let's get started!

UITextField

A text field in the iPhone OS is single line area for entering text. Any time your user needs to enter a small amount of text, such as a username, password, or short description, you should use a text field. In code, text fields are implemented using the `UITextField` class.

When tapped, the software keyboard slides up from the bottom of the screen. You don't have to add any code for this to work; the keyboard is displayed automatically! In fact, almost every aspect of the keyboard is managed by the iPhone OS. If you wish to be notified when buttons are tapped or when the keyboard is dismissed, you must adopt the UITextFieldDelegate protocol and become the text field's delegate. Sound complicated? It's really quite simple. Protocols and delegation are explained in detail later this chapter.

Interface Challenge

Instead of walking you through every step required to build the Tiptacular interface, you are challenged to build the first part yourself using these steps:

1. Create a new View-based Application and name it "Tiptacular."

2. Edit TiptacularViewController.xib so it matches the view shown in the following image:

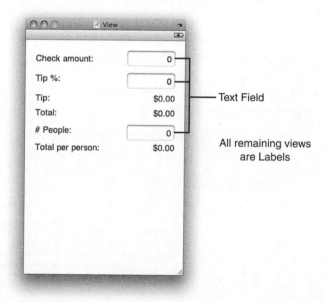

Build your view so it matches the interface shown.

3. Find the Text Field view under the **Library > Cocoa Touch > Inputs & Values** filter in the library window.

4. For each text field, change the font size to **17**.

5. For each text field, use **right** alignment.

6. For each of the "$0.00" labels, use **right** alignment, and resize them so they are as wide as the text fields.

7. Add the following outlets to your `TiptacularViewController` class:

   * `checkAmountTextField` of type `UITextField`

   * `tipPercentTextField` of type `UITextField`

   * `numberOfPeopleTextField` of type `UITextField`

   * `tipLabel` of type `UILabel`

   * `totalLabel` of type `UILabel`

   * `totalPerPersonLabel` of type `UILabel`

THERE'S A TIP FOR THAT

Remember that to add an outlet you must first create the instance variable, then define a property with the `IBOutlet` specifier, and finally synthesize the properties in your implementation file.

8. Release each of your instance variables in the TiptacularViewController.m `dealloc` method.

9. Hook up the outlets as shown in the following image:

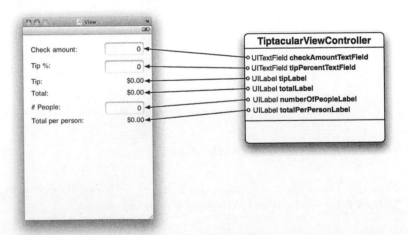

Connect the outlets and actions to the interface.

The previous steps are part of the blueprint you will go through when developing almost any app. Start with the interface, figure out what your outlets and actions are, and hook them up.

Starter code to reach this point is available online at: http://troybrant.net/ iphonebook/chapter8/Tiptacular-starter-code.zip.

ONE MORE THING

Even though the starter code is available on the website, I highly encourage you to try completing the previous steps on your own. The more practice you get writing code, the faster you will become an adept iPhone programmer.

Try It Out

Save your project, build it, and launch it in the iPhone Simulator. If all is well so far, you should see the same interface as the following image:

Tiptacular interface
on launch

Tiptacular after tapping
a text field

When you tap a text field, the keyboard slides up automatically.

Try tapping one of the text fields. With absolutely zero code, the keyboard shows up. Now try to get rid of it. Hmm, it seems you have a problem. After the keyboard shows up, it's there forever, unless you make some changes to the code.

To fix the problem, you need to assign your controller as the delegate for each UITextField. The text field sends messages to its delegate to let it know when certain events take place. To fully understand delegates, however, you need to know a bit about protocols in Objective-C.

Protocols

A *protocol* is a contract that declares a set of methods, which a class must implement. Protocols are equivalent to a Java interface (not to be confused with the Objective-C interface file). In this way, you can ensure that objects of various classes all respond to a particular message.

> **DEFINITION**
>
> A **protocol** defines a set of methods a class must implement. When a class adopts a protocol, it needs to provide a body for each method defined in the protocol or the Xcode compiler will produce a warning. Protocols are used to guarantee that objects of different classes respond to a particular message.

Required Versus Optional Methods

A protocol can contain both required and optional methods. Methods under the @required directive in a protocol *must* be implemented in a class that adopts the protocol. Otherwise, a build warning will result. Methods under the @optional directive in a protocol *can* be implemented, but classes can choose whether they wish to implement them or not.

For example, here is the definition for a protocol named "Edible" that requires the calories method to be defined. The fat, protein, and carbs methods can optionally be defined.

```
// Edible.h

@protocol Edible <NSObject>

@required
```

```
- (float)calories;

@optional
- (float)fat;
- (float)protein;
- (float)carbs;

@end
```

Some notes about the code:

- To declare a protocol, you use the @protocol directive, as shown in the previous code.

- The <NSObject> part of the declaration is the *parent protocol* that the Edible protocol inherits from. That means that any class that implements the Edible methods must also implement the methods for the NSObject protocol. This isn't normally an issue because all objects you deal with in iPhone programming are subclasses of NSObject, and thus implement the required methods.

THERE'S A TIP FOR THAT

This may sound strange, but there is an NSObject *class* and an NSObject *protocol*. The NSObject *class* implements the NSObject *protocol*, in fact. Protocols and classes can share the same name, which can get confusing.

A class can implement a protocol by including it in its declaration. Here is the declaration for a PowerShake class, which promises to implement the Edible methods by including the protocol in its header:

```
// PowerShake.h

#import "<Foundation/Foundation.h>"
#import "Edible.h"

@interface PowerShake : NSObject <Edible>
{
   float calories;
   float protein;
}
@end
```

In the implementation file, you need to fulfill the promise by implementing the protocol methods:

```
// PowerShake.m

@implementation PowerShake

- (float)calories {
    return calories;
}
- (float)protein {
    return protein;
}

// no implementation for optional fat and carbs methods

@end
```

As you can see, you implement the required `calories` method. Because power shakes are used to build muscle and like to brag about how much protein they have, the optional `protein` method is implemented as well. The power shake class would rather not report the astronomical amount of fat and carbs it contains, however. As a result, the compiler is completely happy since it only checks that the required methods are defined.

Protocols, while important in their own right, are especially crucial to understand because they are used in delegation.

Delegation

Delegation at its root is a very simple concept. You can make dinner all by yourself *or* you can delegate the cooking to your deadbeat friends lazing on the couch. You can buy all the party supplies yourself *or* you can delegate buying the drinks to your brother and getting the decorations to your sister. You can build an app all by yourself *or* you can delegate the user interface to your designer friend while you code under the hood.

Delegation on the iPhone OS is no different. Rather than creating a single class with many responsibilities, you can share responsibility among several classes. Delegation makes classes more reusable and maintainable. Many UIKit classes allow customization of their behavior via delegation.

A *delegate* is an object that is notified when it needs to handle a task. The delegate is sent messages by another object that wants to pass off responsibility for a task. How do these two objects agree on which messages to send? That's where protocols come in. The delegating class defines a protocol that its delegate must implement. Then, regardless of the delegate's type, the class instance can safely send the messages to the delegate.

DEFINITION

The **delegate** for a class is notified when key events take place. For instance, the delegate for UITextField is notified when a key is tapped or when the keyboard is dismissed.

It might sound a bit abstract, but you will see exactly how and why to use delegation in the Tiptacular application.

Using the API in Xcode

So how are you supposed to know when a class requires a delegate or not? How do you find out what properties a class supports or even what messages it responds to? What you need is an API to see what havoc you can wreak using these built-in Foundation and UIKit classes.

Of course, the iPhone SDK wouldn't be complete without documentation, and you can conveniently access it both in Xcode and on the web. There are several ways to get to the information you need:

- Find the class or method you're interested in, right-click it, and select **Find Selected Text in API Reference**. This launches the integrated API reference, as shown in the following image.

- In Xcode, select **Help > Documentation** from the top menubar.

- Search for the class or method name from your web browser. Most of the time, the official Apple documentation is in the first few results.

- Finally, you can always access all the SDK materials on http://developer.apple.com/iphone/.

Learning to use the API reference is crucial to developing iPhone and iPad apps. Eventually, this book will end (*sniff*). When it does, you inevitably reach a point where only your wits and the documentation help you. Get used to using it as you go through this book so you can be ready when the day comes where you venture off on your own.

UITextFieldDelegate

Now, let's see delegation in action. You will use delegation in order to dismiss the keyboard for each of the text fields. The general idea is that you assign the controller as the delegate for the text fields. This way you will be notified when the "return" key on the keyboard is tapped.

To achieve this, you must do three things:

1. Add the UITextFieldDelegate protocol to the controller class declaration in the header file.

2. Implement UITextFieldDelegate methods in the controller implementation file.

3. Set the controller as the delegate for each UITextField instance.

After completing these three steps, the text fields will notify the controller when certain events take place—when editing begins or ends and when the return key is pressed, to name a few.

To get started, adopt the UITextFieldDelegate protocol in your class definition in TiptacularViewController.h:

```
// TiptacularViewController.h

// step 1: adhere to the delegate protocol
@interface TiptacularViewController : UIViewController
  <UITextFieldDelegate>
{
```

That takes care of step 1. Next, you need to implement the textFieldShouldReturn delegate method from the UITextFieldDelegate protocol. The textFieldShouldReturn: message is sent to the UITextField's delegate when the return button on the keyboard is pressed. It may be an optional method, but in this case you need to implement it in order to dismiss the keyboard when the user taps the return key.

So add the following code anywhere in the TiptacularViewController.m implementation file:

```
// TiptacularViewController.m

// step 2: implement UITextFieldDelegate methods
- (BOOL)textFieldShouldReturn:(UITextField *)textField
{
    // dismiss the keyboard
    [textField resignFirstResponder];
    return YES;
}
```

What, you expected a dismissKeyboard method or something halfway descriptive to get rid of the keyboard? Don't be silly. The resignFirstResponder method does just the trick, though.

After adding the delegate method, you have taken the first two steps toward adopting the UITextField delegate, but you still have one last bit of wiring to do. For the last step, you need to set the controller as the delegate for each of the text fields. Add the following code to make this change:

```
// TiptacularViewController.m

// Implement viewDidLoad to do additional setup after loading the
    view,
// typically from a nib
- (void)viewDidLoad
{
    [super viewDidLoad];

    // step 3: inform the UITextFields the controller is their delegate
    checkAmountTextField.delegate = self;
    tipPercentTextField.delegate = self;
    numberOfPeopleTextField.delegate = self;
}
```

viewDidLoad is called automatically as part of a view controller's *lifecycle*, which is covered in detail in Chapter 11. In short, the viewDidLoad method is called *after* all the views in your nib file are initialized but *before* the view is actually displayed.

As shown previously, the final step in using delegation for the UITextField is to assign the controller as the delegate object. With this, the wiring is complete, and the keyboard should be dismissed when you tap the return key. Save, build, and give it a try in the simulator. That pesky keyboard will slide away when you tap the return key.

CRASH AND LEARN

If the `textFieldShouldReturn:` method is not called, the most likely cause is that your outlets are not connected to the interface. If the outlets are wired correctly, make sure you didn't misspell the message name. Objective-C is case-sensitive.

Customize the Keyboard

One of the advantages of using a software keyboard is that the iPhone OS can offer any number of specialized key configurations. And in fact, as a developer, you can customize the type of keyboard that slides up for your text fields. There are several custom keyboards available, including the ones shown in the following figure:

Default keyboard   Email keyboard   Number and
                                                  Punctuation keyboard

Three of the software keyboards available in the iPhone OS.

ONE MORE THING

One of the advantages of using a software keyboard is that your application automatically benefits from any future improvements Apple makes to the keyboard. Also, when Apple adds support for new languages, the software keyboard in your app is updated with no effort on your part.

There are also keyboards specially designed for entering URLs, phone numbers, and more.

The text fields for your Tiptacular app are all used for numeric input, so replace the default keyboard with one that has numbers. Also, you customize the return key to display "Done" instead of "return" as well.

You can easily make these changes in Interface Builder:

1. Make sure TiptacularViewController.xib is open in Interface Builder.

2. Select the **Check Amount** text field.

3. In the Attributes tab of the inspector window, you will see a section for Text Input Traits, shown in the image below. For the Keyboard field, select **Numbers & Punctuation**. For the Return Key field, select **Done**.

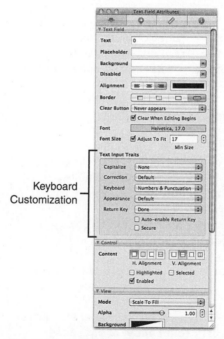

When a text field is selected, the Text Input Traits section allows you to customize the keyboard displayed by the text field.

4. Repeat step 3 for the remaining two text fields.

Save the interface, and launch it again in the iPhone Simulator. Now, when you tap a text field, you will see the Numbers & Punctuation keyboard so you can immediately start entering numbers. You will also see that the grey return key has been replaced with a blue "Done" key, which is better suited for this application.

Computing the Tip

Now, let's add some logic for computing the tip, total price, and price of the meal per person.

Add the following code just below your @synthesize directives in TiptacularViewController.m:

```
// TiptacularViewController.m

// Recalculate tip values, and update the interface
- (void)updateTipTotals
{
    // Get the values from the text fields
    float checkAmount = [checkAmountTextField.text floatValue];
    float tipPercent = [tipPercentTextField.text floatValue];
    int numberOfPeople = [numberOfPeopleTextField.text intValue];

    // Covert from whole numbers (18%) to fraction (0.18)
    tipPercent = tipPercent / 100;

    // recompute the totals
    float tipDue = checkAmount * tipPercent;
    float totalDue = checkAmount + tipDue;
    float totalDuePerPerson = 0;

    // Handle divide by zero
    if (numberOfPeople > 0)
    {
        totalDuePerPerson = totalDue / numberOfPeople;
    }

    // Use a number formatter to generate price strings
    NSNumberFormatter *currencyFormatter =
        [[NSNumberFormatter alloc] init];
    [currencyFormatter setNumberStyle:
        NSNumberFormatterCurrencyStyle];

    // Update the labels
    tipLabel.text =
```

```
        [currencyFormatter stringFromNumber:
                [NSNumber numberWithFloat:tipDue]];
    totalLabel.text =
        [currencyFormatter stringFromNumber:
                [NSNumber numberWithFloat:totalDue]];
    totalPerPersonLabel.text =
        [currencyFormatter stringFromNumber:
                [NSNumber numberWithFloat:totalDuePerPerson]];

    // Remember memory management!
    [currencyFormatter release];
}
```

As you can see, you get the values from the text fields, use them to compute the tip totals, and update the display labels with the computed values. Some parts of the code require a little more explanation, though:

- Notice how you can mix and match dot-syntax with messaging syntax. On the first line of code, you access checkAmountTextField's text property to get the NSString value from the text field. Then send the floatValue message to that NSString object, which—as you may expect—returns a float.

- The NSString floatValue and intValue methods are robust. If the string contains letters or other non-numeric characters, the methods will parse the numbers in the string as best they can.

- To turn the computed values back into strings for display, use the NSNumberFormatter class. Because all the labels display some kind of price value, you just need to set the format style once to NSNumberFormatterCurrencyStyle and use the stringFromNumber: method to generate the strings.

- Remember the golden rule of memory management: if you retain it, you release it. In this case, you use alloc/init to create the NSNumberFormatter, which increments the retain count, so you must balance it out with a release.

After adding the updateTipTotals method, you need to call it in the appropriate place. For Tiptacular, the tip labels should update as soon as the user finishes editing any text field.

One option is to call `updateTipTotals` from `textFieldShouldReturn:`, the delegate method you added earlier. This is actually a nice spot. Every time the Done button is tapped, you update the tip total labels.

However, if you do this, the labels will *not* update if you edit one text field and then tap on another text field. The `UITextFieldDelegate` offers another method you can implement to handle this case. The method is `textFieldDidEndEditing:` and you can add it to your code as shown in the following:

```
// TiptacularViewController.m

// Called when the user finishes editing a text field
- (void)textFieldDidEndEditing:(UITextField *)textField
{
    [self updateTipTotals];
}
```

CRASH AND LEARN

If you call a helper method from within your class, be sure that either the helper method is declared in your header, or that the helper method is defined *above* the method call. Xcode uses a *single-pass compiler* to build your code—just like C—so you either need to declare method signatures or implement the methods above where you reference them.

As the name implies, the `textFieldDidEndEditing:` method is called when the user finishes editing a text field. This can happen either by tapping the Done button or by switching focus to another text field. Since you are already set as the text field's delegate, this method will be called without any further work.

After adding the code, save your project and try it out. If all the connections are made and delegates wired correctly, you should have a fully functioning tip calculator! Why download one of the dozens from the App Store when you can build your own, right?

Full source code for the finished Tiptacular application is available online at http://troybrant.net/iphonebook/chapter8/Tiptacular-done.zip.

Tiptacular Complete

And that's a wrap on Tiptacular. In this chapter, you not only learned how to incorporate text fields into an application, you learned about protocols and how delegation works. You also figured out how to customize the keyboard in Interface Builder and how to get rid of the keyboard when the return key is pressed. These are no small feats! You will find your understanding of delegation especially comes in handy as you use it time and again in the chapters to come.

Next chapter, you learn how to use basic collections, like NSArray and NSDictionary. You will also see how these collections are used to create an application that uses a picker view.

The Least You Need to Know

- A protocol consists of a set of method signatures that your class promises to implement.

- Delegation is a common way for a class to share its responsibilities or allow its behavior to be customized.

- To dismiss the keyboard, call [textField resignFirstResponder] on the active text field.

- You can customize the type of keyboard and other keyboard properties in Interface Builder.

- To be notified when changes are made to a text field, implement methods from the UITextFieldDelegate protocol.

- Use NSNumberFormatter to generate strings from numbers, such as "$2.18" from the float 2.1827469.

Pickers

In This Chapter

- Arrays
- Dictionaries
- Property lists
- Pickers
- Ruralfork app

So you're hungry and feel like eating out. You're tired of your usual haunts, so you want to try something new. You know you don't want to break the bank, and you know the general area where you want to eat. Wouldn't it be nice if there was an app that could pick a place to eat for you? Well, you might say "there's an app for that," and it's called Urbanspoon. Urbanspoon made finding somewhere to eat *fun*. Instead of selecting a restaurant from a list, you use a slot-machine interface to specify your criteria (like cost), and then shake the phone to randomly pick a place to eat.

The slot-machine view is a standard view called a picker, and you learn how to add one to your own app in this chapter. Before you can add a picker, though, you must know how to use arrays and dictionaries. To demonstrate how to use a picker, you will build Ruralfork, an app for browsing some of the most unhealthful meals on the planet.

Collections

The iPhone OS offers two collection classes you will use often in your applications: NSArray and NSDictionary.

NSArray

NSArray is a class provided by the Foundation framework that manages a flat ordered collection of objects. You are likely familiar with arrays in other languages, and NSArrays work in much the same way.

The easiest way to understand collections is to see them in action. Here is a quick sample, showing you how to initialize and iterate through an NSArray:

```
// array initialization (note the nil at the end)
NSArray *numberArray = [NSArray arrayWithObjects:
  [NSNumber numberWithInt:25],
  [NSNumber numberWithFloat:3.14],
  [NSNumber numberWithBool:YES],
  nil];

// fast enumeration
for (NSNumber *num in numberArray)
{
  // %@ calls the description method on each number
  NSLog(@"number = %@", num);
}

// access and convert NSNumber back to primitive C type
int myAge = [[numberArray objectAtIndex:0] intValue];
float pi = [[numberArray objectAtIndex:1] floatValue];
BOOL drinkingCoffee = [[numberArray objectAtIndex:2] boolValue];
```

Some important notes about the preceding code:

- The syntax for arrayWithObjects: has an important detail. As you can see, you specify the objects you want in the array in a comma-delimited list. The end of the list is indicated by nil. Always remember to include the nil at the end, or your app will likely crash and burn at runtime.

- NSNumber is a wrapper class that allows primitive C types (like ints, floats, and BOOLs) to be added to an NSArray. In the previous code, you can see how NSNumber can be used to add a number to an array and then convert it back to its original C type later.

- To iterate through the array, Objective-C offers a convenient mechanism called *fast enumeration*. In the preceding code, each time through the loop, the num variable is set to the next entry in the array. It's much cleaner than writing a for loop and incrementing an index by hand, as you may be used to.

- Just like `toString` in Java, the `description` method in Objective-C returns a helpful `NSString` that describes an object. `NSNumber` implements the description method by returning whatever number it contains in string form. You can override this method in classes you create to help with debugging.

To make your life easier, Apple incorporated the `%@` symbol in the string formatting system. In the `NSLog` statement previously, the `%@` symbol is replaced with the string that results from calling `[number description]`. Most built-in classes implement the `description` method, so you can use this technique to inspect your numbers, arrays, and dictionaries.

NSDictionary

A dictionary is a collection of key-value pairs. In an `NSDictionary`, both the key and the value are `NSObject` types. Unlike `NSArray`, `NSDictionary` does not guarantee that your data is stored in the order it was added. Instead, dictionaries are built for random access. When given a key, the dictionary looks up and returns the value for that key. You may know dictionaries as hash tables from other languages.

Again, the easiest way to see how to use an `NSDictionary` is to see it in action:

```
NSDictionary *workoutDict =
  [NSDictionary dictionaryWithObjectsAndKeys:
      @"running", @"activity",
      [NSDate date], @"date",
      [NSNumber numberWithFloat:6.2], @"distance",
      nil];

// access values using valueForKey:
NSString *activityType = [workoutDict valueForKey:@"activity"];
NSDate *workoutDate = [workoutDict valueForKey:@"date"];
NSNumber *distanceObject = [workoutDict valueForKey:@"distance"];

// convert NSNumber object to primitive float
float distance = [distanceObject floatValue];

// fast enumeration for dicts iterate over keys, not values
for (NSString *key in workoutDict) {
  NSString *value = [workoutDict valueForKey:key];
  NSLog(@"key = %@, value = %@", key, value);
}
```

Important notes about the preceding code:

- The dictionary is initialized with three key-value pairs using the `diction-aryWithObjectsAndKeys:` method. However, pay close attention to the order specified—*value* followed by *key*.

- `NSDate` is another helpful built-in class that holds information about a specific date. The `[NSDate date]` method returns an autoreleased date object containing the current date and time.

- Again, note that the `dictionaryWithObjectsAndKeys:` method is `nil`-terminated. Don't forget to include it.

CRASH AND LEARN

It is very easy to forget that final `nil` when you initialize your arrays and dictionaries. Without it, your app *will* crash at runtime, so get into the habit of including a `nil` at the end when initializing your collections.

- To get the value for a particular key, use the `valueForKey:` method. Also, notice that because `valueForKey:` method returns a generic `id` pointer, you don't need to cast it before assigning to an `NSString`, `NSDate`, or `NSNumber`.

- `NSDictionary` supports fast enumeration just like `NSArray`. Note that the iteration is over the *keys*, not the *values* in the dictionary. If you want to iterate over the dictionary values, use the `allValues` method, which returns an `NSArray` of values in the dictionary.

NSMutableArray and NSMutableDictionary

One important note about instances of `NSArray` and `NSDictionary` is that they are *immutable*. This means you can't add or remove objects after they are created. If you want to be able to modify the contents of an array or dictionary, you need to use the `NSMutableArray` and `NSMutableDictionary` classes.

You can replace the `NSArray` and `NSDictionary` instances in the preceding code with their dynamic counterparts like so:

```
// array initialization
NSMutableArray *numberArray = [NSMutableArray array];
[numberArray addObject:[NSNumber numberWithInt:25]];
[numberArray addObject:[NSNumber numberWithFloat:3.14]];
[numberArray addObject:[NSNumber numberWithBool:YES]];
```

```
// dictionary initialization
NSMutableDictionary *workoutDict =       [NSMutableDictionary
    dictionary];
[workoutDict setObject:@"running" forKey:@"activity"];
[workoutDict setObject:[NSDate date] forKey:@"date"];
[workoutDict setObject:[NSNumber numberWithFloat:6.2]
            forKey:@"distance"];
```

The addObject: method is available *only* for NSMutableArray. An instance of NSArray will not respond to it. The same goes for NSMutableDictionary's setObject:forKey: method. It may take some time to get used to this split between mutable and immutable classes, but you will use both extensively throughout the book.

Property Lists

There is yet another way to initialize arrays and dictionaries. Instead of initializing them in code, you can initialize them using a simple data file called a *property list*, or *plist*. A property list is a simple file format that can be used to describe basic data types—arrays, dictionaries, strings, numbers, dates, booleans, and so on.

DEFINITION

A **property list,** also known as a **plist,** is a simple file format used frequently in iPhone programming. Property lists can store basic data types, including arrays, dictionaries, strings, numbers, dates, booleans, and so on.

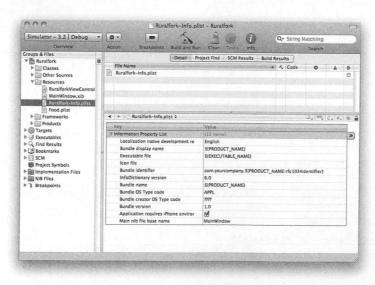

Every Xcode project contains a property list describing the application.

In the previous image, Ruralfork-Info.plist is an example of what a property list might look like. In this case, the property list was generated as part of the project and describes some of the properties of the application. You won't access this particular property list directly, but the system makes use of it when launching your app.

You can define your own property lists and use them to initialize both arrays and dictionaries. To see how it works, take the data in the previous code samples, and create property lists for them:

Key	Type	Value
▼ Root	Array ⬍	(3 items)
Item 0	Number	25
Item 1	Number	3.14
Item 2	Boolean	☑

Number.plist

Key	Type	Value
▼ Root	Dictionary ⬍	(3 items)
activity	String	running
date	Date	Dec 16, 2010 4:17:53 PM
distance	Number	6.2

Workout.plist

On the left, the property list for an array of numbers. On the right, the property list for a dictionary with workout statistics.

In the previous figure, there are two property lists—one for your array and one for your dictionary. Initializing the array and dictionary from the property lists in code is quite simple:

```
// use the bundle object to look up paths for resource files
NSBundle *bundle = [NSBundle mainBundle];

// get the relative file path
NSString *numberPlistPath =
  [bundle pathForResource:@"Numbers" ofType:@"plist"];

// initialize the array
NSArray *numberArray =
  [NSArray arrayWithContentsOfFile:numberPlistPath];

// get the relative file path
NSString *workoutPlistPath =
  [bundle pathForResource:@"Workout" ofType:@"plist"];

// initialize the dictionary
```

```
NSDictionary *workoutDict =
  [NSDictionary dictionaryWithContentsOfFile:workoutPlistPath];
```

As shown in the preceding code, after you have the path of the property list, you can initialize the contents of your collection in a single line.

Also introduced in this code is the NSBundle class. When your app is built, all the different pieces of your apps—binaries, libraries, resource files—are packaged together into a special folder called a *bundle*. You can use the NSBundle class at runtime to find information about your bundle when the app is running. In this case, NSBundle is used to construct a path to your application's resource files.

> **DEFINITION**
>
> A **bundle** is a directory that groups resources together in one place. An **iPhone application bundle** contains the application executable as well as resources used by the application—images, libraries, icons, and so on. Use the NSBundle class to construct paths to these resource files.

Intro to Pickers

Shown below, a *picker* is an interface element for displaying a list of options to a user:

A picker in the Clock app on the iPhone.

In the Clock app, you use a picker to set the amount of time for the timer to run. Pickers are used primarily in situations where you have a list of values a user can choose from. Pickers can be used to specify numeric values—as shown in the previous image—or enumerated strings, such as states or cities.

You use pickers in this chapter's sample app to present a list of food choices to the user.

Ruralfork App

Wouldn't it be great if there was an app for when you have the craving for something monstrously bad for you? I'm talking about fat-laden, artery-clogging conquests the likes from which you might never recover. Well, that app is about to exist because you are going to build it.

In the following figure, the Ruralfork app contains a picker for you to scroll and several labels for displaying the selected food's toxicity.

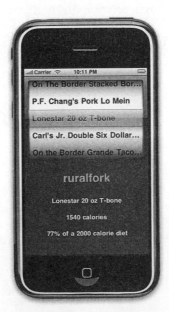

A couple of foods displayed in Ruralfork.

Interface Challenge

Just like last chapter, instead of walking you through every step required to build the interface, you are challenged to build it yourself. Writing these apps from scratch will help you internalize the blueprint for developing iPhone and iPad apps. Start with these steps:

1. Create a new View-based Application and name it "Ruralfork."

2. Edit RuralforkViewController.xib so it matches the following image:

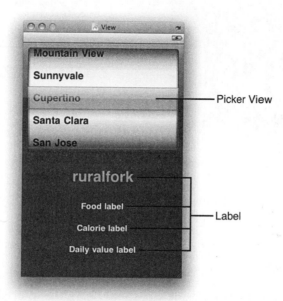

Build your view so it matches the interface shown.

You can find the Picker View using the **Library > Cocoa Touch > Data Views** filter in the library window.

3. Add the following outlets to your RuralforkViewController class:

   - `pickerView` of type `UIPickerView`
   - `foodLabel` of type `UILabel`
   - `calorieLabel` of type `UILabel`
   - `dailyValueLabel` of type `UILabel`

4. Release all the instance variables in the `dealloc` method as usual.

5. Hook up the outlets as shown in the following image:

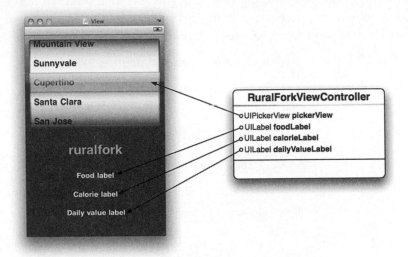

Connect the outlets and actions to the interface.

Starter code to reach this point is available online at: http://troybrant.net/
iphonebook/chapter9/Ruralfork-starter-code.zip.

Here We Go

At this point in your Ruralfork app, you should have the interface laid out, your
controller defined, and your outlets all hooked up to the interface.

ONE MORE THING

From this point forward, every chapter that includes a sample application will
have starter code on my website. You can browse all the starter codes here:
http://troybrant.net/iphonebook/.

To provide data for the picker view, you need to have a collection of food data ready
when the picker asks for it. You will use an array of dictionaries—shown in the following image—to hold all the food data:

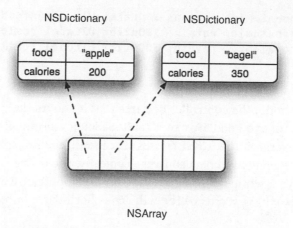

Each element in the array is a dictionary, and each dictionary contains information about a single food item.

This data is stored in a property list, which you should download from the following URL: http://troybrant.net/cig/resources/chapter8/Food.plist. Add the file to the Resources folder of your project. Feel free to poke through the property list to see how the data is structured. You will use the property list in just a bit to initialize the food array.

Adopt the Protocols

To get started programming the picker view, make the changes necessary to your RuralforkViewController.h interface file so it matches the following code:

```
// RuralforkViewController.h

#import <UIKit/UIKit.h>

@interface RuralforkViewController : UIViewController
    <UIPickerViewDelegate, UIPickerViewDataSource>
{
  UIPickerView *pickerView;
  UILabel *foodLabel;
  UILabel *calorieLabel;
  UILabel *dailyValueLabel;
  NSArray *foodArray;
}

@property (nonatomic, retain) IBOutlet UIPickerView *pickerView;
```

continues

```
@property (nonatomic, retain) IBOutlet UILabel *foodLabel;
@property (nonatomic, retain) IBOutlet UILabel *calorieLabel;
@property (nonatomic, retain) IBOutlet UILabel *dailyValueLabel;

@end
```

In the preceding code, the controller declares that it adopts the
`UIPickerViewDelegate` and `UIPickerViewDataSource` protocols. Why do you need
both of them? Several of the `UIKit` classes that use delegation split the delegates into
two categories: delegates and data sources. Typically, the data source provides the raw
data to be displayed, while the delegate controls the appearance and behavior of the
view. The `RuralforkViewController` will act as both data source and delegate.

Initialization

Now, jump to the RuralforkViewController.m file. Override the `viewDidLoad`
method by adding the code below:

```
// Implement viewDidLoad to do additional setup after loading the
   view,
// typically from a nib.
- (void)viewDidLoad
{
  [super viewDidLoad];

  NSBundle*bundle=[NSBundle main Bundle]
  NSString *path =
      [bundle pathForResource:@"Food" ofType:@"plist"];
  foodArray = [[NSArray alloc] initWithContentsOfFile:path];

  pickerView.delegate = self;
  pickerView.dataSource = self;
}
```

In the preceding code, you can see how to use the Food.plist file to initialize the
`foodArray` object. You need the array to be valid for the lifetime of the controller
object, so you wait and release it in the controller's `dealloc` method. You will add this
code in just a moment.

The last lines of code in `viewDidLoad` are crucial: you set the controller as both the
delegate and datasource of the picker view. Now, you need to implement the picker
view delegate and data source methods to customize the picker look and behavior.

dealloc

Because you used alloc/init for the `foodArray` instance variable, you need to release it. It's an instance variable, so you should release it in the controller's `dealloc` method.

Modify your `dealloc` method so it matches the following:

```
// RuralforkViewController.m


- (void)dealloc
{
  [pickerView release];
  [foodLabel release];
  [calorieLabel release];
  [dailyValueLabel release];
  [foodArray release];
  [super dealloc];
}
```

Remember NARC: if you use `new`, `alloc`, `retain`, or `copy`, you *must* release the object. This includes releasing retained instance variables in your class's `dealloc` method. Memory management can be tricky to get right, but following these rules will set you on the right path.

UIPickerViewDataSource

Now, let's move on to the `UIPickerView` data source methods. The protocol has two required methods, which are defined in the following code. You can add the code anywhere in the file:

```
#pragma mark -
#pragma mark UIPickerViewDataSource methods

// Returns the number of columns in the picker
- (NSInteger)numberOfComponentsInPickerView:(UIPickerView *)view
{
  return 1;
}

// Returns the number of rows in each column
- (NSInteger)pickerView:(UIPickerView *)view
  numberOfRowsInComponent:(NSInteger)component
```

continues

```
{
    return [foodArray count];
}
```

In picker view terminology, a *component* is a column. If you want a three-column picker, you just return 3 for the numberOfComponentsInPickerView: method. Your picker will have a single column, so you return 1.

DEFINITION

A **component** in a picker view is simply a column.

Your picker will have a row for each food item, so return the size of your food array in pickerView:numberOfRowsInComponent:.

In the previous code, the #pragma mark directive was introduced for the first time. #pragma mark doesn't affect your code in any way. Instead, it is used by Xcode to make code navigation easier. The text that follows #pragma mark is included in the Xcode editor window symbol browser, as shown in the following:

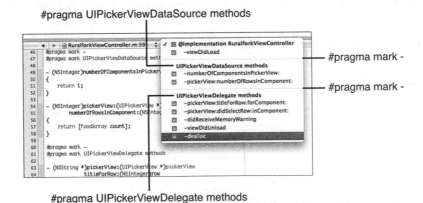

#pragma mark text helps you browse your code using the symbol browser.

When Xcode sees the #pragma mark – line, it draws a line in the symbol editor, which further improves readability. I highly recommend using the #pragma mark directive in your own code to group similar sections of code together.

So that does it for the UIPickerViewDataSource methods. So far, you have specified how many columns and how many rows the picker will have. But how do you tell the picker what title each row should have or what to do when a row is selected? That's where the UIPickerViewDelegate methods come in.

UIPickerViewDelegate

All the methods in the UIPickerViewDelegate protocol are optional, and you will implement the following two:

THERE'S A TIP FOR THAT

Want to see all the methods available in UIPickerViewDelegate? Right-click the "UIPickerViewDelegate" text in Xcode and choose **Find Selected Text in API Reference**.

```
#pragma mark -
#pragma mark UIPickerViewDelegate methods

// Returns the title for a given column and row
- (NSString *)pickerView:(UIPickerView *)pickerView
    titleForRow:(NSInteger)row
    forComponent:(NSInteger)component
{
    NSDictionary *foodInfo = [foodArray objectAtIndex:row];
    return [foodInfo objectForKey:@"name"];
}

// Called when a row is selected
- (void)pickerView:(UIPickerView *)pickerView
    didSelectRow:(NSInteger)row
    inComponent:(NSInteger)component
{
    NSDictionary *foodInfo = [foodArray objectAtIndex:row];

    NSString *name = [foodInfo objectForKey:@"name"];
    NSNumber *calories = [foodInfo objectForKey:@"calories"];

    // assuming a 2000 calorie-a-day diet
    int dailyValue = [calories floatValue] / 2000 * 100;

    foodLabel.text = name;
    calorieLabel.text =
        [NSString stringWithFormat:@"%@ calories", calories];
```

continues

```
dailyValueLabel.text =
    [NSString stringWithFormat:@"%d%% of a 2000 calorie diet",
        dailyValue];
}
```

The first method, `pickerView:titleForRow:forComponent:`, is used to determine the name at the given row in the picker. If you have a multi-column picker, you would need to check the component value to determine the column number. In this case, remember that each element in the `food` array is a dictionary, and you can access the name of the food using the `objectForKey:` method on the dictionary.

The second method, `pickerView:didSelectRow:inComponent:`, is invoked by the picker when a new row is selected. After a new selection is made, you'll update the labels in the interface with the current food information. You can get both the name and calorie count from the dictionary and update the `foodLabel` and `calorieLabel` `text` properties using this information. Based on the calorie count, you can also determine what percentage of a normal 2,000-calorie-a-day diet the food fills up.

Note that when formatting the percentage string, there is the potentially confusing "`%d%%`" format. Because `%` is used as the formatting character, in order to include an actual percent sign in your string, you must escape it using the `%` character. So "`%d%%`" paired with the integer 25 would be replaced with the string "`25%`."

THERE'S A TIP FOR THAT

You can further customize the picker view by implementing more of the delegate methods. Check out the API reference for the `UIPickerViewDelegate` class to see what other methods are available.

Try It Out

The moment of truth approaches: does this all work? Give it a shot—save your project, build it, and launch it in the iPhone Simulator. You should see the picker view populated with the most calorie-packed foods known to man. After you select a particular food, the food details should populate the labels you added to the interface. If all that works, you are done!

Full source code for the finished Ruralfork application is available online at http://troybrant.net/iphonebook/chapter9/Ruralfork-done.zip.

In this chapter, you learned about collections, and you learned how to use the UIPickerViewDelegate and UIPickerViewDataSource protocols to customize the picker to your interface. You also learned about property lists and how to use the #pragma mark directive to keep your code organized.

It took a while to work up to this point, but you made it, and you deserve to celebrate. If you eat out, be sure to bring Ruralfork along so you can choose a suitable meal. You may also want to make sure you have the ICE app installed on your phone in case you end up in a food coma.

After you have sufficiently recovered, be sure to tune in next chapter, where you learn about web views, spinners, toolbars, action sheets, and alert views.

The Least You Need to Know

- Don't forget to include a terminating nil when initializing NSArray using initWithObjects: or NSDictionary using initWithObjectsAndKeys:.
- Use fast enumeration to iterate over the elements of an array or dictionary.
- Use NSBundle's pathForResource:ofType: method to construct the path for your resource files.
- To customize a UIPickerView, your controller should implement both the UIPickerViewDelegate protocol and the UIPickerViewDataSource protocol.
- Use #pragma mark directives to keep your code organized.

Web Views, Spinners, and Alerts

In This Chapter

- Browser app
- Web views
- Alert views
- Toolbars
- Action sheets
- Spinners

Imagine you have written an application that helps people bake cakes. For each ingredient, you have a link to the Wikipedia article describing the ingredient. In the first version of your app, tapping that link closes your application and opens the link in Safari. In order to get back to the cake they were baking, the user has to close Safari, open your app again, and navigate to the cake page, again. As you might imagine, doing this a few times would drive just about anyone insane.

After desperately fending off your users' torches and pitchforks, you decide to use *web views* instead. This time, when the user taps the web link next to the ingredient, the web page is displayed *inside your app*. Your users rejoice because they don't have to constantly jump between Safari and your app over and over again!

In this chapter, you learn how to incorporate web views into your own apps. While the web page is loading, you will display a spinner to give the user visual feedback, and you will use alert views for displaying error messages. After you have everything working, you will add a toolbar and use action sheets for listing bookmarked websites. It might sound like a lot, but the code to build the sample app is simple, as you will find out very shortly.

Web Views

Web views make it extraordinarily easy to display web pages inside your application. In code, web views are implemented via the `UIWebView` class. You can register for the `UIWebViewDelegate` protocol to be notified when certain events happen, such as a URL loading successfully or stopping with an error. In this sample application, you will add a `UIWebView` to your interface and use the `UIWebViewDelegate` to know when it finishes loading a URL.

Web view in
Tweetie

Web view in
Tweeterific

Web view in
Facebook

Web views are used to display a website without making the user leave the app.

One word of warning on web views: they can use quite a bit of memory. If you use a web view in your application, make sure you release the web view when you're done with it, or you could end up with a significant memory leak.

ONE MORE THING

Remember that web views on the iPhone and iPad do not support plugins such as Java and Flash.

To see how simple it is to implement web views, let's build a new sample app, Browser.

Browser App

An app this simple deserves a simple name. The Browser app will have only one view, a `UIWebView`, that will load a web page of your choosing. Over the course of the chapter, you will add more functionality, but for now, you get to start with something easy.

Interface Challenge

To get started, follow these steps:

1. Create a new View-based Application and name it "Browser."

2. Open **BrowserViewController.xib**, and set the background color to white.

3. Add a web view using the **Library > Cocoa Touch > Data Views** filter in the library window. Position it so it takes up the entire view.

4. With the web view selected, check **Scale Page to Fit** in the Attributes tab of the inspector window. By default, the web page is rendered without any zoom, so you usually have to zoom out to see the entire page. This checkbox makes it so you can see the entire page when the page first loads.

5. Add a single outlet named "webView" of type UIWebView to your BrowserViewController class. Remember to add a property for the outlet with IBOutlet in its declaration. Also remember to synthesize your property.

6. Release webView in the dealloc method.

7. Hook up webView in the controller to the web view in the interface.

Your view in Interface Builder should match the one that follows:

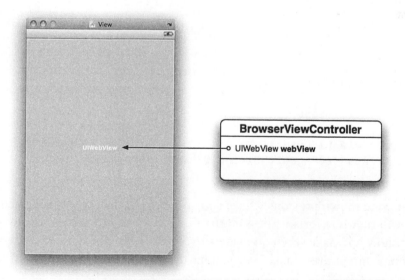

All you have to connect is the webView outlet.

Save your interface, build your project, and give Browser a try in the simulator. If you see a blank white screen, that's perfect. You will load a web page next.

Launching a Web Page

To launch a web page, use the `loadRequest:` method on your `UIWebView` instance. To see how it works, add this helper method near the top of your BrowserViewController.m implementation file:

```
// BrowserViewController.m

// Start loading a new web page in the web view
- (void)loadWebPageWithString:(NSString *)urlString
{
    NSURL *url = [NSURL URLWithString:urlString];
    NSURLRequest *request = [NSURLRequest requestWithURL:url];
    [webView loadRequest:request];
}
```

As shown in the preceding code, the `loadRequest:` method takes in an `NSURLRequest` object. The `NSURLRequest` object is constructed from an `NSURL` object, and the `NSURL` object is initialized using an `NSString`, such as `@"http://troybrant.net"`. As soon as the `loadRequest:` method finishes, the web view will display the requested page.

To try out this nifty little helper method, call it from `viewDidLoad` by adding the following code:

```
// BrowserViewController.m

- (void)viewDidLoad
{
    [super viewDidLoad];
    [self loadWebPageWithString:@"http://troybrant.net"];
}
```

Add the code shown previously, save your project and run it in the simulator. The screen will be white for a while, and then you will see the website. If the web page doesn't show up, make sure you made all your connections and didn't misspell the preceding address. Also make sure you have a working network connection.

Speaking of which, how do you know if the web view fails to load the web page? Remember, the Internet is not a big truck. It's a series of tubes. Tubes can get clogged, and your load request can fail.

It turns out you can be notified when that happens by implementing the `UIWebViewDelegate` protocol. Before covering the protocol, however, let's take a moment to look at *alert views*.

Alert Views

If you have ever seen a low battery message on your iPhone or iPad, then you have seen an alert view. Alert views are primarily used to communicate errors or to verify a destructive action, like deleting data permanently. Several alert views are shown in the following:

Alert view in
Mail

Alert view in
Safari

Alert view in
RunMonster

Alert views are used primarily to display error messages but can be used to verify a destructive action as well.

You can launch an alert view for your own application using the `UIAlertView` class. You can see how to pop up your own alert view in the following code, where you report a loading error to the user.

THERE'S A TIP FOR THAT

Use alert views *only* when it is necessary to interrupt your user with an important notification. Alert views are very jarring to the user experience, and they are overused in many apps.

UIWebViewDelegate

To be notified of failures when the web pages are loading, the controller needs to become the delegate of the UIWebView instance. Remember, there are three steps in becoming a delegate:

1. Adopt the delegate protocol. In this case, you need to register for the UIWebViewDelegate protocol in the BrowserViewController.h file, as shown in the following:

```
// BrowserViewController.h

#import <UIKit/UIKit.h>

@interface BrowserViewController : UIViewController
        <UIWebViewDelegate>
{
  UIWebView *webView;
}
@property (nonatomic, retain) IBOutlet UIWebView *webView;
@end
```

2. Implement the delegate methods. The delegate method you need is webView:didFailLoadWithError:. When this method is called, display an alert view with information about what exactly went wrong. Add the following code to your BrowserViewController.m file to achieve this result:

```
// BrowserViewController.m

// Called when the web page doesn't load
- (void)webView:(UIWebView *)webView
  didFailLoadWithError:(NSError *)error
{
    UIAlertView *alertView =
    [[UIAlertView alloc] initWithTitle:@"Error loading web page"
                              message:[error localizedDescription]
                              delegate:nil
                              cancelButtonTitle:nil
                              otherButtonTitles:@"OK", nil];
    [alertView show];
    [alertView release];
}
```

A few notes about the preceding code:

- To initialize a `UIAlertView`, use the `initWithTitle:message:delegate:` `cancelButtonTitle:otherButtonTitles:` method. What a mouthful!

- You can implement the `UIAlertViewDelegate` protocol if you want to find out what button the user tapped. In this case, you just display a single button titled "OK," so there's no need.

- The "localized" part of the `localizedDescription` method on `NSError` means the error message is translated into whatever language your user is using. Translation isn't done automatically for all the strings in your app, but `NSError` generously translates the error message for you.

- To display the `UIAlertView`, simply send it the `show` message.

- We emphasize this repeatedly because it is important: notice that you used alloc/init to initialize `alertView`, so you must release it.

3. Finally, set the controller as the delegate of the `UIWebView` instance. You should do this in the `viewDidLoad:` method before calling `loadWebPageWithString::`, as shown below:

```
// BrowserViewController.m

- (void)viewDidLoad
{
    [super viewDidLoad];
    webView.delegate = self;
    [self loadWebPageWithString:@"http://troybrant.net"];
}
```

After matching your `BrowserViewController` as shown previously, save your project and run it in the simulator. Looks the same, right? Now, disable your network connection by putting your device into Airplane Mode and run the app again. You should see the following image:

No Internet connection? Excellent! Your alert view works.

If you see the previous alert message, then you have implemented the UIWebViewDelegate protocol and launched a UIAlertView successfully. Don't forget to take your device back out of Airplane Mode!

New Interface Elements

The app in its current form is pretty static. Let's spice things up a bit and add a way to define and access bookmarks in the app. One nice way to allow your user to access bookmarks is by using the system bookmark button. You will add one to a toolbar at the bottom of the Browser view. Also, in order to give the user some crucial visual feedback, you will add a spinner that animates while the web page is loading.

Here is the interface you are shooting for:

Browser app in its final form.

In the previous image, you can see three new interface elements we're going to add: toolbars, action sheets, and spinners. Before you dive into the code, take a look at each of these interface elements.

Toolbars

You have seen toolbars in your desktop applications, typically at the top of a window. A toolbar typically displays buttons used to control the app. On the iPad, toolbars should be placed at the top of the screen while toolbars in iPhone apps should always be placed at the *bottom* of the screen. You can see toolbars in various applications in the following figure.

DEFINITION

A **toolbar** is a rectangular strip that displays a row of buttons used to control the app. On the iPad, toolbars are typically found at the top of your interface. On the iPhone, however, they are always located at the bottom of your interface.

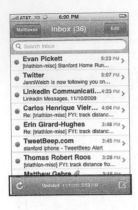

| Toolbar in | Toolbar in | Toolbar in |
| Mail | Twitterific | RunMonster |

Toolbars come in different styles.

In code, toolbars are implemented using the `UIToolbar` class, and buttons on the interface are implemented using the `UIBarButtonItem` class. You will see how to create and control `UIToolbars` in the code to come.

Action Sheets

Action sheet is the term for the menu of buttons that appear vertically when a button is tapped. Action sheets are used, as the name implies, to specify an action of some kind. In the Browser app, you will use the action sheet to list bookmarks. Examples of actions sheets are shown in the following figure:

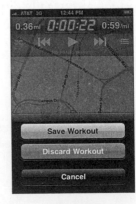

| Action sheet in | Action sheet in | Action sheet in |
| Tweetie | Notes | RunMonster |

Action sheets contain a list of buttons.

DEFINITION

An **action sheet** displays a list of choices to the user when a toolbar button is tapped. An action sheet should be used for presenting multiple ways of completing a task or for confirming a particularly dangerous action.

In code, action sheets are implemented using the `UIActionSheet` class. You will implement the `UIActionSheetDelegate` protocol to determine which bookmark was selected.

Spinners

Spinners are animated indicators that let you know that an app is working on something. The Browser app in its current form just displays a white screen and provides no feedback whatsoever while the web page is loading. Users will see that white screen and think, "Is the app frozen?" Spinners solve this problem by providing subtle feedback that, in fact, the app is working hard to complete the task.

Spinner in
iPod app

Spinner in
Google Earth

Spinner in
RunMonster

Spinners give users reassurance that even though the screen hasn't changed, the app is hard at work.

DEFINITION

A **spinner** is an animated indicator informing the user the app is performing a task in the background. Any time your app can take more than a few seconds to complete a task, a spinner should be displayed to the user.

In code, spinners are implemented using the UIActivityIndicatorView class. Starting and stopping the spinner is very simple, and you will see how it's done in the code in the next section.

Adding Bookmarks

Browser is about to get a serious upgrade. To add the bookmark functionality, you will add the interface elements—toolbars, buttons, spinner—in Interface Builder, then add the code to launch the bookmark list in an action sheet.

Updating the Interface

The first step to adding bookmarks is to update the interface. Follow these steps:

1. In Interface Builder, click and drag a **Toolbar** to the bottom of your interface using the **Library > Cocoa Touch > Windows, Views & Bars** filter in the library window.

2. The toolbar is now covering up the bottom part of the web view. To make sure web content doesn't get clipped at the bottom, select the web view and drag its bottom border up until it is flush with the top of the toolbar.

3. The default toolbar button currently displays the text, "Item." Change it to the system bookmark icon. First, select the **toolbar button**. It will probably take two clicks to select since the first click selects the toolbar. In the Attributes tab of the inspector window, set the Identifier field to **Bookmarks**.

4. Click and drag a **Flexible Space Bar Button Item** just to the left of the bookmark button. You can find the flexible bar button item in the **Library > Cocoa Touch > Windows, Views & Bars** filter in the library window. This will push the bookmark button to the far right of the toolbar.

THERE'S A TIP FOR THAT

When laying out buttons for your toolbar, you typically place the most important action button on the right. The left side of the toolbar is usually reserved for navigation or cancel buttons.

5. Click and drag an **Activity Indicator View**—also known as a spinner—to the far left side of the toolbar. You can find the activity indicator view using the **Library > Cocoa Touch > Inputs & Values** filter in the library window.

6. With the spinner selected, set the Style to White and check **Hide When Stopped** in the Attributes tab of the inspector window.

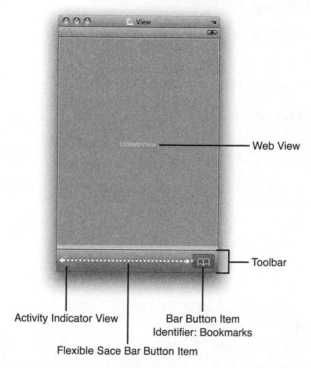

Your interface should match the one shown here.

At this point, your interface should match the one in the previous image. If it doesn't, make sure you didn't skip any of the previous steps. You can always see how it's done in the completed code for this chapter on the book website.

Next, hook up the bookmark button to the controller by adding an action.

Updating Connections

With the addition of new interface elements, you also need to update your controller's outlets and actions. You need outlets for the spinner and toolbar so you can manipulate them in code. You will also need an action method to be called when the bookmark toolbar button is tapped. Add these now:

1. Add the following outlets and actions to your `BroswerViewController` class:

   - `spinnerView` outlet of type `UIActivityIndicatorView`

   - `toolbar` outlet of type `UIToolbar`

   - Action with the following signature:

   ```
   // BrowserViewController.h

   - (IBAction)bookmarkItemTapped;
   ```

   CRASH AND LEARN

   Forgot how to add outlets and actions? See Chapter 4 for instructions on how to add both outlets and actions to your class.

2. In Interface Builder, wire up the outlets and actions as shown in the following image:

   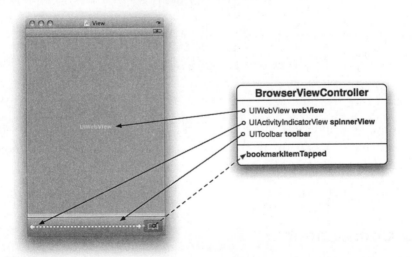

Connect the outlets and actions to the interface.

3. Release the `spinnerView` and `toolbar` outlets in your `dealloc` method.

Save your project. You will now add the code that controls the spinner and launches the action sheet.

Controlling the Spinner

Before getting to the action sheet, you should add the spinner behavior. The spinner will start when the web page begins loading and stop when the page has finished loading. Controlling the spinner is quite simple: you just call `startAnimating` and `stopAnimating` on the `UIActivityIndicatorView` instance to start and stop the spinner.

But how do you know when the web page has started and stopped loading? `UIWebViewDelegate` has just the methods you need. Add the following code to your BrowserViewController.m file to see the delegate methods in action:

```
// BrowserViewController.m

// Called when a web page loads successfully
- (void)webViewDidFinishLoad:(UIWebView *)webView
{
    [spinnerView stopAnimating];
}

// Called when a web page begins to load
- (void)webViewDidStartLoad:(UIWebView *)webView
{
    [spinnerView startAnimating];
}
```

To know when the web view starts loading content, implement the `webViewDidStartLoad:` delegate method. To know when the web view stops loading content, the `webViewDidFinishLoad:` delegate method is called if the load finishes successfully; otherwise, `webView:didFailWithError:` is called.

Starting and stopping the spinner is easy, as you can see. Also, because you checked the "Hide When Stopped" checkbox for the spinner in Interface Builder earlier, the spinner is visible only when a page is loading and conveniently goes away otherwise.

Controlling the Bookmark Button

With the spinner taken care of, the only remaining step is to launch an action sheet when the bookmark button is tapped. Displaying the action sheet is pretty straightforward, and you can launch one by adding the following code to the BrowserViewController.m file:

```
// BrowserViewController.m

- (IBAction)bookmarkItemTapped
{
    UIActionSheet *actionSheet =
        [[UIActionSheet alloc] initWithTitle:nil
                                    delegate:self
                             cancelButtonTitle:@"Cancel"
                        destructiveButtonTitle:nil
                             otherButtonTitles:@"Apple",
                                @"XKCD",
                                @"Dr McNinja", nil];
    [actionSheet showFromToolbar:toolbar];
    [actionSheet release];
}
```

The init method for the action sheet is rather lengthy. The first parameter is the title of the action sheet, which you don't really need. The second parameter is the UIActionSheetDelegate; the action sheet notifies the delegate when the user taps one of its buttons or cancels. You will implement the UIActionSheetDelegate protocol in just a moment.

The third parameter is the name of the cancel button. The cancel button is always displayed at the bottom of the action sheet. The fourth parameter is the destructive button, which is displayed just above the cancel button. The destructive button is always red, and you should use it if the action deletes content or erases data in any way. The bookmark app is harmless and doesn't need a destructive button. The last parameter is a list of the names of buttons that will be displayed on the action sheet. Again, don't forget to add the nil at the end!

To display the action sheet, you use the showFromToolbar: method, though you could have used the showInView: method. The showInView: method should be used if your interface doesn't have a toolbar.

Finally, because you used alloc/init for the action sheet, you must balance it with a release.

UIActionSheetDelegate

So you told the action sheet you were its delegate, but the compiler will complain that you don't implement the UIActionSheetDelegate. Remedy the situation by implementing the delegate protocol now. Follow these steps to add the protocol and delegate method to your class:

1. Add the `UIActionSheetDelegate` protocol to your class header in BrowserViewController.h. After you are done, your protocol definition will include two protocols: `<UIWebViewDelegate, UIActionSheetDelegate>`

2. Add the following delegate code to BrowserViewController.m:

```
// BrowserViewController.m

#pragma mark -
#pragma mark UIActionSheetDelegate methods

// Called when a selection is made on an action sheet
- (void)actionSheet:(UIActionSheet *)actionSheet
  clickedButtonAtIndex:(NSInteger)buttonIndex
{
  if (buttonIndex == 0)
  {
        [self loadWebPageWithString:@"http://www.apple.com"];
  }
  else if (buttonIndex == 1)
  {
        [self loadWebPageWithString:@"http://www.xkcd.com"];
  }
  else if (buttonIndex == 2)
  {
        [self loadWebPageWithString:@"http://www.drmcninja.
com"];
  }
}
```

Add the code somewhere below the `loadWebPageWithString:` method so the compiler doesn't complain about the `loadWebPageWithString:` method not being defined.

The `UIActionSheetDelegate` protocol contains several optional methods, but the only one you need is `actionSheet:clickedButtonAtIndex:`. This method is called when the user taps one of the buttons on the action sheet. The `buttonIndex` parameter corresponds to the order that you specified the button titles when you initialized the `UIActionSheet`. Index 0 means the button at the top of the action sheet was tapped. The cancel button doesn't have an index because tapping it will not invoke this method.

To launch the web pages, use the handy-dandy `loadWebPageWithString:` helper method you wrote earlier in the chapter. Doesn't abstraction make code look nice?

Try It Out

All that's left now is to save your project, cross your fingers, build it, and run it in the iPhone Simulator. Try tapping the bookmark button to see if the action sheet slides up. Select a web page and look for the spinner in the bottom left corner. Try it with your network connection both on and off. If everything goes according to plan, you should have a fully functioning Browser app.

Full source code for the finished Browser application is available online at http://troybrant.net/iphonebook/chapter10/Browser-done.zip.

Browser App Done

To put it lightly, you covered quite a bit in this chapter. You learned about web views for displaying web pages and alert views for displaying error messages. You learned how crucial it is to provide user feedback while long-running tasks are running and how spinners meet this need. The Browser app got a major upgrade by adding a toolbar with bookmark button. That button, when tapped, launches an action sheet that allows the user to specify exactly which action they want to take. It may seem like a lot, but you learned how easy it is to use these interface elements.

You have now completed the second part of this book. This part was all about using interface controls—sliders, text fields, pickers, and web views; in the next part, you are introduced to a new class of applications: multi-view applications. Most of the apps you want to build will have more than one screen, so how do you manage these views? How do you transition between them? What classes can you use to make it easier? Part 3 is kicked off with a detailed look at view controllers, the building blocks of all multi-view apps.

The Least You Need to Know

- To load a web page, add a `UIWebView` to your controller, and send it the `loadRequest:` message.
- `UIAlertView` can be jarring and should be used primarily for displaying error messages.

- Any time you have a long-running task, like loading a web page, provide user feedback by using a view such as `UIActivityIndicatorView`.

- Use `UIActionSheet` to slide up a list of buttons a user can tap to specify a particular action.

Multi-View Applications

By this point, you can write a nice application as long as it only has one screen. More than likely, though, you will need several screens for your app, which means you need a way to manage these screens. Learn how to use view controllers, navigation controllers, and tab bar controllers to control your screens in a multi-view application. Also, see how you can add split views and popovers to your iPad applications.

View Controllers

In This Chapter

- Multi-view applications
- Model-View-Controller
- Tweet sample app
- Modal views
- View controller lifecycle

"You can type in what you're doing, what you're thinking … it's like reverse stalking." Evan Doll, one of the instructors of the iPhone programming class at Stanford, used this excellent description of Twitter while introducing a class project. The project was called Presence, a multi-view Twitter app intended to introduce students to topics such as Model-View-Controller (MVC), delegation, and table views.

There were new challenges for the students to tackle in the Presence app. How do you set up the project to support multiple views? How do you transition between views? How do you keep track of state and pass data between the views?

In this chapter, you learn the answers to all these questions. MVC, modal views, and view controllers are covered. To put these skills to use, you build the Tweet app, so you too can "reverse stalk" yourself to the world.

Multi-View Applications

iPhone apps, as you know, have limited screen real estate when compared to their desktop counterparts. Even iPad apps have a small screen compared to most desktop applications. It's almost inevitable that an app you want to write will need to have multiple screens. When Apple developed the iPhone, they came up with two solutions for managing multiple screens: the *navigation bar* and the *tab bar*. Examples of both are shown in the following:

Navigation bar

Tab bar

Navigation bars are used for hierarchical content. Tab bars are used for separating very different screenfuls of content.

- **Navigation bars:** The navigation bar, casually known as the nav bar, is used to organize hierarchical information. The nav bar typically contains the title of the view and a button to navigate back up to the previous level in the hierarchy.

DEFINITION

A **navigation bar** organizes the screens in your app in an hierarchy. Navigation bars are always found at the top of the screen and often display a title and a back button.

A **tab bar** organizes the screens in your app in a tabbed list. Tab bars are always found at the bottom of the screen.

- **Tab bars:** The tab bar, on the other hand, is used to separate views in your app that don't have an hierarchical relationship. Each tab has a self-contained view, which means that the view for the tab should not have a relationship to any other tab.

You will build applications with navigation bars (Chapter 12) and tab bars (Chapter 13), but first, you need to know what each individual screen is composed of. The purpose of this chapter is to explain exactly what these single screens are made of.

In short, each screen of your app consists of a model containing your application data, a view for displaying the screen, and a controller for managing how your app behaves. To truly understand iPhone programming, you need to understand this MVC relationship. So let's take a moment to explore what MVC is and how it affects how you build iPhone apps.

MVC

Have you ever seen (or written) code that consists of roughly one monster class that does everything? Somehow it just works, but you have no idea how or why. Adding new functionality is an admirable idea, but futile in the end. Everything you do seems to break something else. Good luck trying to find code you can reuse.

MVC is a design pattern used to avoid these "spaghetti-code" situations. In MVC, classes have clearly defined responsibilities, so instead of one class to run your application, you have classes managing data, classes displaying data to the user, and classes gluing it all together. Segmenting the app into these smaller chunks has several advantages, including the fact your code is more reusable, less complex, and easier to understand and maintain.

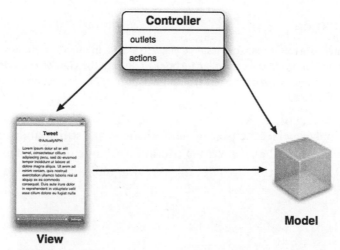

MVC in a nutshell.

MVC, shown in the previous image, splits your application into three components:

- **Model:** Model classes manage your data, and they often map to real-world objects. For instance, in the Twitter app you are going to build, you will create a `TwitterUser` model class for keeping track of the Twitter user's information. Models do not know anything about controllers or views. That is, a `TwitterUser` object will never have an explicit pointer to a `TwitterViewController` object. Because of this, model classes are very reusable.

- **View:** View classes are all about your application's appearance. Every time you customize UI elements with Interface Builder, you are defining the view component of MVC. Views do not know about controllers, but they sometimes can refer to model classes. Views tend to be very reusable as well.

- **Controller:** Controllers are the brains behind your application. They determine what happens when a button is tapped, a switch flipped, or a picker picked. They need to know about both the model—for accessing application state—and the view—for updating the interface.

Controllers are usually paired with a single view they're in charge of, and this is where the term *view controller* comes from. In fact, you have been using view controllers in all your projects so far: `iShockUViewController`, `RuralforkViewController`, and `BrowserViewController` to name a few. View controllers are typically application-specific and not reusable.

DEFINITION

A **view controller** manages a single view. As shown in previous chapters, action methods in the controller are hooked up with the view to respond to certain events. View controllers typically act as the glue connecting views with model objects.

Perhaps this makes perfect sense to you. Perhaps MVC still sounds more like a type of sandwich you order than something useful for iPhone development. Either way, you will see MVC in action by building your first multi-view iPhone application.

Tweet App

It's basically a rite-of-passage to write a Twitter app as one of your first iPhone OS applications. In this chapter, you will get a chance to satisfy this requirement on your way to becoming a full-fledged app developer. The app you will build is called Tweet, a Twitter app that simply displays a user's latest tweet. The interface has two views, which can be seen in the following screenshots:

When the info button is tapped, the view flips to the backside, which contains the settings screen.

So why make such a big deal about MVC for this app? Well, you can see that the application contains two full-screen views. As a rule, each of these screens should be managed by a view controller. Also, you create a `TwitterUser` class to keep track of the user's info and latest tweet. Visually, your app is organized according to MVC as shown in the following image.

In all the previous applications, you have been able to get away with having a single view controller. Now you need to create a second view controller to manage the settings screen. You also need to create the `TwitterUser` model class to manage the data in your application. You will see that having a dedicated model class also makes passing data between the two view controllers very simple.

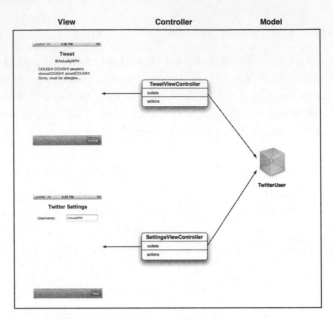

Class diagram and MVC breakdown for the Tweet app.

With this MVC picture in mind, here's the strategy used to build the first version of the Tweet app with two main views:

1. Build the Tweet view using Interface Builder.

2. Add the outlets and actions for the Tweet view and hook them up to the `TweetViewController`.

3. Add the `SettingsViewController` class to the project, and build the Settings view.

4. Add the outlets and actions for the Settings view and hook them up to the `SettingsViewController`.

5. Add code to the `TweetViewController` to flip to the Settings view when the Settings button is tapped.

6. Add code to the `SettingsViewController` to flip back to the Tweet view when the Done button is tapped.

7. Create the `TwitterUser` model class.

8. Store the Twitter username and the latest tweet in the `TwitterUser` model class. You will be provided with a helper class for fetching tweets.

9. Update the Tweet view with the latest tweet when necessary.

> **ONE MORE THING**
>
> Notice how the first step in all these apps is creating the view. This is no accident. Building your interface first is central to creating well-designed applications.

Sound good? Let's get started.

Building Tweet

Much like the apps we've built so far, we'll walk through the app development together. There is code online you can check at regular intervals to make sure you're on track or if you get stuck building it on your own.

Build the Tweet Screen

To get started, follow these steps:

1. Create a new View-based Application and name it "Tweet."

2. Edit TweetViewController.xib so it matches the following image:

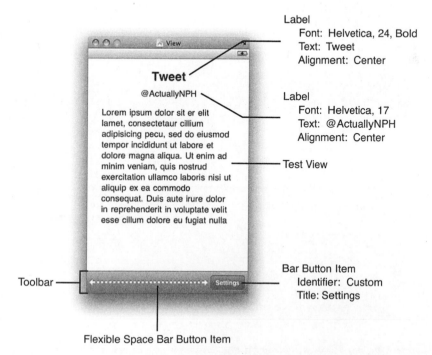

Build your TweetViewController.xib view so it matches the interface shown.

THERE'S A TIP FOR THAT

To get perfectly centered text in your interface, drag the left edge of your text label until it hits the far left guideline. Drag the right edge until it hits the far right guideline. Select center text alignment from the inspector window, and—violà!—you have perfectly centered text.

You can find the Text view using the **Library > Cocoa Touch > Data Views** filter in the library window. You may be admiring my Latin skills, but alas, I can't take credit. The text view displays the Latin text by default.

3. Add the following outlets to your `TweetViewController` class:

   - `usernameLabel` of type `UILabel`

   - `tweetTextView` of type `UITextView`

4. Release these outlets in the `dealloc` method.

5. Add the following action to your `TweetViewController` class:

   `- (IBAction)settingsButtonTapped;`

   Be sure to add the action method to both .h and .m files. The method body in the .m file should be empty.

6. Hook up the outlets and actions as shown in the image below:

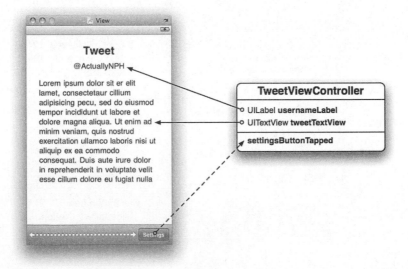

Connect the outlets and actions to the interface.

Add the Settings View Controller

Your Tweet view is set up and ready for action. Now you need to add the view for the settings screen. Adding a new view means adding both a new nib file and a new view controller. Conveniently, you can do both at the same time while adding the new view controller. Follow these steps to add and configure this new view:

1. In Xcode, Ctrl-click on the **Classes** group, then select **Add > New File**.

2. In the iPhone OS > Cocoa Touch Class category, select **UIViewController subclass**. Check the **With XIB for user interface** checkbox so the nib file is created with the view controller. Make sure you match the following image:

Make sure you check the "With XIB for user interface" box so the nib file is created along with the view controller.

3. Click **Next**. Name the file SettingsViewController.m, and click **Finish**.

4. Move the SettingsViewController.xib file to the Resources group, and make sure the .m and .h files are in the Classes group.

Now we're ready to start building the settings interface.

Build the Settings Screen

The steps for building the second interface should feel familiar. You will create the interface and hook it up to the controller exactly like you just did for TweetViewController:

1. Edit SettingsViewController.xib so that it matches the following image:

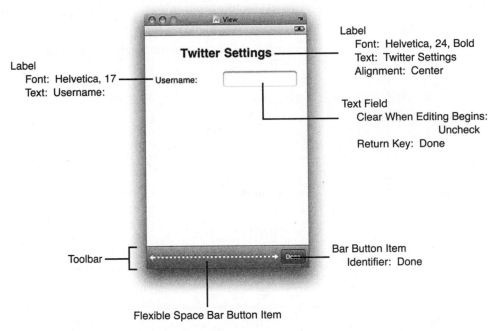

Build your SettingsViewController.xib view so it matches the interface shown.

2. Add the following outlet to your SettingsViewController class:

   usernameTextField of type UITextField

3. Release this outlet in the dealloc method.

4. Add the following action to your TweetViewController class:

   - (IBAction)doneButtonTapped;

   Be sure to add the action method to both .h and .m files. The method body in the .m file should be empty.

5. Hook up the outlets and actions as shown in the image that follows:

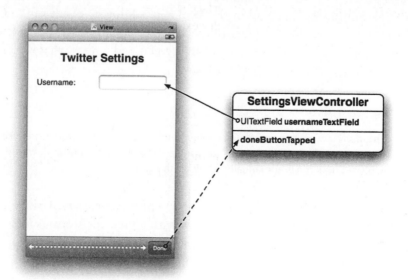

Connect the outlets and actions to the interface.

6. As shown in Chapter 8, modify the SettingsViewController class to conform to the UITextFieldDelegate protocol. Override the viewDidLoad method in SettingsViewController.m, and assign the controller as the text field's delegate. Add the textFieldShouldReturn method, and dismiss the keyboard when the return key is tapped. Chapter 8 shows how to complete these steps if you need a refresher.

Your settings screen is now ready for action.

Starter code to reach this point is available online at: http://troybrant.net/iphonebook/chapter11/Tweet-starter-code.zip.

Modal Views

Save your project, build it, and run it in the iPhone Simulator. You should see the Tweet view with Latin filling up most of the screen. If you try tapping the Settings button, nothing will happen. That's perfectly fine. Your next step is to remedy the situation by displaying the settings screen as a modal view.

A *modal view* is a temporary view in your application that requires the user to perform some action to dismiss it. Many applications use modal views for adding and editing data, such as composing an email in the Mail app, adding an event in the Calendar app, or picking a photo for a contact in the Contacts app. In each of these cases, the modal view slides up from the bottom of the screen and covers whatever screen you were viewing.

DEFINITION

A **modal view** is a temporary view in your application that is used to obtain key information from the user. Like action sheets and alert views, modal views are displayed until the user manually dismisses the view.

Modal views are also used in what Apple terms *utility applications*. Utility apps are simple applications that display a single view with a view for settings *behind* the single view. The Stocks app and Weather app are examples of these kinds of apps. If you open the Weather app and tap the "i" button in the bottom-right corner, the view flips to the Settings view.

DEFINITION

A **utility application** is one that is dedicated to a single task and consists of a single screen. For example, the Stocks and Weather apps for iPhone are utility apps.

The `UIViewController` class has built-in support for displaying views modally. By default, modal views are displayed using the vertical slide animation. The Tweet app falls under the utility app category, however, so you will specify that you want to use the flip transition.

Transition Styles

A view controller's `modalTransitionStyle` property determines how the view appears on screen when displayed modally. There are four transition options:

- **Cover vertical:** The modal view slides up from the bottom of the screen to cover the screen. This is the default transition style.

- **Flip horizontal:** The current view flips to reveal the modal view as if it were behind the current view. You will use this transition to display the Tweet settings screen.

- **Cross dissolve:** The current view fades away while the modal view fades in at the same time.

- **Partial curl:** One corner of the current view curls up to reveal the modal view beneath it. The Maps application uses this transition.

All four of these transitions are available for both iPhone and iPad. See UIViewController's modalTransitionStyle property in the iPhone API documentation for more details.

iPad Presentation Styles

On the iPhone, a modal view always fills the entire screen. On the iPad, however, a modal view can be displayed in a variety of shapes and sizes by setting the modal view controller's modalPresentationStyle property. There are four styles available on iPad:

- **Full screen:** The modal view covers the entire screen. This is the default style for both iPhone and iPad.

- **Page sheet:** The height of the modal view is set to the height of the screen, and the width is set to the width of the view in portrait mode. Uncovered areas are dimmed to prevent user interaction.

- **Form sheet:** The modal view is presented in a box centered in the middle of the interface. Like the page sheet style, uncovered areas are dimmed to prevent user interaction.

- **Current context:** The modal view is presented using the same style as its parent view controller. For instance, if the modal view is displayed in a popover view controller, the modal view fills the popover.

In iPhone apps, the modalPresentationStyle property is ignored since modal views are always presented full screen. For more details on presentation styles, look up the modalPresentationStyle property in the API documentation for UIViewController.

Flip to the Settings Screen

In the Tweet app, you will display the settings screen modally using the flip transition. To make this happen, add the following code to your TweetViewController.m file:

```
// TweetViewController.m

#import "SettingsViewController.h"
...

// Flips to the settings view
- (IBAction)settingsButtonTapped
{
    // Initialize the view controller
    SettingsViewController *settingsViewController =
        [[SettingsViewController alloc] init];

    // Use the flip transition
    settingsViewController.modalTransitionStyle =
        UIModalTransitionStyleFlipHorizontal;

    // Display the settings view
    [self presentModalViewController:settingsViewController
        animated:YES];

    // Memory management
    [settingsViewController release];
}
```

The preceding code creates a new view controller, indicates that it should be displayed using a flip animation, and then tells the `TweetViewController` instance to display it. Some notes on the previous code:

- Be sure to import the SettingsViewController.h file at the top of your TweetViewController.m file. This way, you'll be able to refer to the `SettingsViewController` class from within your `TweetViewController`.

- The first line of `settingsButtonTapped`: shows how to create view controllers programmatically. When the name of the view controller's nib file matches the name of the class, the nib file is loaded automatically on alloc/init. That's how the SettingsViewController class knows to load SettingsViewController.xib. You can also load a nib file with a different name by using the `initWithNibName:bundle:` method.

- Notice that the `modalTransitionStyle` property is set on the *new* view controller, not the current one. That is, set `settingsViewController.modalTransitionStyle`, not `self.modalTransitionStyle`.

- When `presentModalViewController:animated:` is used, it establishes a parent-child relationship between the current view controller and the new one. So no matter what happens on the modal view controller, when it is dismissed, the current view controller is shown again. For Tweet, this means that the Settings button flips to the Settings view, and when the Done button is tapped on the Settings view, the view flips back to the Tweet view.

- As always, notice that you used alloc/init to initialize the `settingsViewController`, so you must release it.

After adding the previous code, save your app, build it, and run it in the simulator. Give that Settings button a tap and see what happens. If you see a gorgeous flip animation, then you're on the right track.

Now, try tapping the Done button on the settings screen. Hmm, nothing happens. Let's do something about that.

Flip Back to the Tweet Screen

When the user taps the Done button on the Settings view, you want it to flip back to the Tweet view. To achieve this, you just need to dismiss the modal view. Add the following code to SettingsViewController.m to flip back to the Tweet view:

```
// SettingsViewController.m

// Dismisses the settings view by flipping back to the tweet view
- (IBAction)doneButtonTapped
{
    [self dismissModalViewControllerAnimated:YES];
}
```

ONE MORE THING

The previous code shows how a modal view can dismiss itself; however, this is not the proper way to dismiss a modal view controller. Convention dictates that the view controller that originally displayed the modal view also dismiss the modal view. In the Tweet app, this means `TweetViewController` should dismiss the settings modal view, but self-dismissal shown above works for now.

Dismissing a modal view, as you can see, is pretty simple. Just call the `dismissModalViewControllerAnimated:` method, and poof! It's gone. Or, in this case, flip! It's gone.

To see whether it works, save your project and launch it in the simulator. Try tapping the Settings button, and then the Done button. Your view should be flipping back and forth like a hot potato. If it doesn't, the most likely reason is your Done button isn't connected to the doneButtonPressed action method in Interface Builder.

Models

So far, you've built the views for your application and successfully hooked them up to the controllers. You have also finished defining how the user will navigate through the app. Now that you have the wiring in place, let's move on toward implementing the Twitter integration in the app. For this phase, you will create a TwitterUser model class to keep track of the user and their latest tweet.

The TwitterUser model class, as you will see, is dead simple. It just contains two properties, one for the username and one for the tweet, and that's it. Model classes are typically very simple like this. Their primary role is keeping track of application data, and as such, they don't need to do much.

To add the TwitterUser model class, follow these steps:

1. In Xcode, right-click the **Classes** group, and select **Add > New File.**

2. In the **iPhone OS > Cocoa Touch Class** category, select **Objective-C** class and make sure "Subclass of" is set to NSObject.

3. Click **Next**. Name the file "TwitterUser.m," and click **Finish**.

4. Edit TwitterUser.h so it matches the following code:

```
// TwitterUser.h

#import <Foundation/Foundation.h>

@interface TwitterUser : NSObject
{
  NSString *username;
  NSString *tweet;
}

@property (nonatomic, copy) NSString *username;
@property (nonatomic, copy) NSString *tweet;

@end
```

5. Edit TwitterUser.m so it matches the following code:

```
// TwitterUser.m

#import "TwitterUser.h"

@implementation TwitterUser

@synthesize username;
@synthesize tweet;

- (void)dealloc
{
    [username release];
    [tweet release];
    [super dealloc];
}

@end
```

Save and build your project to make sure you don't have any typos. It should build cleanly at this point.

One thing to note about the TwitterUser.h file: notice how the properties use the copy attribute? As a rule of thumb, you should use the copy attribute when the object type is NSString. For other object types, you'll usually use retain.

Controlling Models

Now that you have defined your model class, you should use it. The goal of your model class is to keep track of data between the Tweet and Settings views. When the Tweet view is displayed, it will initialize the TwitterUser object with a default username. When the user flips to the Settings view to change the username, the TwitterUser object will also reflect the change. Then, when the user flips back to the Tweet view, it will refresh the latest tweet based on the username stored in the TwitterUser object. If this doesn't make sense, it'll become clearer as you write code.

The first thing you need to do is add support for the TwitterUser model class to the TweetViewController. First, add the TwitterUser to your TwitterViewController.h file, as follows:

```
// TweetViewController.h

#import "TwitterUser.h"

@interface TweetViewController : UIViewController
{
   ...
   TwitterUser *twitterUser;
}
...
@end
```

Now, you will initialize the `twitterUser` variable when the nib file is first loaded. You also will add code to update the interface based on the model object. Add the following code to TwitterViewController.m to make these changes:

```
// TweetViewController.m

#define kDefaultUsername    @"ActuallyNPH"
...

// Updates the interface with the latest user data
- (void)updateInterface
{
   // update the interface using model data
   usernameLabel.text = [NSString stringWithFormat:@"@%@",
                                  twitterUser.username];
   tweetTextView.text = twitterUser.tweet;
}

// Initialize the user when the nib loads
- (void)awakeFromNib
{
   twitterUser = [[TwitterUser alloc] init];
   twitterUser.username = kDefaultUsername;
   twitterUser.tweet = @"";
}
...

- (void)dealloc
{
   [usernameLabel release];
   [tweetTextView release];
   [twitterUser release];
   [super dealloc];
}
```

In the preceding code, if you're not familiar with C, then you may wonder what kDefaultUsername is. The term itself is simply a constant. Take special note that the #define line does *not* end with a semicolon.

Save your project, and make sure it still builds cleanly. At this point, TweetViewController creates the model instance when it starts, but it needs to share this model class with the SettingsViewController. To easily share the model, you will add a twitterUser property on the SettingsViewController so the TweetViewController can pass along a pointer to its TwitterUser instance.

First, make sure you call this property in the right place in TweetViewController.m. After you initialize the SettingsViewController object in the settingsButtonTapped action method, add this line:

```
// TweetViewController.m

- (IBAction)settingsButtonTapped
{
    SettingsViewController *settingsViewController =
        [[SettingsViewController alloc] init];

    settingsViewController.modalTransitionStyle =
        UIModalTransitionStyleFlipHorizontal;

    settingsViewController.twitterUser = twitterUser;

    [self presentModalViewController:settingsViewController
        animated:YES];
    [settingsViewController release];
}
```

Now, you must add the property to the SettingsViewController. Add the following code to SettingsViewController.h:

```
// SettingsViewController.h

#import "TwitterUser.h"

@interface SettingsViewController : UIViewController
    <UITextFieldDelegate>
{
    ...
    TwitterUser *twitterUser;
}
```

continues

```
@property (nonatomic, retain) TwitterUser *twitterUser;
...
@end
```

Then, add this code to SettingsViewController.m:

```
// SettingsViewController.m

// Set the username text just before the view appears
- (void)viewWillAppear:(BOOL)animated
{
    [super viewWillAppear:animated];
    usernameTextField.text = twitterUser.username;
}

// Update the model object with the username before
// dismissing the modal view
- (IBAction)doneButtonTapped
{
    twitterUser.username = usernameTextField.text;

    [self dismissModalViewControllerAnimated:YES];
}
...

- (void)dealloc
{
    [usernameTextField release];
    [twitterUser release];
    [super dealloc];
}
```

viewWillAppear: is one of many view controller lifecycle methods that are called automatically over the span of a view controller's existence. As the name implies, viewWillAppear: is called just before a view controller becomes visible to the user. Let's take a moment to cover what these lifecycle methods are and how you can use them in your applications.

View Controller Lifecycle Methods

View controllers have a number of methods that are automatically invoked over the controller's life span. Sometimes, you want to do some setup when the view controller is first initialized. Or you might want to customize the view programmatically before it's displayed to the user. You can override these lifecycle methods in your view controller subclasses.

Here's a brief description of each view controller lifecycle method:

- **awakeFromNib:** If you built the view for your view controller in Interface Builder, then `awakeFromNib` is called just before the view is unpacked and initialized from the nib file.

- **loadView:** After `awakeFromNib`, `loadView` is called. `loadView` is where you can programmatically add views to the interface.

ONE MORE THING

Here's a little secret you should be aware of: you don't need Interface Builder to build your interface. It is quite possible to create your entire interface programmatically in `loadView`. There is no inherent advantage to writing the code by hand, however. In this book, you will continue to use Interface Builder to visually lay out the interface for each app.

- **viewDidLoad:** Regardless if a view was created programmatically or loaded from a nib, `viewDidLoad` is called after the view has been fully loaded into memory.

- **viewWillAppear:** The `viewWillAppear:` method is called immediately before the view controller's view appears onscreen. However, `viewWillAppear:` can be called multiple times throughout the lifetime of the view controller. In Tweet, every time you flip between the Tweet and Settings view controllers, the `viewWillAppear:` method for each of them is called.

- **viewDidAppear:** The `viewDidAppear:` method is called after the transition animation to the view controller has completed.

- **viewWillDisappear:** The `viewWillDisappear:` method is called—you guessed it—right before the view disappears. Specifically, this is when the user navigates away from the current view, but before any transition animation starts.

- **viewDidDisappear:** The `viewDidDisappear:` method is called after the transition animation away from the current view controller has completed.

- **viewDidUnload:** The `viewDidUnload` method is called in low-memory situations. Specifically, when the view controller is *not* visible and receives a low-memory warning, then the viewDidUnload method is called. You should release all the retained views in this method to free up as much memory as possible. The next time your view controller is displayed, your view will be rebuilt.

CRASH AND LEARN

Never call any of the aforementioned lifecycle methods directly. Each lifecycle method is invoked at the appropriate time automatically by the system. Calling these methods directly will likely have disastrous results.

Don't worry if it doesn't make complete sense right now. It will take time and practice to understand exactly how you can use these lifecycle methods in your own apps. Just pay attention to how these methods are used in the book's example applications, starting with the Tweet app.

Add viewWillAppear: to TweetViewController

In SettingsViewController, you use the viewWillAppear: method to set the username text field string to the value in the model class. By using viewWillAppear:, you guarantee the text field value is set before the SettingsViewController becomes visible.

In TweetViewController, you will use viewWillAppear: to get the user's latest tweet and update the interface with data from the model object. viewWillAppear: is the perfect spot for this, for two reasons:

- When the app is first launched, the viewWillAppear: method is called before the interface becomes visible, which means that the Latin in the text view will be replaced with a real tweet.

- After the user updates the Twitter username on the Settings screen, viewWillAppear: is called just before it flips back to the Tweet view. You can update both the usernameLabel outlet with the new username and grab the latest tweet for that user before the user sees the Tweet view again.

Before you override `viewWillAppear:`, however, you need to download the TwitterHelper files you can use to interact with the Twitter API. Follow these steps to grab and use the TwitterHelper files in your project:

1. Download and unzip the files in http://troybrant.net/iphonebook/chapter11/TwitterHelper.zip.

2. Drag-and-drop the TwitterHelper directory into the Classes group in Xcode. Make sure **Copy items into destination group's folder (if needed)** is checked.

3. Save and build the project. It should build without any problems.

4. Add the following method to TweetViewController.m:

```objc
// TweetViewController.m

#import "TwitterHelper.h"

// Update the interface with a real tweet from the user
// before the view appears
- (void)viewWillAppear:(BOOL)animated
{
    [super viewWillAppear:animated];

    NSString *latestTweet =
            [TwitterHelper fetchLatestTweetForUsername:
                    twitterUser.username];
    twitterUser.tweet = latestTweet;

    [self updateInterface];
}
```

Notice that when you grab the tweet, the first thing you do is update the model with the information. Then, in `updateInterface`, you use the data in the model to update the view. Always update the application in this sequence: model first, then the view.

Time for the moment of truth. Save your project, build it, and give it a whirl in the iPhone Simulator. You should have a fully functioning multi-view Twitter app. Try changing the username to see if the tweet updates. If it does, you have successfully completed your first multi-view application.

THERE'S A TIP FOR THAT

Notice how the interface freezes for a moment when fetching the tweet? Instead of hanging the interface, you *should* flip to the other view immediately and display a spinner while the app retrieves the tweet. To do this properly, you need to fetch the tweet in a background thread. If you are interested right now, take a look at the source code for a version of Tweet that uses a background thread, available online at http://troybrant.net/iphonebook/chapter11/Tweet-spinner.zip.

Full source code for the finished Tweet application is available online at http://troybrant.net/iphonebook/chapter11/Tweet-done.zip.

Tweedle Dee, Tweedle Done

Phew! It took a while, but you finally finished the app. You can finally take a break, watch some TV, catch up on email, and … check your Twitter feed? Of course, you don't have too much time to spare—you can just read one tweet at a time using your new handy-dandy iPhone app.

You covered quite a bit of ground this chapter. After getting a dose of MVC theory, you saw some of its practical use by building the Tweet app. You also read about modal views and discovered how easy it is to flip to a new view controller. Speaking of new view controllers, you built a model class to keep track of the application data, and found it to be a really useful way to pass data between view controllers. Finally, you went over view controller lifecycle methods such as `viewDidLoad` and `viewWillAppear:`.

It's a lot to take in, but the following figure shows how you structured the Tweet app according to MVC:

In the next chapter, you will sink your teeth into using navigation controllers to transition horizontally between view controllers. Push and pop will sound less like an exotic dance move and more like a way of managing view controllers after you finish the chapter. Navigation controllers are built specifically for organizing hierarchical data, and you will build another Twitter app to see exactly how it all works.

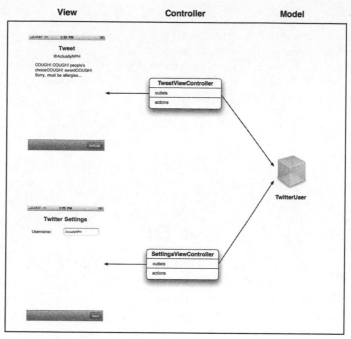

MVC is crucial to iPhone development, and this is precisely what it looks like applied to the Tweet app.

The Least You Need to Know

- In an MVC application, model classes manage data, views deal with how the app looks, and controller classes glue all the parts together.
- To launch a modal view, use `UIViewController`'s `presentModalViewController:animated:` method.
- Use model classes to pass data between your view controllers.
- Never invoke view controller lifecycle methods like `viewWillAppear:` directly. The system takes care of calling them at the right times.

Navigation Controllers

In This Chapter

- Navigation bars and controllers
- Application delegates
- Adding buttons and changing titles on the navigation bar
- Passing data to a new view controller
- CelebriTweets app

When Apple was developing the original iPhone interface, they had several teams working on the built-in applications. One team worked on Mail and Calendar. Another worked on the Phone and SMS apps. Other teams worked on the iPod, Clock, Maps, Settings, and Notes apps. And all of these apps had to solve the same problem: hierarchical navigation. How do you get around in the application? How do you know where you are? There was no iPhone SDK at the time, so each of these groups came up with their own solutions. As you can imagine, every implementation was slightly different, and this got messy in a hurry.

After the teams realized they were all solving the same problem, they consolidated their solutions into the UINavigationController class. Now, instead of 20 different navigation schemes, all the built-in apps use just one navigation class, streamlining the process for both engineers and users alike.

This navigation class Apple wrote for their own use is available to you in the iPhone SDK as well. In this chapter, you will learn about the UINavigationController class and discover how you can use it to move between multiple views in your application.

Navigation Controller Basics

So what exactly is a navigation controller? Well, the textbook definition is that it manages a hierarchy of views as the user moves through an app. However, it's much easier to comprehend visually, and you can see how navigation controllers work in the following image:

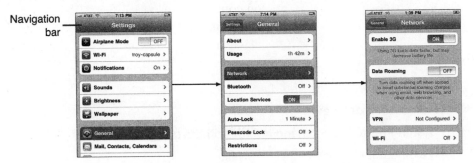

Navigation bar

The Settings app is a prime example of what navigation controllers look like and how they work.

The bar above the view is known as the "navigation bar". The navigation bar displays the current view's title, as well as a back button that returns you to the previous view.

UINavigationController

In code, the navigation controller is represented using the `UINavigationController` class.

ONE MORE THING

For more detailed coverage of `UINavigationController`, look it up in the API documentation. You can do this by accessing **Help > Documentation** in Xcode and then searching for "UINavigationController" in the top right search box.

The `UINavigationController` class has two main elements: a stack of view controllers, and the navigation bar.

DEFINITION

A **stack** is a special collection of items where the last item added is the first item removed—otherwise known as last-in/first-out (LIFO). To add an item to the stack is to **push** the item to the top of the stack. Removing an item from the stack is accomplished by **popping** the item that was most recently added to the stack.

Typically when setting up a navigation controller in your app, you'll provide a view controller to initially display. This view controller is known as the *root view controller*. Let's look at how you might set up a navigation controller when the application launches.

DEFINITION

The **root view controller** is the initial view controller a navigation controller displays.

```
- (void)applicationDidFinishLaunching:(UIApplication *)app
{
    firstViewController *firstViewController =
        [[firstViewController alloc] init];

    navController =
        [[UINavigationController alloc]
            initWithRootViewController:firstViewController];

    [firstViewController release];

    [window addSubview:navController.view];
    [window makeKeyAndVisible];
}
```

In the previous code, you see a new tactic to build your iPhone OS application. Instead of just using the View-based Application template to add a single view controller to the window, you create and add a navigation controller in code.

You may also notice that the previous code is in the applicationDidFinishLaunching: method. Every iPhone and iPad app has an application delegate object that is notified about various application events, such as when the application finishes launching. Up to this point, you have been able to safely ignore the application delegate. However, now that you are going to programmatically add a navigation controller to your main window, you put that code in the application delegate's `applicationDidFinishLaunching:` method.

Pushing View Controllers

When you want to show a new view controller using the navigation controller, you *push* it onto the navigation stack. Let's say that your navigation controller is displaying a view controller called `SettingsViewController`. To display a new view controller, use the `pushViewController:animated:` method, as shown in the following:

```
GeneralViewController *generalViewController =
  [[GeneralViewController alloc] init];

[self.navigationController
  pushViewController:generalViewController
  animated:YES];

[generalViewController release];
```

The `GeneralViewController`—the middle view controller in the previous image—will then slide horizontally onto the screen. Without any additional code on your part, a back button will appear in the navigation bar. When the user taps it, the `GeneralViewController` will be popped off the navigation stack, and the `SettingsViewController` will slide back into view. Notice that view controllers can access their parent navigation controller using the `self.navigationController` property.

CRASH AND LEARN

You will almost never pop view controllers off the navigation stack yourself. Let the built-in back button do the work for you.

Customizing the Navigation Bar

After adding a navigation controller to your interface, the first thing you should do is change the title. Instead of setting the navigation bar's title directly, however, you need to change the title of each view controller's *navigation item*. The navigation controller updates the appearance of the navigation bar with the contents of the current view controller's navigation item before your view controller is displayed. You can customize each view controller's navigation item, as shown in the following:

Navigation Item

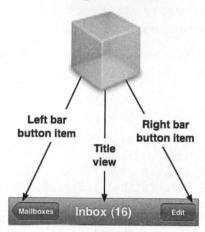

You can customize all three parts of the navigation bar: left button, title, and right button.

DEFINITION

Editing a view controller's **navigation item** allows you to customize the left button, right button, and title of the view controller in the navigation bar. The UINavigationItem class represents a navigation item in code.

In code, a navigation item is represented using the UINavigationItem class. To set the title, set the title on the navigation item in your view controller class:

```
- (void)viewDidLoad
{
    // Set the navigation bar title
    self.navigationItem.title = @"Settings";

    // You can also set the navigation
    // bar title using self.title
    self.title = @"Settings";
}
```

When you update the navigation item, make sure you do it in the viewDidLoad method. viewDidLoad is called after the navigation item itself has been properly initialized.

Alternatively, you can set the title in the navigation bar using the view controller's `title` property. One advantage to setting the title on the view controller instead of the navigation item is the title appears in tab bars as well as navigation bars.

If you want to add a button to the toolbar, you need to create a `UIBarButtonItem` and add it to the navigation item:

```
- (void)viewDidLoad
{
    UIBarButtonItem *editButton =
        [[UIBarButtonItem alloc]
            initWithTitle:@"Edit"
            style:UIBarButtonItemStyleBordered
            target:self
            selector:@selector(editButtonTapped)];
    self.navigationItem.rightBarButtonItem = editButton;
    [editButton release];
}
```

This will display an edit button to the right of the title in the navigation bar whenever this view controller is being displayed. When the button is tapped, the `editButtonTapped` method is invoked.

You can also choose to display a button with a system icon by using `UIBarButtonItem`. For instance, if you want to display the system "+" icon, use the `initWithBarButtonSystemItem:style:target:action:` method instead:

```
- (void)viewDidLoad
{
    UIBarButtonItem *addButton =
        [[UIBarButtonItem alloc]
            initBarButtonSystemItem:UIBarButtonSystemItemAdd
            style:UIBarButtonItemStyleBordered
            target:self
            selector:@selector(addButtonTapped)];
    self.navigationItem.rightBarButtonItem = addButton;
    [addButton release];
}
```

CelebriTweets App

There's something fascinating—and a little morbid—about knowing what's going on in the private lives of celebrities. Instead of resisting this urge, you get to feed your curiosity by building a Twitter app that shows what your favorite celebrities are tweeting about. You'll have a chance to exercise your newfound `UINavigationController` knowledge in building the app. Here is the finished product:

CelebriTweets uses a UINavigationController and uses custom buttons in the navigation bar.

Once again, you will be given some guidance on building the app interface in Interface Builder. Because you have done it a few times now, every little detail won't be provided. Given that you have never used a navigation controller before, on the other hand, you will be given a step-by-step process for adding a `UINavigationController` to your app.

Celebrities View Controller

To get started, follow these steps:

1. Create a new Window-based Application and name it "CelebriTweets." Notice that you are *not* using the View-based Application template like you have in previous chapters. You will add the navigation controller in code to gain a better understanding of how navigation controllers work.

2. Just like you did last chapter, create a new `UIViewController` subclass named "CelebritiesViewController" to the project. Make sure the **With XIB for user interface** checkbox is checked. Also, keep your code organized by moving the .m and .h files to the Classes group and the .xib file to the Resources group.

3. Edit CelebritiesViewController.xib so it matches the following image:

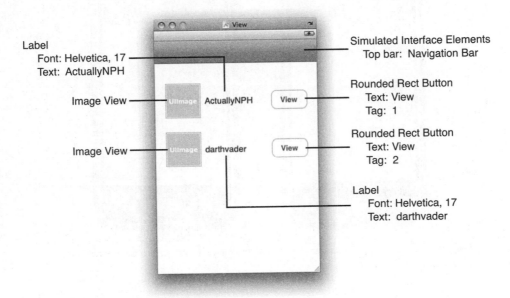

Build your CelebritiesViewController.xib view so it matches the interface shown.

Notice that the navigation bar at the top is simulated while you're in Interface Builder, since the view controller hasn't yet been pushed onto a navigation stack. To get this effect, select the **root view object**, then select the **Attributes tab** of the inspector window. In the Simulated Interface Elements section, select **Navigation Bar** for the Top Bar field.

You can also set the Tag field in the Attributes tab of the inspector window. You will use the tag value later to identify which button was tapped.

4. Add the following outlets to your `CelebritiesViewController` class:

   • `firstUserLabel` of type `UILabel`

   • `secondUserLabel` of type `UILabel`

- `firstUserImageView` of type `UIImageView`

- `secondUserImageView` of type `UIImageView`

Remember, add instance variables to the class for each outlet. Also, remember to use the IBOutlet specifier when adding a property for each outlet.

5. Release these instance variables appropriately in your view controller's `dealloc` method.

6. Add the following action to your `CelebritiesViewController` class:
   `- (IBAction)viewButtonTapped:(UIButton *)sender;`

   Be sure to add the action method to both .h and .m files. The method body in the .m file should be empty.

7. Hook up the outlets and actions as shown in the following image:

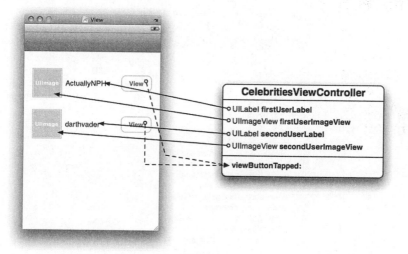

Connect the outlets and actions to the interface.

Notice how both view buttons are connected to the same action method. Remember how you gave each button a unique "tag" in Interface Builder? You will use that value to determine which button was tapped.

Your first view is now ready for action. Save your project, and build it. There should be no build errors, and if that is the case, then you can start building the profile view controller.

Profile View Controller

The profile view controller is the second level of the hierarchy. It will be pushed on the navigation stack and displayed when the user taps one of the "View" buttons in the top level view. Go ahead and build it:

1. Add a `UIViewController` subclass named "ProfileViewController" to the project. Just like the `CelebritiesViewController`, be sure to generate the nib file.

2. Edit ProfileViewController.xib so it matches the following image:

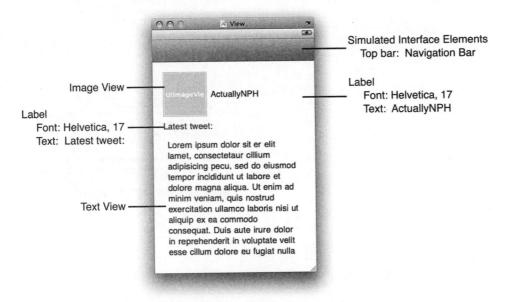

Build your ProfileViewController.xib view so it matches the interface shown.

3. Add the following outlets to your `ProfileViewController` class:

    - `usernameLabel` of type `UILabel`
    - `userImageView` of type `UIImageView`
    - `tweetTextView` of type `UITextView`

4. Release these instance variables appropriately in your view controller's `dealloc` method.

5. Hook up the outlets as shown in the following image:

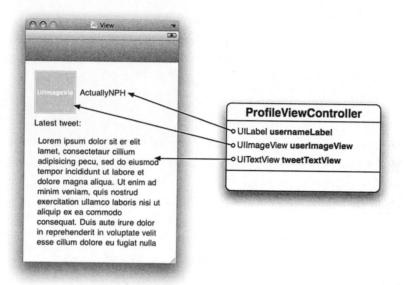

Connect the outlets and actions to the interface.

TwitterUser Model

Just like the previous chapter, you will use a model class to keep track of application data. And, just like the previous chapter, your model will consist of the `TwitterUser` class.

We'll modify the previous `TwitterUser` class to include one more property: the user's image. Use the `UIImage` class to store and modify images. If you reuse the `TwitterUser` class from the last chapter, be sure to add a `UIImage image` instance variable and matching property.

You will use the model class once again to pass data between the view controllers. The `CelebritiesViewController` will contain two `TwitterUser` objects, one for each user in the list. The `ProfileViewController` will display one user at a time, so it only needs a single `TwitterUser` model object reference.

Let's go ahead and set up the project to support the model class. Follow these steps to add `TwitterUser`:

1. Add an Objective-C class to the project, and make sure it is a subclass of `NSObject`. Name it "TwitterUser.m."

2. Add the following instance variables:

   - `username` of type `NSString`

   - `tweet` of type `NSString`

   - `image` of type `UIImage`

3. Add properties for each of these instance variables. Use the `copy` attribute for each `NSString` and `retain` for the `UIImage`. Be sure to synthesize your properties.

4. Add the following instance variables to CelebritiesViewController.h:

   - `firstUser` of type `TwitterUser`

   - `secondUser` of type `TwitterUser`

5. Add a `TwitterUser` instance variable named "twitterUser" to ProfileViewController.h.

6. Add a property for this `twitterUser` instance variable using the `retain` attribute. Be sure to synthesize the property.

7. Add the proper memory management code for the code added previously. Hint: release all your instance variables.

Your view controllers are now ready to make use of `TwitterUser` model objects.

Starter Code

It took a while, but that should do it for app setup. At this point, save your project, and try to build it. You should be error-free and warning-free.

Starter code to reach this point is available online at: http://troybrant.net/iphonebook/chapter12/CelebriTweets-starter-code.zip.

Now, try to run the app in the iPhone Simulator. You will be greeted with a blank white screen. What's going on? Remember that you used the Window-based Template, so it is up to you to set the window's contents. Don't worry: all your hard work to get to this point will pay off just after you add a navigation controller to the window.

Adding a UINavigationController

Up to this point, you have used Interface Builder for your interface needs. Interface Builder is fantastic for designing individual screens of your interface, but when it comes to linking those screens together, doing it in code is much more convenient. So you are going to build your navigation controller entirely in code.

Editing CelebriTweetsAppDelegate

As discussed earlier, you need to create a UINavigationController instance in the applicationDidFinishLaunching: method of the application delegate. For CelebriTweets, the CelebriTweetsAppDelegate is the class you need to modify. This class was created automatically when you used the Window-based Application template to create the project.

The first step in adding the navigation controller is to give the application delegate an instance variable. Match your code to the following:

```
// CelebriTweetsAppDelegate.h

@interface CelebriTweetsAppDelegate : NSObject
  <UIApplicationDelegate>
{
  UIWindow *window;
  UINavigationController *navController;
}
```

Now, you need to create the navigation controller. Do this in the applicationDidFinishLaunching: method:

```
// CelebriTweetsAppDelegate.m

#import "CelebritiesViewController.h"

- (void)applicationDidFinishLaunching:(UIApplication *)application
{
  CelebritiesViewController *celebritiesViewController =
```

continues

```
            [[CelebritiesViewController alloc] init];

    navController =
        [[UINavigationController alloc]
                initWithRootViewController:celebritiesViewController];
    [celebritiesViewController release];

    [window addSubview:navController.view];
    [window makeKeyAndVisible];
}

- (void)dealloc
{
    [window release];
    [navController release];
    [super dealloc];
}

@end
```

Save your project, build, and run it in the simulator. If you see a navigation bar and your CelebritiesViewController, then you're on the right track. If you don't see them, make sure you are adding the navigation controller's view as a subview of the window.

Notice that the CelebritiesViewController object is released after addition to the navigation controller. This is because navigation controllers retain each of the view controllers in their stacks.

Pushing View Controllers

Your next goal is to push a new ProfileViewController when one of the view buttons is tapped. To achieve this goal, add the code below to CelebritiesViewController.m:

```
// CelebritiesViewController.m

#import "ProfileViewController.h"

#define kFirstUserTag            1
#define kSecondUserTag           2

// Display the user profile when the "View" button is tapped
- (IBAction)viewButtonTapped:(UIButton *)sender
{
```

```
// Create the new view controller
ProfileViewController *profileViewController =
    [[ProfileViewController alloc] init];

// Pass the controller the correct user model object
if (button.tag == kFirstUserTag)
{
    profileViewController.twitterUser = firstUser;
}
else if (button.tag == kSecondUserTag)
{
    profileViewController.twitterUser = secondUser;
}

// Push the new view controller
[self.navigationController
        pushViewController:profileViewController
    animated:YES];

// Always remember memory management
[profileViewController release];
}
```

Because both view buttons point to the same action method, the tag property is used to tell which one was tapped. Note that you haven't initialized the firstUser and secondUser objects yet, but for now they are set to nil, which is perfectly fine while you get the navigation controller working.

Test your changes by running your project in the simulator. Now, try tapping one of the view buttons. Voilà! The ProfileViewController slides beautifully into view. Note the automatically built-in back button that takes you back to the list view.

You can now move between the two screens in your app, thanks to the navigation controller. Now, let's see about updating the navigation bar with titles and custom buttons.

Customizing the Navigation Bar

You customize the navigation bar in three ways: by adding a title for each view controller, by customizing the title of the back button, and by adding a new button to the right of the navigation bar title on the profile view.

Setting the Title

Let's set the title of CelebritiesViewController to "Celebrities" and ProfileViewController to "Profile."

To set the CelebritiesViewController's title, override the viewDidLoad method as shown in the following:

```
// CelebritiesViewController.m

- (void)viewDidLoad
{
    [super viewDidLoad];

    // Set the navigation bar title
    self.title = @"Celebrities";
}
```

Add the same code to ProfileViewController, but set the title to "Profile" instead. Save and run the code to make sure the titles appear. Notice that the title in the navigation bar automatically updates as you navigate back & forth.

Changing the Back Button

By default, the back button generated when you push a new view controller is set to the title of the previous view controller. Now, when you tap one of the view buttons, the back button will read "Celebrities."

Sometimes, though, you want to change the title of the back button, especially if your main title is long. It seems like it should be simple enough, right? Just access the backBarButtonItem property and change the title string. Unfortunately, customizing the back button is a bit more involved.

The first part to understand is that the back button is owned by the navigation item in the previous view controller. So when you are viewing the ProfileViewController and the back button is titled "Celebrities," the CelebritiesViewController owns the back button. Now, this may sound strange, but to customize the back button, you need to update the navigation item of the CelebritiesViewController, *not* the ProfileViewController.

Also, instead of simply changing the text property of the back button, you have to create an entirely new button. To see how it works, add the following code to your CelebritiesViewController class:

```
// CelebritiesViewController.m

- (void)viewDidLoad
{
  [super viewDidLoad];

  // Set the navigation bar title
  self.title = @"Celebrities";

  // Back button to use when SettingsViewController is on screen
  UIBarButtonItem *backButton = [[UIBarButtonItem alloc]
      initWithTitle:@"Back"
      style:UIBarButtonItemStylePlain
      target:nil
      action:nil];
  self.navigationItem.backBarButtonItem = backButton;
  [backButton release];
}
```

Notice how the target and action fields are both set to nil. If you don't specify the target and action fields, the back button pops the view controller by default.

Adding a Compose Button

Let's also add a button for composing a new tweet. Instead of using boring text or painstakingly creating a new icon, you will use the built-in system composition icon. Match the following code to add the button to your navigation bar:

```
// ProfileViewController.m

- (void)viewDidLoad
{
  [super viewDidLoad];

  self.title = @"Profile";

  // Set the right item in the navigation bar
  UIBarButtonItem *composeButton =
      [[UIBarButtonItem alloc]
```

continues

```
        initWithBarButtonSystemItem:UIBarButtonSystemItemCompose
        target:self
        action:@selector(composeButtonTapped)];
    self.navigationItem.rightBarButtonItem = composeButton;
    [composeButton release];
}

#pragma mark -
#pragma mark Action methods

// You could display a view for entering a new tweet here
- (void)composeButtonTapped
{
    NSLog(@"You could launch a new tweet modal view here");
}
```

Run the code in the iPhone Simulator to see your custom back button and new compose button. The composeButtonTapped method is where you can present a modal view for composing tweets. In fact, you can go ahead and add a Tweet composition view if you're feeling adventurous, but the method will be left empty for now.

You can find the code with all the preceding steps implemented at http://troybrant. net/iphonebook/chapter12/CelebriTweets-nav-done.zip.

That is the last update to the navigation controller you will make in this app. Now, you can turn your attention to getting and displaying some real Twitter data.

Twitter Data

All that remains is populating your model objects with Twitter data and updating the interface using these model objects. You have done this a few times now, so instead of giving you the code directly, we'll give you an outline of the steps to use real Twitter data.

Your general strategy will be to use the TwitterHelper class to populate the model objects and then update the interface based on these model objects in viewWillAppear:. You will do this for both CelebritiesViewController and ProfileViewController. Follow these steps to update CelebritiesViewController:

1. Download the TwitterHelper folder from http://troybrant.net/iphonebook/ chapter12/TwitterHelper.zip, and add it to your project.

2. In `CelebritiesViewController`, initialize the `firstUser` and `secondUser` model object in `viewDidLoad:`.

   - Set the first object's username to `@"ActuallyNPH"` and the second to `@"darthvader"`.

   - Use `TwitterHelper`'s `fetchLatestTweetForUsername:` class method to initialize the `tweet` property of both users.

   - Use `TwitterHelper`'s `fetchProfileImageForUsername:` class method to initialize the `image` property of both users.

3. Add `- (void)updateInterface` to CelebritiesViewController.m. Update the following interface elements:

   - Set `firstUserLabel.text` to `firstUser.username`

   - Set `firstUserImageView.image` to `firstUser.image`

   - Set `secondUserLabel.text` to `secondUser.username`

   - Set `secondUserImageView.image` to `secondUser.image`

4. Add `- (void)viewWillAppear:(BOOL)animated` to CelebritiesViewController.m. Call the `updateInterface` method in `viewWillAppear:`. Remember to call the superclass `viewWillAppear:` method, as you did last chapter.

Now, make the following changes to `ProfileViewController` so it can properly display a `TwitterUser`:

1. Add `- (void)updateInterface` to ProfileViewController.m. Update the following interface elements:

   - Set `usernameLabel.text` to `twitterUser.username`

   - Set `userImageView.image` to `twitterUser.image`

   - Set `tweetTextView.text` to `twitterUser.tweet`

2. Add `- (void)viewWillAppear:(BOOL)animated` to ProfileViewController.m. Call the `updateInterface` method in `viewWillAppear:`.

And that should do it. Save your project, build, and run in the iPhone Simulator. As your reward for your hard work this chapter, you should see little thumbnail images for Neil Patrick Harris and Darth Vader. Okay, maybe that's a crummy reward, but you can take pride in putting together your first honest-to-goodness navigation-based application.

Full source code for the finished CelebriTweets application is available online at http://troybrant.net/iphonebook/chapter12/CelebriTweets-done.zip.

All Done

Over the course of this chapter, you learned about navigation controllers and how to add them to your applications. You finally learned how to use the application delegate, adding the navigation controller directly to the window in `applicationDidFinishLaunching:`. You also learned how to customize the navigation bar's appearance based on the currently displayed view controller. Finally, you put it all together in building the CelebriTweets app, and now you can sit back, relax, and check out what Darth Vader is tweeting about.

The focus of this chapter was on navigation controllers, which organize your views hierarchically. In the next chapter, you learn an alternate way to organize your views: tabs. `UITabBarController` is used to present these tabs, and you will work up to combining both navigation and tab bar controllers in a single application.

The Least You Need to Know

- Navigation controllers manage a hierarchy of view controllers.
- To display a new view controller using the navigation controller, use `pushViewController:animated:`.
- Edit the `UINavigationItem` in your view controller's `viewDidLoad` method to customize the appearance of the navigation bar while the view controller is displayed.
- The back button displayed belongs to the *previous* view controller in the navigation stack.
- Use a model class to pass information to a new view controller before you push it on the navigation stack.

Tab Bar Controllers

In This Chapter

- UITabBarController
- UITabBarItem
- Tab overflow
- Combining navigation and tab bar controllers
- Chweeter app

What happens when you slide to unlock your iPhone or iPad? You hear the *click* of a latch unlocking. When you open the Camera app, what do you see? You see a closed shutter, as if you were using an old-timey, nondigital camera. When you type using the software keyboard, what do you hear? The tap-tap-tap of a physical keyboard spurts out of the device speakers.

One of the reasons both iPhone and iPad are so intuitive is because they use these *physical metaphors*. A physical metaphor recreates the properties of a real-world object in software. These metaphors help users feel familiar and comfortable while using various applications. These features also help communicate exactly how you use the apps without needing an instruction manual.

This chapter covers another physical metaphor used extensively in the iPhone OS: tabs. The UITabBarController class is used to organize your views in a flat list, one for each tab. You learn how to add both an icon image and a text label to each tab, and you see how you can combine navigation controllers and tab bar controllers in a single application.

Intro to Tab Bar Controllers

A tab bar controller presents a list of tabs at the bottom of the application view. Each tab corresponds to a single view controller, which is loaded and displayed when the user selects the tab. For example, see the App Store app, which uses a tab bar controller to organize its views:

Each tab corresponds to a different view controller.

For iPhone apps, the maximum number of tabs a tab bar can display is five. For iPad apps, the maximum is seven tabs. If you have more than the maximum, the tab bar controller will automatically display a "More" tab, which lists the rest of the items. You will see exactly how this works in a few sections.

Initializing the Tab Bar Controller

The UITabBarController class is used to add tab bars to your apps. To initialize a tab bar controller, create an array of view controllers, and assign it to the tab bar's viewControllers property. You add the tab bar controller's view to the window in applicationDidFinishLaunching:. See the sample code that follows for an example:

```
- (void)applicationDidFinishLaunching:(UIApplication *)app
{
    // Initialize the view controllers
    SomeViewController *firstViewController = ...;
    AnotherViewController *secondViewController = ...;
    YetAnotherViewController *thirdViewController = ...;

    // Initialize the array
    NSArray *viewControllers = [NSArray arrayWithObjects:
```

```
          firstViewController,
          secondViewController,
          thirdViewController,
          nil];

      // Initialize the tab bar controller
      tabBarController = [[UITabBarController alloc] init];

      // Set the view controllers
      tabBarController.viewControllers = viewControllers;

      // Add the tab bar controller's view to the window
      [window addSubview:tabBarController.view];

      // Display the window
      [window makeKeyAndVisible];
  }
```

The tab bar controller creates tabs for the view controllers in the order that you add them. In the previous code, the firstViewController is displayed on the first tab, the secondViewController on the second, and the thirdViewController on the third.

ONE MORE THING

Check out the Apple documentation for the UITabBarController class. When you finish this book, Apple's docs will be your best friend for learning new iPhone programming topics. It is good to get into the habit of looking at the docs any time you come across a new class or concept in this book. Your future self will thank you later for being so disciplined.

Customizing the Tab Bar Buttons

Tabs themselves can be customized by editing your view controller's tabBarItem property. In the previous chapter, you needed to edit the navigationItem property to customize the navigation bar for each view controller, and tab bar items work the same way.

There are two properties you can edit for each tab: the icon and the text. When setting the icon image, there are a few rules to keep in mind:

- The image should be roughly 30×30 pixels in size. If it is too large, the image is automatically scaled to fit.

- The *alpha values* of your image are used to determine the shape of the icon. Areas of your image with an alpha value of 1 will be completely filled in. Areas of your image with alpha values of 0 will be empty. Colors in your image are ignored, so to produce a particular shape, you need to adjust your image's alpha values.

> **DEFINITION**
>
> The **alpha value** of an image determines the image's transparency. Alpha values range from 0—completely invisible—to 1—completely visible.

- PNG is the best image format to use for tabs—and everywhere else in your application.

> **CRASH AND LEARN**
>
> JPEG images do not support transparency, so they should not be used for tab icons.

Instead of editing an existing `tabBarItem` property, you need to create a new `UITabBarItem` when the view controller is first initialized. To see how to set a custom tab bar item, check out the following code:

```
// Initialize the image
UIImage *tabImage = [UIImage imageNamed:@"webIcon.png"];

// Initialize a new tab bar item
UITabBarItem *tabBarItem = [[UITabBarItem alloc]
  initWithTitle:@"Web"
  image:tabImage
  tag:0];

// Set the view controller's tab bar item
self.tabBarItem = tabBarItem;

// Gotta remember memory management
[tabBarItem release];
```

When initializing an image in code, you use the `UIImage` class and `imageNamed:` method, as shown previously. `imageNamed:` is very convenient because you just pass it the name of your image, and it hunts down the image in your project for you. All you have to do is make sure the image has been added to your project.

Provided the webIcon.png image is part of the project, the previous code will produce a custom tab that displays both the image and the title "Web."

Too Many Tabs

As mentioned earlier, there is only room for a maximum of five tabs in the tab bar view. Instead of leaving you out to dry if you have more than five tabs, however, the tab bar controller automatically inserts a More tab at the end of the tab list. When the More tab is selected, it lists all your extra view controllers in a table view. You can see the More tab in the following iPod app screenshots:

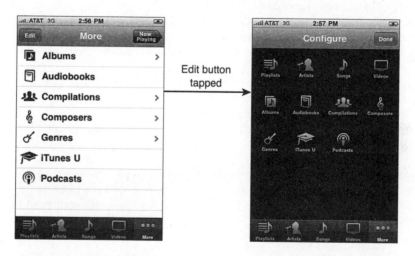

Tab overflow view controller   Tab layout view controller

The More tab is displayed automatically when you have six or more view controllers in your tab bar. You can customize the tab order after tapping the Edit button.

There is nothing you need to do to enable the More tab. This overflow behavior comes for free.

In fact, the user can even edit the order of the tabs by tapping the Edit button in the overflow view. The resulting organizing view is shown on the right in the image above. This, too, comes for free when you use the `UITabBarController` class. All you have to do is add six or more view controllers when you initialize the tab bar controller.

Combining Tab Bar and Navigation Controllers

Because navigation controllers are a subclass of `UIViewController`, you can add them to a tab bar just as easily as your own `UIViewController` subclasses. Just wrap your custom view controller in a `UINavigationController`, and add the navigation controller to the tab bar. For example, let's take the same tab bar initialization code shown previously and put one of the custom view controllers in a navigation controller:

```
- (void)applicationDidFinishLaunching:(UIApplication *)app
{
    // Initialize the view controllers
    SomeViewController *firstViewController = ...;
    AnotherViewController *secondViewController = ...;
    YetAnotherViewController *thirdViewController = ...;

    // Wrap the first view controller in a nav controller
    UINavigationController *navController =
        [[UINavigationController alloc]
            initWithRootViewController:firstViewController];

    // Initialize the array
    NSArray *viewControllers = [NSArray arrayWithObjects:
                                    navController,
                                    secondViewController,
                                    thirdViewController,
                                    nil];

    // Memory management
    [navController release];

    // Continue with tab bar initialization like normal
    ...
}
```

Any time you combine tab bars and navigation bars, you should always have the tab bar controller at the root of the view hierarchy. Here is an easy way to remember this rule: your app can have several navigation controllers—one for each tab—but there should only ever be one tab bar controller.

Chweeter App

To see how easy it is to add tab bar controllers to your apps, you are going to build the latest-and-greatest Twitter app that uses them. Up to this point, both of your previous Twitter applications have used the `TwitterHelper` class to grab data from the Twitter API. Instead of making the effort to use the `TwitterHelper` class again, you "chweet" by using a web view to display a user's Twitter profile. (Cheat + tweet = chweet, get it?)

By the time you're done the app will look like this:

You will "chweet" by using a web view instead of the Twitter API to display a user's profile.

As you can see in the previous figure, the interface consists of a tab bar controller with two tabs: one for the web view and another for a settings screen. The app works by taking the username entered on the settings screen and using it to open the mobile web page for the Twitter user.

To build the app, you do the normal app setup and then add the tab bar controller to the window in the application delegate. After customizing the tabs themselves, you will wire up the `TwitterUser` model object so that both tabs have access to the user's username.

Interface Challenge

Set up your application as usual, following along with the steps below. If you get lost or stuck, look to the previous chapters for more detailed explanations on the app setup. Also, at the end of this section, the completed starter code will be available for download on my website as usual.

First Steps

To get started, follow these steps:

1. Create a new Window-based Application and name it "Chweeter." You will build the tab bar controller in code, so ignore the conveniently placed Tab Bar Application template.

2. Add a class named "WebViewController" to your project, and edit the nib file so it matches the following image:

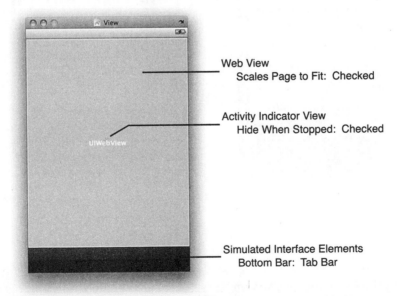

Build your WebViewController.xib file so it matches the interface shown.

Simulating the tab bar is just as easy as simulating the navigation bar in the previous chapter. Select the Attributes tab of the inspector window, then choose **Tab Bar** for the Bottom Bar field in the Simulated Interface Elements section.

3. First, add the outlets shown in the following image to your
   `WebViewController` class. Then, hook them up as shown in the image:

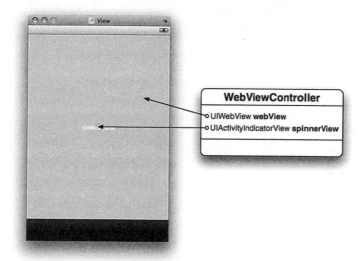

First, add the outlets shown to your WebViewController code files. Then, connect these outlets to the interface elements as shown here.

4. Add a class named "SettingsViewController" to your project, and edit the nib
   file so it matches the following image:

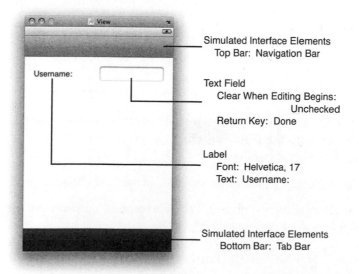

Build your SettingsViewController.xib file so it matches the interface shown.

5. Add and hook up these outlets to your `SettingsViewController` class:

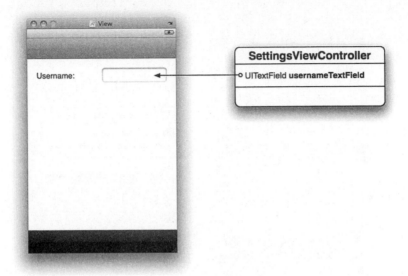

First, add the outlets shown to your SettingsViewController code files. Then, connect these outlets to the interface elements as shown here.

Hopefully, these setup steps are becoming second nature. You always start each project the exact same way: building the interface first and then hooking up the outlets and actions.

Add the Model

Again, the model will consist of the trusty `TwitterUser` class. And again, `TwitterUser` is used to pass data between the view controllers. Or, more accurately, both view controllers will point to the same `TwitterUser` object.

If you have your `TwitterUser` class from the previous two chapters, you can just drag-and-drop it into the Classes group of your project. Otherwise, you can write a new `TwitterUser` class as follows:

1. Add an `NSObject` subclass named "TwitterUser" to the project.

2. Add an instance variable and the corresponding property for a variable named "username" of type `NSString`.

The TwitterUser class is very simple this time around. If you are using a TwitterUser class you wrote in a previous chapter, it doesn't hurt to have the other instance variables and properties defined. You just won't use them.

Now you need to add the model class to your view controllers. You also need to add a property for each of these references so you can point both view controllers to the same TwitterUser object. To set up and use the model class, follow these steps:

1. Add a TwitterUser instance variable named "twitterUser" to both WebViewController.h and SettingsViewController.h.

2. For both classes, add a property for twitterUser. Be sure to synthesize the property.

You set these properties when you initialize the WebViewController and SettingsViewController objects. For now, though, your model references are defined and ready for action.

Starter Code

Starter code to reach this point is available online at: http://troybrant.net/iphonebook/chapter13/Chweeter-starter-code.zip.

Save your code, build it, and make sure it is both error- and warning-free. Run the code in the iPhone Simulator, and if you see a blank white screen, then you're ready to add the tab bar controller.

Adding a UITabBarController

Just as you did in Chapter 12 when adding navigation controllers, you will add the tab bar controller to the window directly in the app delegate.

The tab bar will manage two view controllers: the WebViewController and the SettingsViewController. To see how navigation controllers and tab bar controllers work together, you will wrap the SettingsViewController in a navigation controller. You can see how the tab bar organizes the views in the following image.

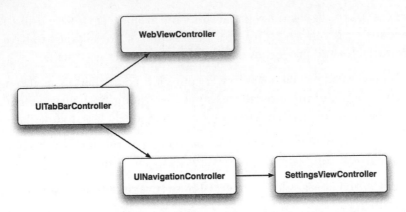

When combining tab bar controllers and navigation controllers, always put the tab bar controller at the root of the hierarchy.

To add the `UITabBarController`, edit your `ChweeterAppDelegate` class so it matches the following:

```
// ChweeterAppDelegate.h

@interface ChweeterAppDelegate : NSObject
  <UIApplicationDelegate>
{
  UIWindow *window;
  UITabBarController *tabBarController;
}
```

And now you must initialize and set the tab bar controller's array of view controllers:

```
// ChweeterAppDelegate.m

#include "WebViewController.h"
#include "SettingsViewController.h"

- (void)applicationDidFinishLaunching:(UIApplication *)application
{
  WebViewController *webViewController =
      [[WebViewController alloc] init];
  SettingsViewController *settingsViewController =
      [[SettingsViewController alloc] init];
```

```
// Wrap the settings view controller in a nav controller
UINavigationController *settingsNavController =
    [[UINavigationController alloc]
        initWithRootViewController:settingsViewController];

// Create an array of controllers the tab bar will use
NSArray *viewControllers = [NSArray arrayWithObjects:
    webViewController, settingsNavController, nil];

// Init the tab bar controller
tabBarController = [[UITabBarController alloc] init];
[tabBarController setViewControllers:viewControllers];
[tabBarController setSelectedIndex:1];

// Memory management
[webViewController release];
[settingsViewController release];
[settingsNavController release];

[window addSubview:tabBarController.view];
[window makeKeyAndVisible];
}
```

You can control which view controller is displayed first by using the
setSelectedIndex: method.

After adding the previous code, save your project, and give it a go in the simulator.
You should see your tab bar controller—hooray!—but unfortunately the tabs themselves are quite empty. You remedy this problem by setting the UITabBarItem for
each view controller.

Adding UITabBarItem to WebViewController

Each tab displays an icon and a title. You can download the icons from the book
website:

- The Web tab icon is at http://troybrant.net/iphonebook/chapter13/webIcon.
  png.

- The Settings tab icon is at http://troybrant.net/iphonebook/chapter13/
  settingsIcon.png.

After downloading the icons, add them to the Resources group of your project.

To customize the look of the tab for each view controller, you need to set the controller's tabBarItem property. This should be set in the view controller's life cycle *before* the view controller is added to the tab bar's array of tabs. The only place you can set the tab bar item to be certain it is initialized is in the init method. You will override the initWithNibName:bundle: method to create and set the tab bar item for each view controller.

CRASH AND LEARN

You can try initializing the tab bar item in viewDidLoad or viewWillAppear:, but unfortunately, this does not work. The problem is that these methods are not called on view controllers in your tab array until the user selects the tab.

Let's start with the WebViewController. Add the following code to the WebViewController.m file to customize its tab button:

```
// WebViewController.m

- (id)initWithNibName:(NSString *)nibName
    bundle:(NSBundle *)bundle
{
    if (self = [super initWithNibName:nibName bundle:bundle])
    {
        // Initialize this controller's appearance in the tab bar
        UIImage *tabImage = [UIImage imageNamed:@"webIcon.png"];
        UITabBarItem *tabBarItem = [[UITabBarItem alloc]
                initWithTitle:@"Web"
                image:tabImage
                tag:0];
        self.tabBarItem = tabBarItem;
        [tabBarItem release];
    }
    return self;
}
```

Any time you override an init method, you should follow the style shown previously. Also, note that the method returns an id object, not void.

Adding UITabBarItem to SettingsViewController

Customizing the tab button for the SettingsViewController is exactly the same process, except you should use the settingsIcon.png image and use "Settings" as the title of the tab. Go ahead and make these changes now:

- In SettingsViewController.m, override the `initWithNibName:bundle:` method.

- Set the view controller's `tabBarItem` to a `UIBarButtonItem` with the settingsIcon.png image and the title "Settings."

After making these changes, save your code, build it, and run it in the simulator. Both tabs should be properly labeled when the view first appears. And believe it or not, if they show up as expected, you are completely done with the tab bar controller part of the Chweeter app. The only part that remains is actually using the model object and wiring up the views. But, as you can see, adding a tab bar controller to your app and customizing the tabs is pretty easy to do.

You can download the reference solution with the finished tab bar controller online: http://troybrant.net/iphonebook/chapter13/Chweeter-tabs-done.zip.

Getting the Rest of the App Working

So, your web view doesn't display anything, and the settings view sits there. Although it may seem like it will take a good bit of work to get these two views working at all, you have already written both of these controllers in previous chapters. In Chapter 10, you wrote a web view controller, and this web view will work in much the same way. In Chapter 11, you wrote exactly the same settings view controller.

Because you can flip back to these chapters for assistance, you are given an outline of the code you need to add instead of showing you every line. And even though you can copy-and-paste code from the earlier chapters, I encourage you to try to write these files from scratch to better learn the material.

Without further ado, let's get started.

WebViewController

Flip back to Chapter 10 or check out the reference solution at the end of the chapter if you get stuck. Otherwise, follow these steps to update the `WebViewController` class:

1. Add the `UIWebViewDelegate` protocol to the class header.

2. Override `viewDidLoad`, and set your controller as the `webView` delegate.

3. Override `viewWillAppear:`, and have the web view display the user's Twitter page. You can accomplish this using the following:

- Access any user's Twitter page by loading the URL, http://mobile.twitter.com/[username]. For instance, my username is tbrant, so the URL for my online Twitter page is http://mobile.twitter.com/tbrant.

- Use the twitterUser model object to determine the Twitter username to load.

THERE'S A TIP FOR THAT

To combine two strings into one, you have several options, but I recommend using NSString's stringWithFormat: method. For instance, [NSString stringWithFormat:@"%@%@", @"Complete", @" Idiot's Guide"] produces the string "Complete Idiot's Guide."

- Construct an NSURLRequest, and load the request using the web view's loadRequest: method.

4. Override viewWillDisappear:, and tell the webView to stopLoading.

5. Implement the following UIWebViewDelegate methods:

   - webViewDidStartLoad: to start animating the spinnerView.

   - webViewDidFinishLoad: to stop animating the spinnerView.

   - webView:didFailLoadWithError: to stop animating the spinnerView, and create and show a UIAlertView with title "Error loading web page" and message [error localizedDescription]. It should display a single button labeled "OK."

After making all of these changes, test out your web view. Try entering some static twitter usernames, such as "the_real_shaq" or "darthvader." Also, try killing your network connection to see if the error alert pops up.

When you have the web view working, you can move on to implementing the SettingsViewController.

SettingsViewController

Again, you are given just a rough outline of what needs to be done to implement the settings view controller since you have written it once before. Refer to the Tweet app in Chapter 11 if you get stuck.

Make the following changes to your `SettingsViewController` class:

1. Add the `UITextFieldDelegate` protocol to the class header.

2. Override `viewDidLoad`, and set `self` as the `usernameTextField` delegate.

3. Override `viewWillAppear:`, and set the navigation item title to "Settings." Also, set the `text` property of the `usernameTextField` to the username of the `twitterUser` model object.

4. Implement the `textFieldShouldReturn:` text field delegate method. In the method, update the model object's username with the text in the text field. Dismiss the keyboard in this method as well. Don't forget the method returns a boolean, so you should return `YES`.

After making the previous changes, try it out in the iPhone Simulator. Make sure you can display and dismiss the keyboard. If you enter a username, however, note that it disappears if you switch between the Web and Settings tabs. What's the problem? One last critical piece is missing: initializing the model object.

One Final Step

Somehow, the Web tab needs to know what username is entered on the Settings tab. Instead of passing the username from the Settings view to the Web view, you will instead point both view controllers to the same model object. For instance, here is an example of how the process works::

- The user types in "ActuallyNPH" and taps **Done**.

- The `twitterUser` model object's username is set to "ActuallyNPH."

- The user selects the Web tab, and the Web view controller checks the contents of the model object for the username.

- The web view controller loads the web page for "ActuallyNPH."

The key to this process is that both tabs must point to the same model object. You can achieve this by initializing and setting the `TwitterUser` object when the view controllers are first created in `applicationDidFinishLaunching:`. Go ahead and initialize the model object by following these steps:

1. In `applicationDidFinishLaunching:` in ChweeterAppDelegate.m, alloc/init a new `TwitterUser` model object. You can decide whether you want to provide a default username or not.

2. Set the `twitterUser` property to this instance for both web and settings view controllers.

3. Properly manage memory for the `TwitterUser` model object you initialized in step 1.

These changes need to be made *after* you initialize the view controllers but *before* you add them to the tab bar controller.

Now, test your code again. After you enter a username, it should launch the online Twitter page for the user in the Web tab. Then, when you switch back to the Settings tab, the text field should display the username you entered. If all works as expected, then you are done!

Full source code for the finished Chweeter application is available online at http://troybrant.net/iphonebook/chapter13/Chweeter-done.zip.

All Done

As you just found out, tab bar controllers are easy to add to your applications. The part that takes the most time is writing the view controllers for each tab. Just as you did with navigation controllers, you created the tab bar controller in code. Setting the tabs was as easy as creating and assigning an array of view controllers. Because navigation controllers are just a view controller subclass, you can add them to the array as well. To customize the tabs themselves, you needed to override the `initWithNibName:bundle:` method, but then it was just a matter of setting the `self.tabBarItem` property to a new `UIBarButtonItem`. All in all, it's not much work, allowing you to focus on the behavior of each view controller rather than reinventing the wheel for your overall application structure.

The next chapter covers one of the all-time most important topics in iPhone programming: table views. "All-time most important" is a weighty claim, but you will find out just how true it is. Table views are used absolutely *everywhere* in iPhone and iPad apps. You learn how to display data in tables, but perhaps more importantly, you see how they can be combined with navigation controllers to provide a very powerful navigation mechanism.

The Least You Need to Know

- To initialize the tabs for a UITabBarController, you need to set the viewControllers property to an array of view controllers.
- Use 30×30 pixel PNG images for tab icons.
- Setting tab bar items in viewDidLoad will not work; instead, you must initialize them in initWithNibName:bundle:.
- Share data between view controllers by pointing them to the same model object.

Table Views

In This Chapter

- Table views
- Populating table view data using delegation
- NSIndexPath
- Row selection
- Integrating table views and navigation controllers
- Frenemies app

What user interface element are you most likely to use in your app? A button? Possibly. A text field? Perhaps. An image of a cat pleading, "I can haz cheezburger?" More than likely. But there is one interface element that you will undoubtedly use time and again in your apps: the table view.

Consider this statistic: all but one of Apple's built-in applications use table views (that one being the Calculator app). Table views are a flexible and effective way to display lots of data. In this chapter, you learn how to use UITableView in your own apps to display lists of content.

Intro to Table Views

Visually, you can think of a table view as a scrollable list. Like a list, the table consists of a single column with multiple rows. Table views are very scalable, supporting large data sets of up to 10,000 items. You can use them to display flat lists of information, such as grocery or to-do lists.

Multiple table views are often chained together to display an information hierarchy, with each displaying a single level. For example, a sports application may use a table view to display a list of teams. When a team is selected, a new table view slides into view displaying a list of players on the selected team. When a player is selected, a table view slides into view displaying the selected player's individual statistics.

To enable these types of interactions, table views are often combined with navigation controllers. The Frenemies sample app you build later in this chapter demonstrates how to combine the two.

Table View Breakdown

Table views come in two styles: plain and grouped. Check out the Mail app to see examples of the plain table view style. You can see the grouped style at work in the Settings app. Here is a visual breakdown of the two styles and their components:

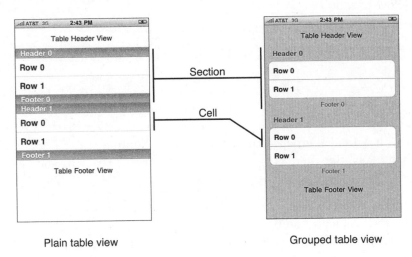

Plain table view   Grouped table view

You cannot change the table view style after it has been initialized.

As you can see in the previous image, tables consist of sections, which in turn consist of rows. Each section can have a header and footer. The table as a whole can also have header and footer views. In the image, a UILabel is used to display the text at the top and bottom of the table.

Populating the Table

In code, a table view is represented using the UITableView class. The UITableView class gives you a lot of control over what the table looks like, but it doesn't give you a direct way to set the data the table displays. Instead, table views use delegation to populate the table data.

THERE'S A TIP FOR THAT

I highly recommend looking through the `UITableView` API documentation provided by Apple. As a reminder, you can access the API by selecting **Help > Documentation** in Xcode.

To populate the table cells, the table needs its `dataSource` property set to a class that implements the `UITableViewDataSource` protocol. There are three primary methods the table calls on its data source to determine what data is displayed:

```
// This method is optional. The default number of sections
// is set to 1 if not implemented.
- (NSInteger)numberOfSectionsInTableView:(UITableView *)tableView;

// This method is required. The method passes you the section
// number, and you need to return the number of rows in that
// particular section.
- (NSInteger)tableView:(UITableView *)tableView
   numberOfRowsInSection:(NSInteger)section;

// This method is required. In addition to the setting the
// number of sections and rows in the table, you are responsible
// for generating and returning the table view cells themselves
// using this method.
- (UITableViewCell *)tableView:(UITableView *)tableView
   cellForRowAtIndexPath:(NSIndexPath *)indexPath;
```

The table view itself has no idea what it will display before asking the data source. One of the benefits of this approach is a spectacular performance boost. Instead of having to create 10,000 rows up front, the table view can just ask the data source for the 10 rows that are currently on the screen. By offloading the cell creation to the data source, you can also customize the table on the fly by returning your own `UITableViewCell` subclasses.

ONE MORE THING

Although the table view data source may seem new and exotic, you have already seen the data source pattern once before: in Chapter 9 when covering picker views, which also use a data source. So if you're having trouble grasping the idea of a data source, look back at how data sources were used in Chapter 9.

In `tableView:cellForRowAtIndexPath:`, you are probably wondering what the heck an index path is. Despite its nonobvious name, it is actually quite simple to understand. An `NSIndexPath` object contains the section and row of a cell requested by the `UITableView`. To access the requested section, use the `section` property of `NSIndexPath`. To access the row, use the `row` property.

An Example

To see how the data source works, let's take a look at an example:

```
- (void)viewDidLoad
{
    // Tell the table view you are its data source
    tableView.dataSource = self;
}

// Sets the number of sections in the table
- (NSInteger)numberOfSectionsInTableView:(UITableView *)table
{
    return 2;
}

// Sets the number of rows in a particular section of the table
- (NSInteger)tableView:(UITableView *)table
    numberOfRowsInSection:(NSInteger)section
{
    // This method is called twice, once for each section
    return 2;
}

// Give the table view the cell to display for a single row
- (UITableViewCell *)tableView:(UITableView *)table
    cellForRowAtIndexPath:(NSIndexPath *)indexPath
{
    // Create the cell
    UITableViewCell *cell =
        [[UITableViewCell alloc]
            initWithStyle:UITableViewCellStyleDefault
            reuseIdentifier:nil];
```

```
    // Set the text for the cell
    cell.textLabel.text =
        [NSString stringWithFormat:@"Row %d",
                indexPath.row];

    // Since you alloc/init the object, you must release it.
    // But, if you release it now, it will be deallocated.
    // So, you must autorelease it so it is released later.
    [cell autorelease];

    return cell;
}
```

The preceding code will create a table with two sections and four total rows. The rows themselves will either display "Row 0" or "Row 1", the same as in the table view image shown earlier. tableView:cellForRowAtIndexPath: is called four times, once for each row in the table.

Table Cell Styles

In the previous code, the cell is initialized using the default style. There are actually four styles to choose from, and you can see the differences between them in the following image:

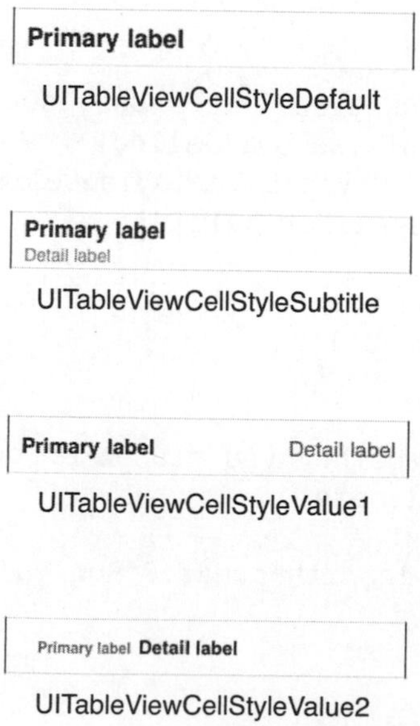

Primary label

UITableViewCellStyleDefault

Primary label
Detail label

UITableViewCellStyleSubtitle

Primary label   Detail label

UITableViewCellStyleValue1

Primary label **Detail label**

UITableViewCellStyleValue2

You can access the detail text label using the cell.detailTextLabel property.

Cell Reuse

In the previous code, a new UITableViewCell is created every time the cellForRowAtIndexPath: method is called. This can make scrolling particularly sluggish, and it turns out there's a better way: cell reuse. If your table has a variable number of rows, you should always use the cell reuse mechanism.

THERE'S A TIP FOR THAT

Reusing cells is one of the best ways to guarantee smooth table view scrolling performance.

To see how it works, let's rewrite the cellForRowAtIndexPath: method to reuse table view cells:

```
- (UITableViewCell *)tableView:(UITableView *)table
  cellForRowAtIndexPath:(NSIndexPath *)indexPath
{
    // define a string (any string) as the cell id
    static NSString *cellId = @"standard row";

    // try to reuse an existing cell
    UITableViewCell *cell =
        [table dequeueReusableCellWithIdentifier:cellId];

    if (!cell)
    {
        // couldn't find a cell to reuse, so create a new one
        cell = [[UITableViewCell alloc]
                initWithStyle:UITableViewCellStyleDefault
                reuseIdentifier:cellId];

        // autorelease the newly created cell
        [cell autorelease];
    }

    // regardless of whether you reused or created a new cell,
    // update the cell data
    cell.textLabel.text =
        [NSString stringWithFormat:@"Row %d", indexPath.row];

    return cell;
}
```

As you can see, the code gets slightly more complex, but the performance benefit is more than worth it. The crux of the entire cell reuse system hinges on UITableView's dequeueReusableCellWithIdentifier: method. This method checks the table view's cell cache to see if there is a spare cell that isn't currently being shown. If so, you can reuse. If there isn't a cell available, the method returns nil, in which case you need to create a new cell. If your table consists of a single type of cell, then the same 10 or so cells will be reused for every one of the 10,000 items in your list. When rapidly scrolling through a large amount of data, creating and destroying objects repeatedly can end up impacting performance, so the more you can reuse existing cells, the better.

Row Selection

UITableView has built-in support for row selection. To be notified when the user taps one of the rows in your table, you must assign self as the table view's delegate (in addition to the data source), and override the following UITableViewDelegate method:

```
// Called when a row is tapped
- (void)tableView:(UITableView *)tableView
    didSelectRowAtIndexPath:(NSIndexPath *)indexPath;
```

Using the indexPath object, you can determine the selected cell by checking its section and row properties.

Cell Accessory Types

Sometimes cells in tables are selectable, and other times they aren't. How does the user tell the difference? When a cell is selectable, you can display a visual indicator in the cell by setting an accessory view. The accessory view lives on the far right side of the cell. There are three types of built-in accessory views you can see in the following image:

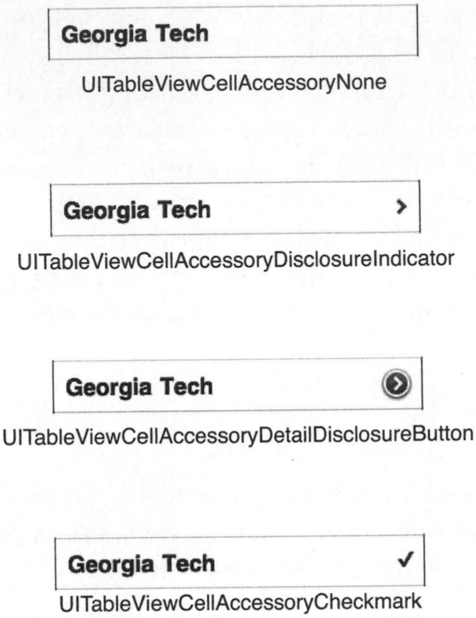

Georgia Tech

UITableViewCellAccessoryNone

Georgia Tech   >

UITableViewCellAccessoryDisclosureIndicator

Georgia Tech   ⊙

UITableViewCellAccessoryDetailDisclosureButton

Georgia Tech   ✓

UITableViewCellAccessoryCheckmark

After you create a cell in cellForRowAtIndexPath:, you can set its accessory type using the cell.accessoryType property.

You set the accessory type when you make the table view cells selectable in the Frenemies sample app. Speaking of which ....

Frenemies

The term frenemy has recently become popular to describe someone who is part friend, part enemy. This person could be your neighbor who *always* has to one-up you with Christmas decorations. Or maybe it's that Facebook friend who never responded when you spammed your friend list for numbers since you lost your phone. You know the type.

The way Twitter is structured, you can follow someone, but they do not have to follow you back. For the Frenemies application, this situation defines a frenemy: someone you follow who doesn't follow you back. You create an app that identifies these supposed friends (jerks!) while at the same time demonstrating how to use table views in a real application.

Discover all the people on Twitter you follow who don't follow you back using the Frenemies app.

As shown in the previous image, the interface consists of two views: the frenemies list and a detailed profile view. A navigation controller manages these views, and when a row in the table is selected, the profile view—with the user model data—will be pushed onto the navigation stack.

Like previous applications, you are challenged to set up the project from scratch.

Interface Challenge

As part of the app setup, you create the project, design the interface, hook up the controllers, and add the navigation controller to manage it all. There is starter code available at the end of this section if you need it.

First Steps

To start building the Frenemies app, follow these steps:

1. Create a new Window-based Application and name it "Frenemies."

2. Add a view controller named "FrenemiesViewController" to your project, and edit the nib file so it matches the following image:

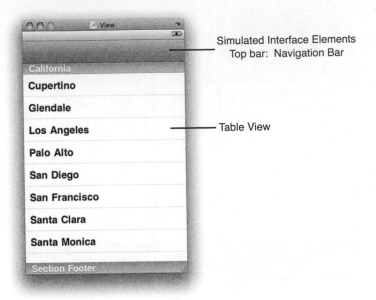

Build your FrenemiesViewController.xib file so it matches the interface shown.

3. Add and hook up the outlets shown in the following image to your `FrenemiesViewController` class:

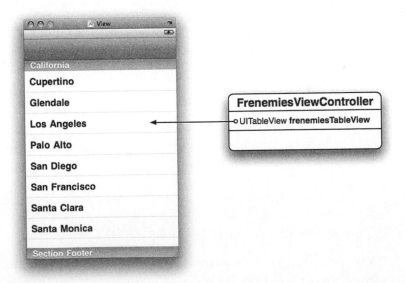

First, add the outlets shown to your FrenemiesViewController code files. Then, connect these outlets to the interface elements as shown here.

4. Add a view controller named "ProfileViewController" to your project, and edit the nib file so it matches the following image:

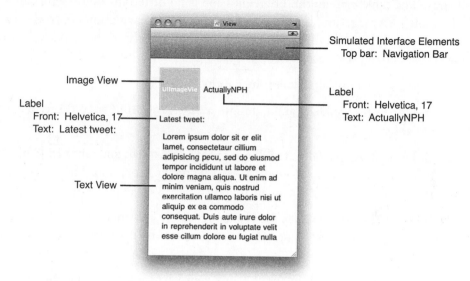

Build your ProfileViewController.xib file so it matches the interface shown.

5. First, add the outlets shown in the following image to your ProfileViewController class. Then, hook them up as shown in the image:

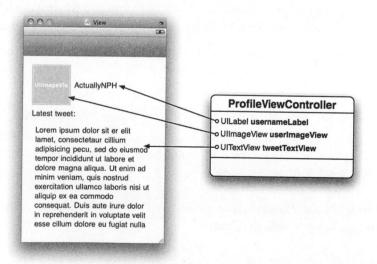

First, add the outlets shown to your ProfileViewController code files. Then, connect these outlets to the interface elements as shown here.

Add the Navigation Controller

As mentioned earlier, table views are often used for navigation in iPhone and iPad apps. The table view in the Frenemies app is no different. Before you can use the table for navigation, however, you need to add a navigation controller to the interface. Just like you did in Chapter 12, add it directly to the window in the FrenemiesAppDelegate class.

Follow these steps to initialize your navigation controller:

1. In FrenemiesAppDelegate.h, declare a UINavigationController instance variable.

2. In FrenemiesAppDelegate.m's applicationDidFinishLaunching: method, initialize an instance of FrenemiesViewController. This will be the navigation controller's first view controller.

3. Next, initialize the UINavigationController instance variable you declared in step 1, and set the FrenemiesViewController instance as the root view controller.

4. Add the UINavigationController's view as a subview of the window.

5. Add any code necessary for correct memory management. Hint: there should be one release in applicationDidFinishLaunching: and another in dealloc.

6. Save, build, and run your code. The FrenemiesViewController should appear, but you will notice that both the table and navigation bar are empty. You populate the table a bit later on, but you can set the navigation titles now.

7. Override the viewDidLoad method in FriendsViewController, and set the navigation item title to "Frenemies."

THERE'S A TIP FOR THAT

To set a navigation controller's title, you need to modify the view controller's navigation item. For a refresher on setting navigation bar titles and navigation controllers in general, see Chapter 12.

8. Override the viewDidLoad method in ProfileViewController, and set the navigation bar title to "Profile."

Save and run your project in the iPhone Simulator. You should see the navigation bar and an empty table view on the FrenemiesViewController. Your next task is to add and initialize the TwitterUser model class that will keep track of your application data.

Add the Model

For this Twitter-based project, you once again make use of the TwitterUser model class. Notice how you can reuse the same model class for four different Twitter applications? That is the power of MVC: write a class once and reuse it over and over again.

If you have your TwitterUser class from previous chapters, you can just drag-and-drop it into the Classes group of your project. You need to add a new array to hold the list of the user's frenemies, however. Make sure your class matches the one described in the following instructions for creating a new TwitterUser class.

If you need to write a new TwitterUser class, follow these steps:

1. Add an NSObject subclass named "TwitterUser" to the project.

2. Add the following instance variables:

   - username of type NSString
   - tweet of type NSString
   - image of type UIImage
   - frenemies of type NSArray

3. Add properties for these instance variables.

Now, regardless of whether you reused one of your earlier TwitterUser classes or wrote a new one, you need to add the model reference to your view controllers:

1. Add a rootUser instance variable also of type TwitterUser to the FrenemiesViewController class.

2. Add a property for this instance variable.

3. Add a user instance variable of type TwitterUser to the ProfileViewController class.

4. Add a property for this instance variable.

5. Now, initialize the `rootUser` object. Make the following changes to properly initialize the object:

   • Add the TwitterHelper folder to your project: http://troybrant.net/ iphonebook/chapter14/TwitterHelper.zip.

   • In `applicationDidFinishLaunching:` in FrenemiesAppDelegate.m, alloc/ init a new `TwitterUser` model object.

   • Set its `username` to @"ActuallyNPH" or another Twitter username of your choosing.

   • Use `TwitterHelper`'s `fetchFrenemiesForUsername:` class method to initialize the `rootUser`'s `frenemies` property.

   • Leave the `rootUser`'s other properties unchanged.

   • Set the `frenemiesViewController`'s `rootUser` property to the `TwitterUser` instance you just initialized.

   • Properly manage memory for the `TwitterUser` object.

You will initialize the `ProfileViewController`'s `TwitterUser` model object later, but for now, your controllers are ready to use the model class.

ProfileViewController

Let's go ahead and finish the `ProfileViewController`. The class is very simple and looks almost exactly the same as the `ProfileViewController` you built in Chapter 12. If you have trouble with any of the instructions that follow, refer back to the navigation controller chapter to see how it was done there.

1. Add an `updateInterface` helper method to the `ProfileViewController` class, and update the `usernameLabel`, `profileImageView`, and `tweetTextView` instance variables with the data in the `user` model object.

2. Override `viewWillAppear:`, and call `updateInterface`.

And that's it! The `ProfileViewController` simply displays the user data stored in the model object and doesn't have to do any hard work itself. Pretty nice how that worked out, right? Again, you can thank MVC for the simplicity of updating the interface based on a model object.

Save, build, and give your code another go in the simulator. You should see an empty table view with the title "Frenemies" in the navigation bar. If your interface matches the one described, then you are ready to start modifying the table view.

Starter Code

Starter code to reach this point is available online at: http://troybrant.net/ iphonebook/chapter14/Frenemies-starter-code.zip.

With the starter code complete, you can now focus on getting the table view to work.

UITableViewDatasource

Your interface currently displays an empty, sad table view. To populate the table, you need to implement two UITableViewDatasource methods: tableView:numberOfRowsInSection: and tableView:cellForRowAtIndexPath:. You also need to tell the table view that your FrenemiesViewController class is both its data source and its delegate. Add the following code to populate the table:

```
// FrenemiesViewController.h

@interface FrenemiesViewController : UIViewController
  <UITableViewDataSource, UITableViewDelegate>
{
   TwitterUser *rootUser;
   UITableView *frenemiesTableView;
}
```

Update the implementation file, too:

```
// FrenemiesViewController.m

- (void)viewDidLoad
{
   [super viewDidLoad];

   self.navigationItem.title = @"Frenemies";

   // Tell the table view you both delegate and data source
   frenemiesTableView.dataSource = self;
   frenemiesTableView.delegate = self;
```

continues

```
}

#pragma mark -
#pragma mark UITableViewDataSource methods

// Sets the number of rows in a particular section of the table
- (NSInteger)tableView:(UITableView *)table
  numberOfRowsInSection:(NSInteger)section
{
    return [rootUser.frenemies count];
}


// Give the table view the cell to display for a single row
- (UITableViewCell *)tableView:(UITableView *)tableView
  cellForRowAtIndexPath:(NSIndexPath *)indexPath
{
    // Reuse existing cells for optimal scrolling performance
    static NSString *cellId = @"cellId";
    UITableViewCell *cell =
        [tableView dequeueReusableCellWithIdentifier:cellId];
    if (!cell)
    {
        // Create a cell only if one couldn't be reused
        cell = [[UITableViewCell alloc]
                initWithStyle:UITableViewCellStyleDefault
                reuseIdentifier:cellId];

        // Memory management
        [cell autorelease];
    }

    // Display the frenemy's name in the cell
    NSDictionary *frenemyDict =
        [rootUser.frenemies objectAtIndex:indexPath.row];
    cell.textLabel.text = [frenemyDict objectForKey:@"name"];

    return cell;
}
```

Some explanation about the previous code:

- Unless otherwise specified, tables have only one section, so you don't need to check the section in tableView:numberOfRowsInSection:.

- What happens if `rootUser.frenemies` is nil? In `tableView:numberOfRows InSection:`, the `count` message would be sent to `nil`, which is perfectly fine in Objective-C (as explained in Chapter 5). The result of the method is then zero, which means the `tableView:cellForRowAtIndexPath:` method is not called at all.

- The static keyword used in declaring the `cellId` variable causes the `cellId` variable to be initialized only once—regardless of how many times `tableView:cellForAtIndexPath:` is called.

- Since it's possible there are many, many rows in the table, you should use the cell reuse mechanism shown in the previous code.

- You may be wondering why the object returned from the `frenemies` array is a dictionary. The dictionary is the raw response from the Twitter API. You can—and should—`NSLog` the `frenemyDict` to see what information the Twitter API supplies about the user. As shown previously, there is a "name" field that contains the user's username, which is then set as the cell's text.

After adding the previous code, save your project and try running it in the simulator. Provided you selected a Twitter user who has frenemies, your table should be populated with data. You can always test with "tbrant" since I have no shortage of back-stabbing acquaintances on Twitter.

Now that you can display data in your table view, let's take a crack at making it interactive.

Row Selection and UITableViewDelegate

When the user taps a row in the table, the app will display the profile view of the selected frenemy. Lucky for you, the table view notifies its `UITableViewDelegate` when a row is selected. You hook into this method and then push a new `ProfileViewController` onto the navigation stack so it slides into view.

When a row is selectable in a table view, it should be indicated using a disclosure indicator (which looks like a right arrow). Later in the chapter, you will add a disclosure indicator to each cell.

To make the rows in your table selectable, add the following code:

```objc
// FrenemiesViewController.m

#include "ProfileViewController.h"

#pragma mark -
#pragma mark Helper methods

// Convert a frenemy dictionary to a TwitterUser model object
- (TwitterUser *)frenemyForUserDict:(NSDictionary *)frenemyDict
{
    // Initialize the TwitterUser with data from the JSON dictionary
    TwitterUser *frenemy = [[TwitterUser alloc] init];
    frenemy.username =
        [frenemyDict objectForKey:@"screen_name"];
    frenemy.tweet =
        [[frenemyDict objectForKey:@"status"]
                objectForKey:@"text"];
    frenemy.image =
        [TwitterHelper
                fetchProfileImageForUsername:frenemy.username];

    // Returning an object you alloc/init, so autorelease
    [frenemy autorelease];

    return frenemy;
}

#pragma mark -
#pragma mark UITableViewDelegate methods

// Display the profile view controller when a row is tapped
- (void)tableView:(UITableView *)tableView
    didSelectRowAtIndexPath:(NSIndexPath *)indexPath
{
    ProfileViewController *profileViewController =
        [[ProfileViewController alloc] init];

    // Get the frenemy JSON dictionary for this row
    NSDictionary *frenemyDict =
        [twitterUser.friends objectAtIndex:indexPath.row];

    // Convert the JSON dictionary to a model object
    TwitterUser *frenemy =
```

```
        [self frenemyForUserDict:frenemyDict];

    // Tell the profile which user to display
    profileViewController.user = frenemy;

    // Display the user's profile screen
    [self.navigationController
        pushViewController:profileViewController
        animated:YES];

    // Memory management
    [profileViewController release];
}


- (UITableViewCell *)tableView:(UITableView *)tableView
    cellForRowAtIndexPath:(NSIndexPath *)indexPath
{
    // Reuse existing cells for optimal scrolling performance
    static NSString *cellId = @"cellId";
    UITableViewCell *cell =
        [tableView dequeueReusableCellWithIdentifier:cellId];
    if (!cell)
    {
        // Create a cell only if one couldn't be reused
        cell = [[UITableViewCell alloc]
            initWithStyle:UITableViewCellStyleDefault
            reuseIdentifier:cellId];

        // Show the right arrow to indicate the row
        // is tappable
        cell.accessoryType =
            UITableViewCellAccessoryDisclosureIndicator;

        // Returning an object you alloc/init, so autorelease
        [cell autorelease];
    }

    // Display the frenemy's name in the cell
    NSDictionary *frenemyDict =
        [rootUser.frenemies objectAtIndex:indexPath.row];
    cell.textLabel.text = [frenemyDict objectForKey:@"name"];

    return cell;
}
```

A few notes about the preceding code:

- Notice again the use of `autorelease` in the `frenemyForUserDict:` method. You can't just release it, because the frenemy would be deallocated before it could be returned by the method. See Chapter 6 for a refresher on autorelease and memory management if this seems confusing.

- The `tableView:didSelectRowAtIndexPath:` method makes it very simple to determine which row was selected. It is simply `indexPath.row`. Since the table is just a reflection of the `rootUser.frenemies` array, you can use the `indexPath.row` index to directly grab the correct frenemy.

- Once the row is selected, you push the new `ProfileViewController` onto the navigation stack, which slides the view controller onto the screen. Since you have already written the `ProfileViewController` to update its interface based on the model object, you should see the user's profile information when the controller is displayed.

After adding the code, save your project, and give it a shot in the iPhone Simulator. You should see the gray disclosure arrows, which indicate the rows are selectable. Try selecting a row. If the profile view slides into view displaying the frenemy information, then you are all set!

On the profile view controller, though, try tapping the back button so the frenemy list is displayed again. Notice something strange? Apparently your row-selection code worked a little *too* well: the row is still highlighted in blue. The last step you need to take to finish the project is deselecting the selected row when the `FrenemiesViewController` comes into view.

Deselecting Rows

Deselecting the row is quite simple and requires just a couple lines to implement:

```
// FrenemiesViewController.m

// Begin deselecting a row just before the view appears
- (void)viewWillAppear:(BOOL)animated
{
    [super viewWillAppear:animated];
```

```
    // Get the path to the currently selected row
    NSIndexPath *selectedRow =
        [friendsTableView indexPathForSelectedRow];

    // Deselect the row
    [friendsTableView deselectRowAtIndexPath:selectedRow
                                    animated:YES];
}
```

Add the preceding code to your `FrenemiesViewController`, and try to run the project again. When you go back to the frenemy list from the profile view this time, the row gently animates from selected to deselected. And with that last change, you are done with the Frenemy app! Try changing the `rootUser`'s `username` to see Twitter users who have some explaining to do.

ONE MORE THING

It may seem like a small, inconsequential action, but that deselection animation is crucial for users of your application. The animation reminds the user exactly which row in the table was selected and helps them stay oriented inside your application. Take away the animation, and your users will have a much harder time getting around your app and could likely just give up in frustration. Moral of the story: always animate your row deselection.

Full source code for the finished Frenemies application is available online at http://troybrant.net/iphonebook/chapter14/Frenemies-done.zip.

All Done

The Frenemies app was a fun opportunity to learn how table views work. After specifying the number of rows in the table, you created—and reused—the table cells in `tableView:cellForRowAtIndexPath:`. Displaying data in the table was neat, but you kicked it up a notch by making the rows selectable. You fixed the last nagging problem by deselecting the highlighted row after the profile view slid off to reveal to the frenemy table.

There is much, much more you can do with table views. To see what the table view API has to offer, I encourage you to check out Apple's API documentation for `UITableViewDataSource` and `UITableViewDelegate`. Here are a few ways you can further customize table views:

- Subclass table cells to more directly customize the cell look and behavior.

- Specify titles or completely new views for table headers and footers.

- Specify titles or completely new views for *section* headers and footers.

- Add and remove rows using sweet animations.

- Reorder rows.

Check out the documentation for more details.

ONE MORE THING

If your view consists of a single table view, you may find it convenient to use a `UITableViewController`. `UITableViewControllers` are specialized view controllers that come prebuilt with a table view set up and ready to use. Look up `UITableViewController` in the API documentation for usage details.

For iPad developers, you won't want to miss the next chapter. Learn how to use split views and popovers, two new interface elements only available in iPad apps, not on iPhone. You will put your iPad skills to the test by building TweetPad, your first iPad Twitter app.

The Least You Need to Know

- A table view consists of a single column but can have any number of rows and sections.

- To populate the table view with data, set your controller class as the data source of the table.

- Use the `section` and `row` properties of the `NSIndexPath` object to determine the cell in your table view data source and delegate methods.

- Any time you have a variable number of rows in your table view, use the `dequeueReusableCellWithIdentifier:` table view method to reuse cells and improve performance.

- To determine when a row is selected, override the `UITableViewDelegate` method `tableView:didSelectRowAtIndexPath:`. Don't forget to clear the selection with animation later!

Split Views and Popovers

In This Chapter

- Split views
- Split view rotation
- Popovers
- TweetPad app

Is an iPad just a giant iPod Touch? Tech bloggers and journalists far and wide have described it as such. Even though the iPad looks and behaves much like the iPhone, using an iPad is a drastically different experience than using an iPhone. An iPhone can be held in one hand while an iPad requires two. An iPhone is used in short bursts while an iPad is used for longer periods of time. And of course, the iPad screen size is "giant" compared to the iPhone display.

With the new iPad experience comes new interface elements. This chapter is dedicated to two views that are only available on iPad: split views and popovers. Both of these elements simplify your iPad apps by requiring the user to navigate fewer screens than they would on an iPhone app. To get some hands-on practice with these elements, you will build TweetPad, an iPad Twitter client that leverages both split views and popovers.

Split Views

A split view is a full-screen view that consists of two side-by-side panes. The first pane has a fixed width of 320 pixels and typically contains a table view. The second pane fills the rest of the screen and usually displays a detail view of the item currently selected in the first pane. This particular arrangement is known as a *master-detail* design. The iPad Mail app, shown in the following figure, demonstrates how to use master-detail design with split views:

The Mail app for iPad uses a split view to display your inbox and message details at the same time.

DEFINITION

Master-detail is design pattern where one view displays a list of items while a second view displays the details of the currently selected item in the master view. Although it's not strictly required, most split views use the master-detail pattern.

A split view consists of two view controllers, one for the left pane and one for the right. The split view itself manages the display of these two view controllers and is represented using the UISplitViewController class.

Adding a Split View Controller

There are multiple ways to add a split view to your interface. The different options are listed here:

- Create a new project using the **Split View-based Application** template. This template is good if you are creating a new application with the split view as the primary view.

- Add a **Split View Controller** object to your nib file. Adding the controller to your nib file is a good option if you have an existing iPad project.

- Add a `UISplitViewController` to your interface programmatically. Creating the split view controller in code provides a great exercise for understanding exactly how the split view system works.

In building the TweetPad app, you will use the third option to programmatically add a split view to the interface. You can always use the first and second methods to more easily create split views in the future, but adding them in code is a good exercise to see at least once.

Rotation

When the iPad is being held in landscape orientation, the split view displays both its left and right panes. However, when the device is rotated to portrait mode, the split view automatically hides the first pane so that the detail view fills the entire screen.

CRASH AND LEARN

The built-in rotation behavior for split views only works if both left and right view controllers override `shouldAutorotateToInterfaceOrientation:` and return `YES` for all orientations.

If the left pane is hidden in the portrait interface orientation, how does your user access its contents? The most common solution is to add a button to the toolbar of the second pane that, when tapped, presents the contents of the first pane in a popover.

Popovers

A popover is a temporary view that is revealed when the user taps a control or onscreen area. Popovers can contain any view of your choosing, including labels, images, and buttons. In the following image, a `UITableView` is displayed in a popover:

When the Plays button is tapped, the popover appears.

The `UIPopoverController` class manages the presentation of the content for the popover. To display a content view, you set the `contentViewController` property on the popover to a view controller of your choice.

Displaying a Popover

There are two ways to display a popover. First, when a button in a toolbar is tapped, you can call `presentPopoverFromBarButtonItem:permittedArrowDirections:animated:` on the `UIPopoverController` object. This method will display a popover pointing to the `UIBarButtonItem` you provide as the first parameter.

The following code demonstrates how to initialize and display a popover when a toolbar button is tapped:

```
- (IBAction)toolbarItemTapped:(UIBarButtonItem *)buttonItem
{
  // Create popover's content view controller
  TheContentViewController *content = ...;
  // Create the popover itself
  UIPopoverController *popoverController =
      [[UIPopoverController alloc]
```

```
                         initWithContentViewController:content];
    // Keep track of the popover for later use
    self.popoverController = popoverController;
    // Display the popover
    [self.popoverController
        presentPopoverFromBarButtonItem:buttonItem
        permittedArrowDirections:UIPopoverArrowDirectionAny
        animated:YES];
}
```

Alternatively, you can call
presentPopoverFromRect:inView:permittedArrowDirections:animated: on
the UIPopoverController object. Unlike the bar button presentation method, you
can use this method to display a popover pointing to any arbitrary rectangle in your
interface. See the following code for an example of how to use this method:

```
// Define the rectangle with top-left point (100, 100)
// with a width and height of 200
CGRect myRect = CGRectMake(100, 100, 200, 200);
// Display the popover in the current view
  [self.popoverController
    presentPopoverFromRect:myRect
    inView:self.view
    permittedArrowDirections:UIPopoverArrowDirectionAny
    animated:YES];
```

When the popover is displayed, an arrow points to the element you specify as
the first argument. For instance, when presentPopoverFromBarButtonItem:
is called with the buttonItem object, an arrow points to buttonItem. When
presentPopoverFromRect: is called with myRect, an arrow points to the rectangle
defined by myRect. You can limit where the popover is displayed by specifying one of
the direction values in UIPopoverArrowDirection. However, you should generally
use UIPopoverArrowDirectionAny.

To dismiss a popover, the user simply needs to tap outside the bounds of the
popover. If you wish to dismiss the popover programmatically, call the
dismissPopoverAnimated: method on the popover controller. This is why it can be
useful to hold on to a reference to the popover controller in an instance variable.

TweetPad

In following with tradition, you will build a Twitter app to get some practice using split views and popovers. Dubbed TweetPad, this iPad app uses a split view to display both the people you follow and profile information for a single person. Once complete, TweetPad will look as follows:

TweetPad displays your friends and their profile information using a split view.

TweetPad's interface is composed using a split view controller. When viewed in landscape mode, the left pane displays the list of friends. In portrait mode, the list of friends is displayed in a popover when the "Friends" button is tapped in the top bar.

 CRASH AND LEARN

You must have iPhone SDK 3.2 or later installed to build iPad applications.

Interface Challenge

Building an iPad app is very similar to building an iPhone app. All of the UIKit classes available for iPhone are also available for iPad. The main difference is that there are classes available for iPad that aren't available on iPhone, like split views and popovers. Just like the iPhone apps built in earlier chapters, you will start building the TweetPad app by creating the view controllers and data model used in the app.

If you get lost at any point, there is starter code available at the end of this section if you need it.

First Steps

To start building the TweetPad app, follow these steps:

1. Create a new Window-Based Application and name it "TweetPad." When selecting the project template, set the Product field to **iPad**.

2. Add a view controller named "FriendsViewController" to your project. When selecting the file template, check the **Targeted for iPad** box. Edit the nib file so it matches the following image:

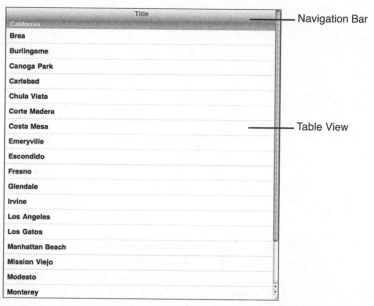

Build your FriendsViewController.xib file so it matches the interface shown.

The first time you open a nib targeted for iPad, the view will be in landscape mode. To rotate to portrait mode, click the arrow in the top-right corner of the view window in Interface Builder. Remember that this is only for the purposes of designing in Interface Builder. You must override the −shouldAutorotateToInterfaceOrientation: method in your view controller subclasses to allow interface rotation.

THERE'S A TIP FOR THAT

Unlike previous chapters where you simulate the navigation bar, you need to add a real Navigation Bar to the top of your interface.

3. Add and hook up the outlets shown in the image below to your
   `FriendsViewController` class:

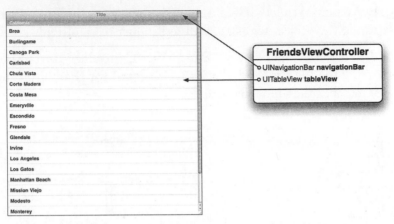

*First, add the outlets shown to your FriendsViewController code files. Then, connect
these outlets to the interface elements as shown here.*

4. Add a view controller named "ProfileViewController" to your project. Again,
   make sure **Targeted for iPad** is selected. Edit the nib file so it matches the
   following image:

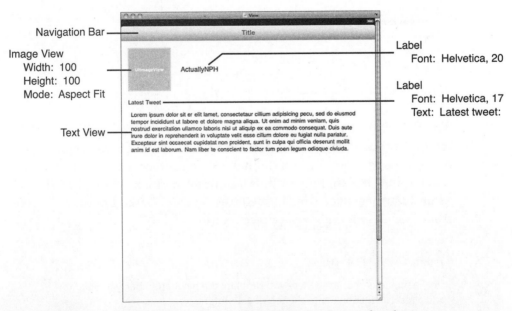

Build your ProfileViewController.xib file so it matches the interface shown.

5. Add and hook up the outlets shown in the image below to your
   ProfileViewController class:

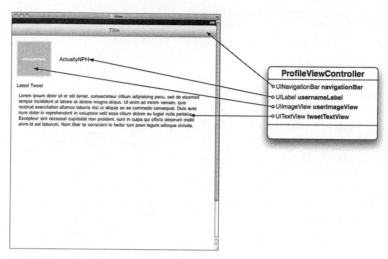

*First, add the outlets shown to your ProfileViewController code files. Then, connect
these outlets to the interface elements as shown here.*

Add the Model

If you have already written the TwitterUser class in Chapters 11 through 14, you can
just drag and drop it into the Classes group of the TweetPad project. If you do use an
existing TwitterUser class, however, you will need to add a new property, an NSArray
named "friends."

To create the TwitterUser class from scratch, follow these steps:

1. Add an NSObject subclass named "TwitterUser" to the TweetPad project.

2. Add the following instance variables:

   • username of type NSString

   • tweet of type NSString

   • image of type UIImage

   • friends of type NSArray

3. Add properties for these instance variables.

4. Add the following custom init method header to TwitterUser.h:

```
// TwitterUser.h
- (id)initWithDict:(NSDictionary *)dict;
```

5. Add the body for the `initWithDict:` method to TwitterUser.m:

```
// TwitterUser.m
#import "TwitterHelper.h"
// Convert a friend dictionary to a TwitterUser model object
- (id)initWithDict:(NSDictionary *)dict
{
  if (self = [super init])
  {
  // Initialize the TwitterUser with data from the JSON dictionary
    self.username = [dict objectForKey:@"screen_name"];
    self.tweet =
          [[dict objectForKey:@"status"] objectForKey:@"text"];
    self.image =
          [TwitterHelper fetchProfileImageForUsername:self.
  username];
  }

  return self;
}
```

Now, regardless of whether you reused one of your earlier `TwitterUser` classes or wrote a new one, you need to add model references to your view controllers:

1. Add a `TwitterUser` instance variable named "rootUser" to the `FriendsViewController` class, and add a property for this instance variable.

2. Add a `TwitterUser` instance variable named "user" to the `ProfileViewController` class, and add a property for this instance variable as well.

3. Download and add the TwitterHelper folder to the TweetPad project. The TwitterHelper folder is online at http://troybrant.net/iphonebook/chapter15/ TwitterHelper.zip.

Save and build the project. There should be no warnings or build errors. You will initialize these model objects later, but for now, both controllers are ready to use the `TwitterUser` model object.

FriendsViewController

FriendsViewController will look nearly identical to the FrenemiesViewController class from Chapter 14. Just like the FrenemiesViewController, FriendsViewController uses a table view to display a list of users.

The main difference lies in what happens when a row in the table is selected. Instead of pushing a view controller on the navigation stack, the right pane of the split view will be updated with the selected user's information. To accomplish this, FriendsViewController will store a reference to the right pane's view controller. You will use this reference to update the displayed person each time the user selects a new person from the friends list.

To add support for updating the right pane, modify your FriendsViewController.h file so it matches the following:

```
// FriendsViewController.h
#import <UIKit/UIKit.h>
#import "TwitterUser.h"
#import "ProfileViewController.h"
@interface FriendsViewController : UIViewController
  <UITableViewDelegate, UITableViewDataSource>
{
  UITableView *tableView;
  UINavigationBar *navigationBar;
  TwitterUser *rootUser;
  ProfileViewController *profileViewController;
}
@property (nonatomic, retain) IBOutlet UITableView *tableView;
@property (nonatomic, retain) IBOutlet UINavigationBar
  *navigationBar;
@property (nonatomic, retain) TwitterUser *rootUser;
@property (nonatomic, retain) ProfileViewController
  *profileViewController;
@end
```

The implementation file will use the rootUser to determine which friends should be displayed in the table view. In addition, the user property of the ProfileViewController object will be updated each time a row is selected.

To make these changes, update your FriendsViewController.m file so it matches the following:

```objc
// FriendsViewController.m
#import "FriendsViewController.h"
#import "TwitterHelper.h"
@implementation FriendsViewController
@synthesize tableView;
@synthesize navigationBar;
@synthesize rootUser;
@synthesize profileViewController;
#pragma mark -
#pragma mark Lifecycle methods
- (void)viewDidLoad
{
    [super viewDidLoad];
    // Set the title of the navigation bar
    navigationBar.topItem.title = @"Friends";

    // Tell the table view you both delegate and data source
    tableView.delegate = self;
    tableView.dataSource = self;
}
- (void)dealloc
{
    [tableView release];
    [navigationBar release];
    [rootUser release];
    [profileViewController release];
    [super dealloc];
}
#pragma mark -
#pragma mark UITableViewDataSource methods
// Sets the number of rows in a particular section of the table
- (NSInteger)tableView:(UITableView *)aTableView
    numberOfRowsInSection:(NSInteger)section
{
    return [rootUser.friends count];
}
// Give the table view the cell to display for a single row
- (UITableViewCell *)tableView:(UITableView *)aTableView
    cellForRowAtIndexPath:(NSIndexPath *)indexPath
{
    // Reuse existing cells for optimal scrolling performance
    static NSString *cellId = @"cellId";
    UITableViewCell *cell =
        [tableView dequeueReusableCellWithIdentifier:cellId];
    if (!cell)
```

```objc
{
        // Create a cell only if one couldn't be reused
        cell =
            [[UITableViewCell alloc]
                    initWithStyle:UITableViewCellStylePlain
                    reuseIdentifier:cellId];
        // Memory management
        [cell autorelease];
    }
    // Display the friend's name in the cell
    NSDictionary *friendDict =
        [rootUser.friends objectAtIndex:indexPath.row];
    cell.textLabel.text = [friendDict objectForKey:@"name"];

    return cell;
}


#pragma mark -
#pragma mark UITableViewDelegate methods
- (void)tableView:(UITableView *)aTableView
    didSelectRowAtIndexPath:(NSIndexPath *)indexPath
{
    // Get the friend JSON dictionary for this row
    NSDictionary *friendDict =
        [rootUser.friends objectAtIndex:indexPath.row];
    // Convert the JSON dictionary to a model object
    TwitterUser *friend =
        [[TwitterUser alloc] initWithDict:friendDict];
    // Tell the profile which user to display
    profileViewController.user = friend;
    // Memory management
    [friend release];
}
@end
```

The table view code is almost identical to the code used to construct the FrenemiesViewController in the previous chapter. It's likely that if you're developing iPhone and iPad versions of your app, you'll be able to share significant amounts of code between the two. The main difference is in tableView:didSelectRowAtIndexPath:. Instead of pushing a view controller, the split view's right pane is updated by setting the profileViewController's user property. In the next section, you will make the changes to ProfileViewController so the selected user's data shows up in the interface.

THERE'S A TIP FOR THAT

If the table view code is confusing, take a look at Chapter 14 for a full discussion on table views.

ProfileViewController

The `ProfileViewController` class will display the currently selected user's username, profile image, and latest tweet. As explained in the previous section, `FriendsViewController` communicates with `ProfileViewController` by updating the `user` property when a row is selected. In order to display the new user's content, you will implement the `setUser:` method to update the interface.

To make the changes described above, add the following code to ProfileViewController.m:

```
// ProfileViewController.m
#pragma mark -
#pragma mark Helper methods
- (void)updateInterface
{
  usernameLabel.text = user.username;
  profileImageView.image = user.image;
  tweetTextView.text = user.tweet;
}
#pragma mark -
#pragma mark Getters and setters
- (void)setUser:(TwitterUser *)aUser
{
  if (user != aUser)
  {
      [aUser retain];
      [user release];
      user = aUser;

      [self updateInterface];
  }
}
#pragma mark -
#pragma mark Lifecycle methods
- (void)viewDidLoad
{
  [super viewDidLoad];

  navigationBar.topItem.title = nil;
```

```
    [self updateInterface];
}
```

You implement the `setUser:` method yourself so you can trigger an interface update if needed. There are a few things to note about the `setUser:` method:

- The `if` statement makes sure the new user is different from the previous user.

- The sequence of retain, release, and assignment of the user is equivalent to a synthesized property with the retain attribute. This sequence – retain the new object, release the old object, then assign the new object – should be used to properly manage memory any time you implement a setter method that uses the retain attribute.

You can choose to implement your own getter or setter methods for any property. See Chapter 6 for more details.

At this point, you have finished laying the groundwork for the TweetPad app. Save your project, and continue reading to see how to connect these two view controllers together with a split view controller in the app.

Starter code to reach this point is available online at: http://troybrant.net/ iphonebook/chapter15/TweetPad-starter-code.zip.

Adding a Split View

Like a tab bar controller, a split view controller should be added to the top level of your view hierarchy. As in the navigation and tab bar controller chapters, you will initialize and set the split view controller in the app delegate.

Add a reference to the split view controller by editing TweetPadAppDelegate.h to match the following:

```
// TweetPadAppDelegate.h
#import <UIKit/UIKit.h>
@interface TweetPadAppDelegate : NSObject
  <UIApplicationDelegate>
{
  UIWindow *window;
  UISplitViewController *splitViewController;
}
@property (nonatomic, retain) IBOutlet UIWindow *window;
@end
```

The split view is then initialized in the app delegate's
application:didFinishLaunchingWithOptions: method. Edit
TweetPadAppDelegate.m so it matches the following:

```objc
// TweetPadAppDelegate.m
#import "TweetPadAppDelegate.h"
#import "FriendsViewController.h"
#import "ProfileViewController.h"
#import "TwitterHelper.h"
#define kDefaultUsername    @"ActuallyNPH"
@implementation TweetPad2AppDelegate
@synthesize window;
- (void)applicationDidFinishLaunching:(UIApplication *)application
{
    // Initialize the left/master pane
    FriendsViewController *friendsViewController =
        [[FriendsViewController alloc] init];

    // Initialize the right/detail pane
    ProfileViewController *profileViewController =
        [[ProfileViewController alloc] init];


    // Initialize the model
    TwitterUser *rootUser = [[TwitterUser alloc] init];
    rootUser.username = kDefaultUsername;
    rootUser.friends =
        [TwitterHelper fetchFriendDictsForUsername:rootUser.username];
    // Set the references for the left/master pane
    friendsViewController.rootUser = rootUser;
    friendsViewController.profileViewController =
        profileViewController;
    // Initialize the split view
    splitViewController = [[UISplitViewController alloc] init];
    splitViewController.viewControllers =
        [NSArray arrayWithObjects:
                friendsViewController,
                profileViewController,
                nil];
    splitViewController.delegate = profileViewController;
    // Memory management
    [friendsViewController release];
    [profileViewController release];
    [rootUser release];
    // Don't forget to add the view!
```

```
    [window addSubview:splitViewController.view];
    [window makeKeyAndVisible];
}
- (void)dealloc
{
    [window release];
    [splitViewController release];
    [super dealloc];
}
@end
```

A few notes about the code above:

- `fetchFriendDictsForUsername:` fetches the 100 people that the user has most recently begun following. The first user in this list is the person the user started following most recently. These dictionaries can be converted to `TwitterUsers` by using `TwitterUser`'s `initWithDict:` method.

- The array of `viewControllers` passed to the split view controller must contain two items. The first item is set as the left pane and the second item is set as the right pane.

- Notice that `profileViewController` is set as the delegate of the split view controller. The split view controller informs its delegate of rotation events. You will add code to `ProfileViewController` momentarily for handling these delegate methods.

With that chunk of code finally typed in, save, build, and run your project. You will see a warning that the `ProfileViewController` does not implement the split view delegate protocol, but ignore this warning for now. By default, the iPhone Simulator launches in portrait mode, so you will see an empty detail pane. There is currently no way to access the master pane in portrait view. To fix this problem, you will add a button to the navigation bar that presents the list of friends in a popover.

UISplitViewDelegate

The split view takes care of a lot of the work in displaying the master pane in a popover. When the master pane is hidden or displayed as the device rotates, the split view notifies its delegate object. The split view provides the delegate with both the bar button item and the popover controller that should be used to display the master pane. All the delegate has to do is add and remove the bar button item to the top bar.

You don't have to do anything else since the split view takes care of displaying the popover when the bar button item is tapped.

In TweetPad, `ProfileViewController` will be the split view's delegate. This requires the class conform to the `UISplitViewDelegate` protocol, which you can do by making the following changes to ProfileViewController.h:

```
// ProfileViewController.h
@interface ProfileViewController : UIViewController
  <UISplitViewControllerDelegate>
{
  ...
  UIPopoverController *popoverController;
}
...
@property (nonatomic,retain) UIPopoverController *popoverController;
@end
```

You will also keep a reference to the popover controller so you can dismiss it programmatically when a row in the friends table is selected.

To hide and display the split view's bar button item, edit ProfileViewController.m so it matches the following:

```
// ProfileViewController.m
...
@synthesize popoverController;
...
- (void)dealloc
{
  [user release];
  [usernameLabel release];
  [profileImageView release];
  [tweetTextView release];
  [navigationBar release];
  [popoverController release];
  [super dealloc];
}
#pragma mark -
#pragma mark UISplitViewControllerDelegate methods
// Display the friends list button when rotating to portrait mode
- (void)splitViewController:(UISplitViewController *)svc
  willHideViewController:(UIViewController *)aViewController
  withBarButtonItem:(UIBarButtonItem *)barButtonItem
```

```
    forPopoverController:(UIPopoverController *)pc
{
    // Set the button's title
    barButtonItem.title = @"Friends";
    // Add the button to the left side of the navigation bar
    [navigationBar.topItem setLeftBarButtonItem:barButtonItem
        animated:YES];
    // Remember the popover controller provided by the split view
    self.popoverController = pc;
}

// Remove the friends list button when rotating to landscape mode
- (void)splitViewController:(UISplitViewController *)svc
    willShowViewController:(UIViewController *)aViewController
    invalidatingBarButtonItem:(UIBarButtonItem *)barButtonItem
{
    // Remove the friends list button
    [navigationBar.topItem setLeftBarButtonItem:nil animated:YES];
    // The popover controller is now invalid
    self.popoverController = nil;
}
@end
```

When FriendsViewController is hidden due to interface rotation, splitViewController:willHideViewController:withBarButtonItem:forPopoverController: is called. Inside this method, you can see that the bar button item passed via the delegate is then added to the navigation bar. The split view takes care of displaying the hidden view in a popover when the user taps this button. In a moment, you will see why you want to keep a reference to this controller.

If the user rotates the screen back to landscape mode, splitViewController:willShowViewController:invalidatingBarButtonItem: is then called. At this point, you need to remove the bar button item since the master pane will be visible once again.

Save the modified files, and run TweetPad in the simulator in portrait mode. You should see the "Friends" button in the top-left corner this time. Click on it, and the list of friends will appear in a popover! Select a friend, and the profile view updates with that user's data.

But there's a problem. The popover controller doesn't go away when you select a user. By default, the popover controller only dismisses when the user taps outside its bounds. You also want to dismiss the popover after the user selects an item in the popover's list. To dismiss the popover programmatically, make the following changes to your setUser: method in ProfileViewController.m:

```
- (void)setUser:(TwitterUser *)aUser
{
  if (user != aUser)
  {
      [aUser retain];
      [user release];
      user = aUser;

      [self updateInterface];
  }
  [popoverController dismissPopoverAnimated:YES];
}
```

After making the change, run the TweetPad project again. This time, when you select a user, the popover dismisses automatically.

THERE'S A TIP FOR THAT

If you wish to change the size of the popover, you can override the contentSizeForViewInPopoverView method in FriendsViewController. Look up the method in the API documentation for more details.

Rotation Support

If you tried rotating the iPhone Simulator up to this point, the interface may or may not have rotated automatically. A split view will only rotate if *both* left and right panes enable automatic rotation. So to add support for automatic rotation, add the following method to both FriendsViewController.m and ProfileViewController.m:

```
// Add this code to both FriendsViewController
// and ProfileViewController
#pragma mark -
#pragma mark Rotation support
- (BOOL)shouldAutorotateToInterfaceOrientation:
    (UIInterfaceOrientation)interfaceOrientation
{
  return YES;
}
```

By returning YES, you are telling the device that the view controller can be viewed in portrait and landscape mode, upside down or right side up. Add the code, and run it in the iPhone Simulator. Rotate the device, and you can now view the app in landscape mode. Notice how the bar button item appears and disappears as the orientation changes from portrait to landscape.

CRASH AND LEARN

Does your profile image look distorted or disappear after rotating the simulator? To fix this problem, you need to edit the Autosizing field of the image view in Interface Builder. To make this change, open ProfileViewController.xib, select the image view, and select the tab with a ruler icon in the inspector window. In the Autosizing section, click on the arrows in the center of the box so that both are grayed out. In the window on the right, the red square that was previously growing and shrinking should be stationary in the top-left corner. This setting forces the image to stay the same size regardless of how the parent view resizes.

With that final change, you have now finished building your first iPad application! As you can see, the skills you learned in building iPhone applications are easily applied to iPad development. The biggest difference is in how the pieces are put together, hence the need for popovers and split views. Next chapter, you will resume building iPhone applications, but you now know the process for building iPad variants if you so choose.

Full source code for the finished TweetPad application is available online at http://troybrant.net/iphonebook/chapter15/TweetPad-done.zip.

Done with Multi-View Applications

You are now done building Twitter apps, and coincidentally, you are also done with the part on multi-view applications. At this point, you know enough to be a fairly dangerous iPhone (or iPad) developer. However, there are still some core concepts no iPhone developer should be without, including data management, networking, custom views, and animation. These juicy topics are covered in the following chapters, so take a break, and come back ready to pump out more iPhone apps!

The Least You Need to Know

- Split views display two views: a master view, which typically displays a list of items, and a detail view, which typically shows more details for the currently selected item.

- When a split view rotates to portrait mode, the master (left) view is shown in a popover that is triggered by a button bar item.

- To display a UIPopoverController when a toolbar item is tapped, use the present PopoverFromBarButtonItem:permittedArrowDirections:animated: method.

- The delegate for a split view controller is notified when the interface rotates from portrait to landscape mode and back.

- A split view controller will only allow interface rotation if both its left and right view controllers override `shouldAutorotateToInterfaceOrientation:` to return YES.

The APIs You Can't Wait to Use

Part 4

Now is your chance to go wild and explore the unique APIs the iPhone and iPad have to offer. Animate views in your app to add a bit of fun and surprise for your users. Add the ability for users to take pictures or videos in your app using the built-in camera. Report your user's location using the Core Location framework. Add background processing support to your app, and make money displaying ads—two great features of iPhone OS 4.0.

Animation

In This Chapter

- Animation blocks
- UIView properties that can be animated
- CGPoint, CGSize, and CGRect
- Animation curves
- Rotating a view
- Animotion app

What are some of the first reactions people have when they use an iPhone or an iPad? "It's so smooth," they say with childlike wonder as they slide their finger across the screen. "Look at that," can be heard as the interface smoothly rotates to match their orientation. "Can I have one?" is usually heard a short time later.

What is it that makes using the iPhone so *nice*? High on the list of answers is its use of animations. Nearly every interaction on the iPhone is animated, from scrolling tables, to opening apps, to sliding up a modal view. And almost all of these animations serve a purpose. All the sliding, flipping, fading, and zooming helps your user construct a mental map for intuitively getting around your apps. However, animations can add a bit of fun and surprise to your apps as well.

You, too, can easily add animations to your own apps. In this chapter, you learn how to use the UIView class to animate your views.

Intro to Animations

The easiest way to add animations to your application is using the `UIView` animation class methods. For instance, the following code demonstrates how to fade out a view:

```
// Start building the animation
[UIView beginAnimations:nil context:nil];

// Run the animation for 2 seconds
[UIView setAnimationDuration:2];

// Fade out the label over 2 seconds
label.alpha = 0;

// Run the animation
[UIView commitAnimations];
```

The default `alpha` value for a view starts at 1, which means the view is not transparent at all. Over the course of two seconds, the view will fade out until it is completely invisible.

ONE MORE THING

Note that all the `UIView` methods above are called directly on the `UIView` class itself—*not* on a `UIView` instance. That's because `beginAnimations:contentxt:`, `setAnimationDuration:`, and `commitAnimations` are all class methods, not instance methods. Class methods were covered in Chapter 5, though this is one of the first times you have seen class methods used in practice.

So what's up with the weird begin-commit syntax? What other properties can you animate? Is there a way to know when the animation ends? These questions are addressed in the following sections, starting with the strange `begin` and `commit` method calls.

CRASH AND LEARN

Although they sure are nice to look at, adding animation purely for its own sake is not useful. The iPhone SDK makes animating so easy that you may be tempted to add animations everywhere. However, always ask yourself if an animation is really needed before adding one on a whim.

Animating UIViews

UIView animations use what are known as *animation blocks*. Everything between the beginAnimations:context: and commitAnimations method calls is animated based on the animation settings you declare within the block. For instance, if you wanted to fade out an image view along with the label, all you have to do is add it to the animation block and set its alpha value to zero.

> **DEFINITION**
>
> An **animation block** defines how a view should animate. A UIView animation block begins by calling beginAnimations:context: and ends by calling commitAnimations. The lines of code between these two methods describe the animation, such as the duration, start time, and animation curve.

There are a few constraints about what can be animated, though. If your animations aren't working, you might want to check the following rules regarding UIView animation blocks:

- All animated objects must be UIView subclasses.

- All animated objects must be part of the view hierarchy—that is, you have to remember to add the view.

- Only animatable UIView properties can be animated.

What are these animatable properties? The properties in the list below can be animated using a UIView animation block:

Properties Animatable in UIView Animation Blocks

Property	Description
frame	The view's rectangle, in superview coordinates
bounds	The view's rectangle, in view coordinates
center	The center of the view's frame
transform	A matrix you can set to change the view's scale, rotation, and offset
alpha	Determines the view's transparency
backgroundColor	Background color of the view

THERE'S A TIP FOR THAT

You can actually animate more properties than the ones shown in the table, but you will need to drop down to lower-level animation techniques offered by the supremely powerful Core Animation framework. Animating using the Core Animation API is a lot more work, but you should check it out if you are looking for fine-grained control of your animations. Search online for "Core Animation," "CALayer," and "CAAnimation" to learn more.

The center property—along with frame and bounds—moves your view to a new position. To use these properties, you need to learn how to use the CGPoint, CGSize, and CGRect types. These types are covered later this chapter in the section on Core Graphics.

Customize the Animation

In the previous animation sample code, you set the length of the animation using the setAnimationDuration: class method. Setting the duration is just one of many ways you can customize the animation. You can also …

- Delay before starting.

- Start at a specific time.

- Specify the *animation curve*.

DEFINITION

The **animation curve** defines the speed at which the animation progresses. Options include animations that run at a constant speed, animations that start fast and end slow, and animations that start slow and end fast. The default animation curve is a slow-fast-slow option that starts slowly, quickly accelerates, and decelerates to end slowly.

- Repeat the animation multiple times.

- Set whether or not it autoreverses (ping-pong back and forth).

You see how to use these properties when animating your view in the sample application.

Knowing When an Animation Ends

If you add an animation to your application, it is likely you would like to know when the animation finishes. Maybe you want to trigger an action, like displaying an alert box. Or maybe you want to start a *second* animation when the first one completes. Luckily, `UIView` provides just such methods via an animation delegate.

The way you add the delegate is a bit strange, but it works the same as the previous times you have used delegation. After you assign yourself as the animation's delegate, your delegate methods will be called automatically.

To learn when the animation finishes, you need to have the following method implemented:

```
// Called when the animation stops
- (void)animationDidStop:(NSString *)animationID
   finished:(NSNumber *)finished
   context:(void *)context;
```

Here's the strange part: when you assign the delegate for the animation block, you must also specify the method to be called when the animation finishes. Here is what the sample code earlier in the chapter looks like with the addition of a delegate:

```
// Start building the animation
[UIView beginAnimations:nil context:nil];
[UIView setAnimationDuration:2];

// Be informed when the animation stops
[UIView setAnimationDelegate:self];
[UIView setAnimationDidStopSelector:
  @selector(animationDidStop:finished:context:)];

// Fade out the label over 2 seconds
label.alpha = 0;

// Run the animation
[UIView commitAnimations];
```

THERE'S A TIP FOR THAT

If your delegate method for animation completion is not being called, make sure you specify the selector as shown in the previous sample code.

You will use the delegate to chain multiple animations together in the sample app.

Core Graphics

To move a view, you need to either set its `center` property—a `CGPoint` type—or set its `frame` property—a CGRect type. These types are defined in the Core Graphics framework, a framework that provides the basic building blocks for drawing and positioning views. Views use three data types from Core Graphics to determine their shape and size: `CGPoint`, `CGSize`, and `CGRect`.

CGPoint, CGSize, and CGRect

If someone asked you to draw a box, you would need to know at least two pieces of information about it: where it goes and what size it is. In Core Graphics, to specify the *where*, you use `CGPoint`. To specify *what size*, you use `CGSize`. And to specify *both* where and what size, you use `CGRect`.

ONE MORE THING

The CG prefix is short for Core Graphics.

All three structures consist of two fields:

- CGPoint = {x, y}
- CGSize = {width, height}
- CGRect = {origin, size}

There are also built-in macros for creating each of these types:

```
CGPoint point = CGPointMake(10, 20);
CGSize size = CGSizeMake(30, 40);
CGRect rect = CGRectMake(10, 20, 30, 40)

// point: x = 10, y = 20
// size: width = 30, height = 40
// rect: origin.x = 10, origin.y = 20,
//       size.width = 30, size.height = 40
```

If you look closely, you will see that point, size, and rect do not have a "*" indicating they are pointers. What's the deal?

The reason for this change is that Core Graphics is a C API. If you remember from Chapter 5, Objective-C is a superset of C, which means you can mix and match C and Objective-C in your code as much as you like. Many iPhone OS applications are written entirely in Objective-C, but in the case of Core Graphics—and other frameworks like AddressBook and CFNetwork—you must use C.

Frame and Bounds

A CGRect describes the rectangle a UIView lives in. This rectangle is defined using the *frame* property of UIView. The exact same rectangle, however, is also defined using the *bounds* property.

DEFINITION

A view's **frame** is a rectangle positioned from the perspective of the parent view. A view's **bounds** is a rectangle positioned from the perspective of the view itself, usually at (0, 0).

Why are there two properties defining the same rectangle? The difference is the coordinate space used for each rectangle. A view's frame rectangle is described from the perspective of the parent view's coordinate system. Its bounds rectangle is described from within the view's own coordinate system.

ONE MORE THING

The coordinate system on iPhone OS devices is set up so that the point (0, 0) is in the top-left corner, and y values grow bigger going down the screen. This is the opposite of what you learned in geometry class, but it's very useful for laying out text and other graphics that flow from the top of the screen to the bottom.

Your eyes must be glazing over. The image that follows illustrates the difference between frame and bounds more visually:

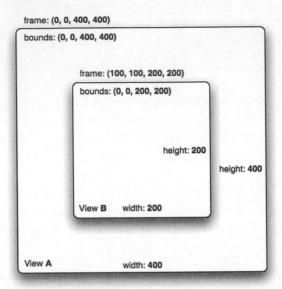

If you are writing code that lives within a custom view that needs to know its size, use its bounds. If you want to resize or reposition a view, manipulate its frame.

Undoubtedly, you need to experiment with frame and bounds to figure out which one to use in your code. However, there are a couple of fairly simple rules for determining which one to use:

- Use bounds when you are inside a view—that is, writing code inside a UIView subclass.

- Use frame when you are outside a view. For instance, use frame to position a UIView instance.

From this point forward, you will use frames and bounds in a variety of situations, so you have plenty of chances to figure them out along the way.

To see how you can animate a view's position, let's build the Animotion app.

Animotion App

Building the Animotion app will give you the chance to play with several ways to animate views.

By building Animotion, you will animate a view in just about every way possible.

The premise of the app is simple: after adding a toy view programmatically to the interface, you will "play" with the toy by moving, spinning, and scaling it in the interface. Eventually, you add an animation delegate to start a second animation after the first one completes.

Interface Challenge

There isn't much of a challenge to the Interface Challenge portion of this chapter. Follow these steps to get started:

1. Create a new View-based Application and name it "Animotion."

2. Edit AnimotionViewController.xib, and set the view's background color to white.

3. Add an instance variable of type `UIView` named "toyView" to `AnimotionViewController`.

4. Add the following constants to AnimotionViewController.m.

```
// AnimotionViewController.m

#define kToyViewStartX  20
#define kToyViewStartY  20
#define kToyViewWidth   50
#define kToyViewHeight  50
```

5. Override `loadView`, and initialize the `toyView` as follows:

   • Programmatically alloc/init `toyView` using the constants you just defined.

   • Set the `toyView`'s `backgroundColor` property to a color, such as `[UIColor orangeColor]`.

   • Use `addSubview:` to add the `toyView` to the AnimotionViewController's view.

6. Properly manage memory in `AnimotionViewController`.

And that is all the setup you have to do for this project. After you have completed the previous steps, save and run your Animotion project. You should be able to see the toy view in the middle of the screen, anxiously waiting to see what your next move will be.

Starter code to reach this point is available online at: http://troybrant.net/iphonebook/chapter16/Animotion-starter-code.zip.

Start Animating

You will do most of your experiments in the `viewDidAppear:` method of the `AnimotionViewController`. In fact, let's go ahead and look at some code that will move the view across the screen:

```
// Animate the toy view as soon as the view appears
- (void)viewDidAppear:(BOOL)animated
{
  [super viewDidAppear:animated];

  // Start building the animation
  [UIView beginAnimations:nil context:nil];
  [UIView setAnimationDuration:2];

  // Move the label from its current position to
```

```
// (200, 300) over 2 seconds
toyView.center = CGPointMake(200, 300);

// Run the animation
[UIView commitAnimations];
}
```

Add the previous code to your own project, run it, and see what it looks like. Perhaps it would be nice for it to start just a bit later so you can see where the toy view begins. You can achieve this by adding a delay using setAnimationDelay:. Add the following code to your animation block to delay the slide across the screen by one second:

```
[UIView setAnimationDelay:1];
```

That's better. The animation now starts after waiting for a second.

Animation Curves

Do you notice how the animation starts slow, gathers speed as it moves across the screen, and then gently puts on the brakes as it comes to a stop? This is a result of the default animation curve being set to UIViewAnimationCurveEaseInOut. The animation curves you have to choose from are described in the following image:

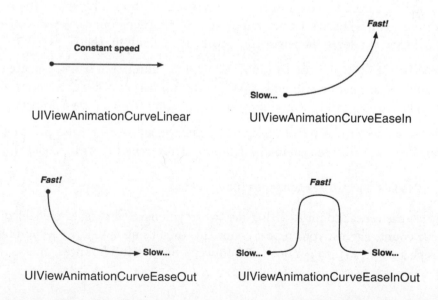

The "ease" direction in the animation curve's name describes which end of the animation is the slow part.

Try each of the four curves to see what each looks like:

- **UIViewAnimationCurveLinear**: Keep the same speed the entire way.

- **UIViewAnimationCurveEaseIn**: Start slow, end fast.

- **UIViewAnimationCurveEaseOut**: Start fast, end slow.

- **UIViewAnimationCurveEaseInOut**: Start slow, speed up, then end slow. This is the default animation curve.

Use the `setAnimationCurve:` method to choose an animation curve. For instance, the code below uses the "ease out" curve:

```
[UIView setAnimationCurve:UIViewAnimationCurveEaseOut];
```

Reverse and Repeat

After moving across the screen, you can animate back to your original spot by enabling the animation's auto-reverse. Add the following code to return to your original spot:

```
[UIView setAnimationRepeatAutoreverses:YES];
```

After adding the code, save and run your project. See how it reverses direction, slides back home, and whoa! What just happened? Right when your view was almost to its original spot, it teleported across the screen. Why did it do that?

When you set `view.center` to `(200, 300)` in the animation block, you are setting the value the animation will end at. When the animation is done, the view will be centered at `(200, 300)`, even if it means teleporting from another position.

There is one way to keep from teleporting after an auto-reverse: keep the animation going! You can easily repeat an animation by adding the following code:

```
[UIView setAnimationRepeatCount:2];
```

Why set the repeat count to 2? Because when you have auto-reverse enabled, each reverse counts against your repeat count. So when using auto-reverse, you must set the repeat count to 2 to get one full bounce, 4 for two full bounces, and so on.

You will notice that even after repeating, the view still teleports. The real is to detect when the animation finishes and reset the position of the view. To detect when the animation completes, you need to become the delegate of the animation.

Figuring Out When the Animation Is Done

To detect when the animation completes and reset the toy view position, add the following delegate method:

```
// Update the toy view's position when the animation stops
- (void)animationDidStop:(NSString *)animationID
    finished:(NSNumber *)finished
    context:(void *)context
{
    // Instantly move the toy view to its original position
    toyView.frame = CGRectMake(kToyViewStartX, kToyViewStartY,
        kToyViewWidth, kToyViewHeight);
}
```

Then, arrange for the method to be called when the animation ends by adding the code in bold to the animation bock in `viewDidAppear:`.

```
// Animate the toy view as soon as the view appears
- (void)viewDidAppear:(BOOL)animated
{
    [super viewDidAppear:animated];

    // Start building the animation
    [UIView beginAnimations:nil context:nil];
    [UIView setAnimationDuration:2];

    // Be informed when the animation stops
    [UIView setAnimationDelegate:self];
    [UIView setAnimationDidStopSelector:
        @selector(animationDidStop:finished:context:)];

    // Move the label from its current position to
    // (200, 300) over 2 seconds
    toyView.center = CGPointMake(200, 300);

    // Run the animation
    [UIView commitAnimations];
}
```

Now, save your code, and run it to see what happens. As you can see, the view stays put this time because you reset its position to where it was when the animation started.

ONE MORE THING

You may have noticed that there are a few different ways to position a view. Sometimes it's frame and other times it's center. You can set a UIView's position in many ways (frame, bounds, center, transform), and the UIView will respond to any and all of them.

Combining Animations

Now that you know when the animation stops, you can start another animation if you want to. Let's try something different this time, though. Add the following code to add a second animation that spins the view 180 degrees:

```
// Convert degrees to radians
- (CGFloat)degreesToRadians:(CGFloat)degrees
{
    return degrees * M_PI / 180;
}

// Start a second animation when the first one completes
- (void)animationDidStop:(NSString *)animationID
    finished:(NSNumber *)finished
    context:(void *)context
{
    toyView.frame = CGRectMake(kToyViewStartX, kToyViewStartY,
        kToyViewWidth, kToyViewHeight);

    // Start building the animation
    [UIView beginAnimations:nil context:nil];
    [UIView setAnimationDuration:1];
    [UIView setAnimationCurve:UIViewAnimationCurveLinear];

    // Convert 180 degrees to radians
    CGFloat rotationAngleInRadians =
        [self degreesToRadians:180];

    // Rotate the view 180 degrees
    toyView.transform =
        CGAffineTransformMakeRotation(
```

```
                rotationAngleInRadians);

    // Run the animation
    [UIView commitAnimations];
}
```

ONE MORE THING

CGFloat is defined as either a `float` or `double`, depending on your system. However, it is more likely to resolve to a `double` on modern systems.

In the preceding code, you modify the view's `transform` property, which is of type `CGAffineTransform`. Affine transforms won't be covered in too much detail in this book, but just know `CGAffineTransform` allows you to rotate, scale, and translate your view. Here are some of the constants and macros you can use to create and modify a `CGAffineTransform`:

- **CGAffineTransformIdentity:** A constant you can assign to completely reset the transform.

- **CGAffineTransformMakeRotation():** Returns a transform you can use to rotate your view.

- **CGAffineTransformMakeScale():** Returns a transform you can use to change your view's size.

- **CGAffineTransformMakeTranslation():** Returns a transform you can use to move your view.

- **CGAffineTransformConcat():** Combines two transforms, and returns the resulting transform. For instance, you can combine rotation and scaling transforms to create a single transform that can both rotate and scale your view.

All Done

And that's a wrap for the Animotion application. Full source code for the finished application is available online at http://troybrant.net/iphonebook/chapter16/Animotion-done.zip.

As you discovered, using `UIView`'s animation block class methods makes adding animations to your application easy to do. Over the course of the chapter, you found what objects can be animated (views in the view hierarchy) and what properties of those views can be animated (`frame`, `center`, `alpha`, and `transform`, to name a few). By adding yourself as the animation delegate, you can find out exactly when animations end, which turns out to be crucial in the event that you have auto-reverse animations enabled. To top it off, you played with a little toy application to see exactly what these animations look like.

In the next chapter, you learn how to integrate with the phone's media capabilities. You will access the phone's camera to record video and take pictures inside your application. You will also see how to save images and video to the shared photo album that your user can access from the built-in Photos app. You will also play video and audio files. If you want to create a photo-editing application or add sound effects to your app, for instance, the next chapter is a must-read.

The Least You Need to Know

- To animate your views, use `UIView`'s `beginAnimations:context:` and `commitAnimations` to create an animation block.
- The following properties can be animated in a `UIView` animation block: `frame`, `bounds`, `center`, `alpha`, `backgroundColor`, and `transform`.
- The "easeIn" part of an animation curve name means the animation starts slowly.
- To be notified when an animation ends, you must call both `setAnimationDelegate:` and `setAnimationDidStopSelector:` class methods on the `UIView` class.
- To rotate a view, use `CGAffineTransformMakeRotation` and apply its result to the `transform` property of a view.

Video, Images, and Audio

In This Chapter

- Taking pictures and recording video
- Saving to the shared Camera Roll
- Playing video
- Notifications
- Playing audio

iPhones and iPads are media machines. Using an iPhone, you can take pictures and record video. The iPad is the perfect device for showing photos to your friends. Both iPhone and iPad play crisp, clear audio.

You can utilize all these multimedia tools in your own applications. This chapter covers how to record, view, and save photos and videos in your apps. You also learn how to play sound clips and vibrate the phone.

Intro to Media on the iPhone OS

The three types of media presented in this chapter are video, pictures, and audio. Specifically, the following topics are covered:

- Taking pictures and recording video
- Saving pictures and videos to the Camera Roll
- Playing video
- Playing audio

Let's get started by accessing the phone's camera for taking pictures and video.

THERE'S A TIP FOR THAT

The Camera Roll is where your photos are stored after you take them with the Camera app. Despite its name, videos are also stored in the Camera Roll on 3GS models and later.

Using the Camera for Pictures and Video

From a developer's point of view, the name UIImagePickerController can be very misleading. You might think that using UIImagePickerController, you would just be able to, well, pick images. Would you have guessed, though, that the UIImagePickerController is used for the following tasks?

- Picking images from your Camera Roll

- Taking pictures

- Recording video

The following image shows the different flavors of the UIImagePickerController:

 UIImagePickerControllerSourceTypeSavedPhotosAlbum

 UIImagePickerControllerSourceTypeCamera
on iPhone 3GS or later

 UIImagePickerControllerSourceTypeCamera
on iPhone 3G or earlier

Setting the sourceType property determines which UIImagePickerController you get.

Let's see how you can use this class to take pictures and videos.

Initializing the Camera Controller

Following is the code to initialize and display a `UIImagePickerController`:

```
#import <MobileCoreServices/MobileCoreServices.h>

// Make sure the device has a camera you can access
if ([UIImagePickerController isSourceTypeAvailable:
    UIImagePickerControllerSourceTypeCamera])
{
    // Initialize the controller
    UIImagePickerController *imagePickerController =
        [[UIImagePickerController alloc] init];

    // Use the camera interface
    imagePickerController.sourceType =
        UIImagePickerControllerSourceTypeCamera;

    // Display camera and video controls
    imagePickerController.mediaTypes =
        [NSArray arrayWithObjects:
                (NSString *) kUTTypeImage,
                (NSString *) kUTTypeMovie,
                nil];

    // Find out when the picture or video is ready
    imagePickerController.delegate = self;

    // Slide up the camera interface as a modal view
    [self presentModalViewController:imagePickerController
        animated:YES];

    // Good ol' memory management
    [imagePickerController release];
}
else
{
    NSLog(@"Cannot access the camera");
}
```

ONE MORE THING

You can set `allowsEditing` to YES on the `UIImagePickerController` to enable editing controls in the camera interface as well. After taking a picture, these controls allow your user to crop and scale the photo. See the `UIImagePickerController` class in the Xcode API reference for more properties to customize the camera interface.

The previous code, when executed, displays a camera view that can be used to take pictures or video. On devices where video is not available, the controller is smart enough to not display the video controls.

CRASH AND LEARN

You must add the `MobileCoreServices` framework to your project for the code in this section to work. See Chapter 21 for instructions on how to add a framework to your project.

When setting the `mediaTypes` property of the image picker, you reference the `kUTTypeImage` and `kUTTypeMovie` strings. Unfortunately, in order to reference these strings, you must import the `MobileCoreServices` framework, which is referenced at the top of the code snippet.

After the user has finished taking a photo or recording a video, the `UIImagePickerController` sends a messages to its delegate, passing along the newly captured media. In the next section, you learn the two methods you must define as the `UIImagePickerControllerDelegate` to get access to these newly minted photos and videos.

Getting Video and Photos from the Camera

`UIImagePickerController` notifies its delegate of two events:

- When the user finishes using the camera
- When the user cancels using the camera

When successful, the delegate is provided with a dictionary that contains the media from the camera. When the delegate has finished handling the information from the camera, it is the delegate's responsibility to dismiss the modal view controller. It may seem strange, but it is an iPhone programming convention that the class that launches a modal view controller should also be the one to dismiss the controller.

ONE MORE THING

To become the picker's delegate, your class must adopt the
`UIImagePickerControllerDelegate` protocol. Remember, this means adding
the protocol name as part of the `@interface` definition in the .h file.

The following code implements the two camera delegate methods. You can see how
to determine whether the user took a video or a picture and how to properly dismiss
the camera controller:

```
#pragma mark -
#pragma mark UIImagePickerControllerDelegate methods

// Called after successfully taking a picture or video
- (void)imagePickerController:(UIImagePickerController *)picker
   didFinishPickingMediaWithInfo:(NSDictionary *)info
{
    // The media type determines whether it was a
    // picture or video
    NSString *mediaType =
        [info objectForKey:UIImagePickerControllerMediaType];

    // Check to see if they took a picture or a video
    if ([mediaType isEqualToString:(NSString *)kUTTypeImage])
    {
        // The original, unmodified image from the camera
        UIImage *originalImage =
            [info objectForKey:
                UIImagePickerControllerOriginalImage];

        // The final, edited image (if editing was enabled)
        UIImage *editedImage =
            [info objectForKey:
                UIImagePickerControllerEditedImage];

        //
        // Now, do something with the images
        //
    }
    else if ([mediaType isEqualToString:(NSString *)kUTTypeMovie])
    {
        // The URL to the video location on disk
        NSURL *url =
```

continues

```
                    [info objectForKey:
                        UIImagePickerControllerMediaURL];


        //
        // Now, do something with the video
        //
    }

    // Since you launched it, you dismiss the camera modal view
    [self dismissModalViewControllerAnimated:YES];
}

// Called when the user taps the "Cancel" button in
// the camera view
- (void)imagePickerControllerDidCancel:
    (UIImagePickerController *)picker
{
    // Since you launched it, you dismiss the camera modal view
    [self dismissModalViewControllerAnimated:YES];
}
```

As shown in the previous code, you get the media type from the input dictionary to determine whether the user snapped a photo or recorded a video. Because the media type is a string, you use the isEqualToString: method to decide whether the user took a photo (kUTTypeImage) or a video (kUTTypeMovie). Then, you can access the image or video URL from the info dictionary and do whatever you want with the image or video. Finally, in each delegate method, you dismiss the camera modal view.

After you have access to the image and video URL, you can save, upload, or play back the media. In the next section, you will see how to save both images and videos to the phone's shared Camera Roll.

THERE'S A TIP FOR THAT

If you want a user to select an existing photo from the Camera Roll, use the UIImagePickerControllerSourceTypeSavedPhotosAlbum source type property. When the user selects one of the photos from the album, the imagePicker Controller:didFinishPickingMediaWithInfo: method will be called.

Saving Photos and Videos

To save images to the shared Camera Roll, you can use
`UIImageWriteToSavedPhotosAlbum`. After saving these photos to the Camera Roll,
you can access them using the built-in Photos app like any other photo you take using
the phone.

Since it may take a while to process the image, the function uses the *target-action*
pattern to notify when it is done saving the image. In the following code, you can see
how to go about saving a `UIImage` and how to know when it has finished saving to the
Camera Roll:

```
// Assume the image is valid
UIImage *image = ...;

// Save the image to the Camera Roll
UIImageWriteToSavedPhotosAlbum(image,
  self,
  @selector(image:didFinishSavingWithError:contextInfo:),
  nil);
...

#pragma mark -
#pragma mark Camera Roll saving callbacks

// Called when the save operation has completed
- (void)image:(UIImage *)image
  didFinishSavingWithError:(NSError *)error
  contextInfo:(void *)contextInfo
{
  if (!error)
  {
      NSLog(@"Image saved successfully to Camera Roll.");
  }
  else
  {
      NSLog(@"Error saving image: %@",
            [error localizedDescription]);
  }
}
```

> **DEFINITION**
>
> **Target-action** is a form of communication in which one object sends a single message—the **action**—to another object—the **target**.

If your image was saved successfully, the error parameter of the image: didFinishSavingWithError:contextInfo: method will be set to nil. Otherwise, you can check the error object to see exactly what went wrong. It is a good idea to notify the user of the error, perhaps using a UIAlertView.

Saving video to the Camera Roll involves more steps, but it is also quite simple to do. The UISaveVideoAtPathToSavedPhotosAlbum function is provided to save the video, but you should call UIVideoAtPathIsCompatibleWithSavedPhotosAlbum first to make sure the video can be saved to the album. You can also be notified when the video is finished saving to disk using the target-action pattern.

The following code demonstrates how to save a video at a particular URL to disk:

```
// Assume video URL is valid
NSURL *videoURL = ...;

// Convert URL to a string
NSString *videoPath = [videoURL path];

// Not all devices can save video to Camera Roll, so check first
if (UIVideoAtPathIsCompatibleWithSavedPhotosAlbum(videoPath))
{
    // Save the video to the Camera Roll
    UISaveVideoAtPathToSavedPhotosAlbum(pathToVideo,
        self,
        @selector(video:didFinishSavingWithError:contextInfo:),
        nil);
}
...

#pragma mark -
#pragma mark Camera Roll saving callbacks

// Called when the save operation has completed
- (void)video:(NSString *)videoPath
    didFinishSavingWithError:(NSError *)error
    contextInfo:(void *)contextInfo
{
    if (!error)
```

```
    {
        NSLog(@"Video saved successfully to Camera Roll.");
    }
    else
    {
        NSLog(@"Error saving video: %@",
              [error localizedDescription]);
    }
}
```

CRASH AND LEARN

The video URL must be a URL to a file on disk, not online.

Because the `UIImagePickerController` returns a URL to the video file on disk, you can use the previous code verbatim to save the video to disk. After the video is done saving, the selector you provide will be called, and again, a `nil` error parameter means it was saved successfully.

Playing Video

Now that you have covered how to save photos and video, let's take a look at how to display these media to the user. A photo is simply a `UIImage`, which can be displayed using a `UIImageView`. Playing videos, however, requires that you use the `MPMoviePlayerController` class for playback.

`MPMoviePlayerController` is a controller that handles movie playback. All you have to do is give it a movie URL and tell it to play. The class can play any movie you can already play on your phone. This typically means files with extensions .mov, .mp4, .mpv, and .3gp are supported.

CRASH AND LEARN

You must add the `MediaPlayer` framework to your project for the code in this section to work. See Chapter 21 for instructions on how to add a framework to your project.

The following code demonstrates how you can launch a MPMoviePlayerController, play a video, and be notified when the video has ended:

```
#import <MediaPlayer/MediaPlayer.h>

// Assume video URL is valid
NSURL *videoURL = ...;

// Initialize the video at the given URL
MPMoviePlayerController *moviePlayerController =
  [[MPMoviePlayerController alloc]
      initWithContentURL:videoURL];

// Scale the video so it fits entirely in the view
moviePlayerController.scalingMode = MPMovieScalingModeAspectFit;

// Register to be notified when playback finishes
[[NSNotificationCenter defaultCenter]
  addObserver:self
  selector:@selector(myMovieFinishedCallback:)
  name:MPMoviePlayerPlaybackDidFinishNotification
  object:moviePlayerController];

// Movie playback is asynchronous, so
// this method returns immediately
[moviePlayerController play];

// DO NOT release the moviePlayerController now.
// Instead, release it in the notification
// callback when playback is complete.
...

#pragma mark -
#pragma mark Movie player notification methods

// Called when the movie finishes playing
- (void)myMovieFinishedCallback:(NSNotification *)notification
{
    // Get the movie controller from the notification
    MPMoviePlayerController *moviePlayerController =
        [notification object];

    // Stop receiving movie notifications
    [[NSNotificationCenter defaultCenter]
```

```
          removeObserver:self
          name:MPMoviePlayerPlaybackDidFinishNotification
          object:moviePlayerController];

     // *Now* release the movie controller we
     // alloc/init'ed earlier
     [moviePlayerController release];
}
```

Some notes about the preceding code:

- If you want to show a video with the controls hidden—say, for an intro video for a game—you can set the `movieControlMode` property on the `moviePlayerController` to `MPMovieControlModeHidden`.

- Notice how the `MPMoviePlayerController` displays itself when the `play` method is called. This is a very different way of displaying a view than you have seen up to this point. Why is it different? The MPMoviePlayerController is just a controller, not a view controller, so it doesn't adhere to view controller conventions.

- To manage memory properly, you need to know when the movie player finishes so you can release your reference to it. Instead of delegate or target-action, the `MPMoviePlayerController` sends out a *notification* when playback is done. You register to receive the notification, and when the movie finishes, you correctly manage memory by releasing your reference to the movie player.

DEFINITION

A **notification** is a callback mechanism that can inform multiple objects when an event occurs. The notification system is similar to delegation except delegation informs a *single* object of an event while notifications can inform *multiple* objects of the event at once.

So what is this notification business? How does it work, and why isn't delegation used? Notifications are another way to communicate between objects, and you can learn more about them in the next section.

THERE'S A TIP FOR THAT

You can also provide a movie-editing interface to your users using the `UIVideoEditorController` class. Search the Xcode API reference or search online for examples of how to use this class.

Notifications

In iPhone programming, there are four common patterns for objects to communicate. Here they are, each with a short summary:

- **Target-Action:** Specify a *single* object and a *single* method to call on that object when a *single* event happens. You have seen this used by buttons and other controls.

- **Delegation:** Specify a *single* object which responds to *numerous* methods to modify or add behavior. You have seen this used by table views, text editing, the location manager, and many others.

- **Notification:** Register to be one of *many* objects notified when an event happens.

- **Key-Value Observing (KVO):** Register to be one of *many* objects notified when a single *property* of another object changes.

ONE MORE THING

KVO will not be covered in this book, but you can learn more about how it works by reading through Apple's guide to Key-Value Observing in the Xcode API documentation.

Target-action and delegation are used when a single object needs to be notified of an event. However, what do you do when an event happens that a lot of objects need to know about? That is when the notification pattern proves most useful.

How It Works

The notification system works by using a centralized class—NSNotificationCenter—to manage the notification process. The NSNotificationCenter keeps a list of objects who are interested in receiving a particular notification. When an object wants to send out the notification, it tells the notification center, which in turn sends out the notification to all the objects in its list.

You can think of NSNotificationCenter as a Twitter server. To start following someone, you give Twitter the name of the person you want to follow. Similarly, you give NSNotificationCenter the name of the notification you want to receive. To post a tweet, you tell Twitter what you want to post, and Twitter sends the message to all your followers. Similarly, you tell NSNotificationCenter to post a notification, and the center sends the notification to all objects that registered for that notification.

In the preceding movie playing code, here is the full notification sequence:

1. Your class registers myMovieFinishedCallback: with the NSNotificationCenter to be called when the notification named MPMoviePlayerPlaybackDidFinishNotification is fired.

2. When the video is done playing, the player tells the NSNotificationCenter to broadcast the notification named MPMoviePlayerPlaybackDidFinishNotification. The player doesn't know which objects have registered for this notification.

3. NSNotificationCenter goes through the list of objects that want to know about MPMoviePlayerPlaybackDidFinishNotification and tells them the event happened by calling the selector they registered. Your class is in this list, and myMovieFinishedCallback: gets called.

4. In myMovieFinishedCallback:, unregister from the NSNotificationCenter so that you are no longer notified about the MPMoviePlayerPlaybackDidFinishNotification.

This is the basic template for using notifications. You won't always unregister in the callback method, but the other steps are largely the same.

NSNotifications

Notifications themselves are represented by the NSNotification class and consist of the following important properties:

- **name:** A string that is used to uniquely identify a notification. In the movie player sample code, the name of the notification was the constant MPMoviePlayerPlaybackDidFinishNotification.

- **object:** An id type that is usually set to the object that posts the notification. In the movie player sample code, the object is indeed set to the MPMoviePlayerController instance that initiated the notification.

- **userInfo:** This dictionary can contain any additional information the object posting the notification wants to send to recipients. You typically need to see the documentation for the class posting the notification to know if there is any useful data in this dictionary.

ONE MORE THING

To be notified of all notifications with a given name, pass nil as the final parameter when calling addObserver:selector:name:object:. Instead, if you want to be notified only when a single object generates the notification, pass the object as the final parameter.

Notifications are used in a variety of situations in iPhone development. Look out for them in the sample code you encounter.

Playing Audio

Up to this point, you have seen several ways of manipulating images and video using the iPhone SDK. You will now turn your attention toward audio. There are many ways to control audio on the iPhone OS, with some approaches much easier to learn than others. The range of options is displayed in the following figure:

Options for Playing Audio

System Sound API

AV Foundation

Audio Toolbox

OpenAL

The system sound API is the easiest to use. The Audio Queue Services package in Audio Toolbox is more difficult to use, but it gives you fine-grained control over audio.

In this section, you see how to do two simple things: make the phone vibrate and play a short audio file. If you want to add distortions, record audio, stream music from the Internet, or do some other more complex task, Apple provides in-depth documentation on manipulating audio in the Xcode API reference.

THERE'S A TIP FOR THAT

As of iPhone OS 3.0, you can access your user's iPod Library using the same MediaPlayer framework used for video playback.

Vibration

Making the phone vibrate takes very little code:

```
#import <AudioToolbox/AudioToolbox.h>

// Vibrate the phone
AudioServicesPlaySystemSound(kSystemSoundID_Vibrate);
```

Simply pass the kSystemSoundID_Vibrate constant to the system sound function, and the phone will buzz. One important thing to note: vibration only works on the iPhone, not the iPad or iPod Touch.

CRASH AND LEARN

You must add the AudioToolbox framework to your project for the code in this section to work. See Chapter 21 for instructions on how to add a framework to your project.

AVAudioPlayer

You can also use the AudioServicesPlaySystemSound function to play audio clips shorter than 30 seconds. However, the function is not as robust as the AVAudioPlayer class, which you will use to play an audio file in the sample code to come.

THERE'S A TIP FOR THAT

You can use the afconvert command-line tool on a Mac to convert a wide range of audio data formats to an iPhone-friendly format.

The iPhone OS is capable of playing a large number of audio formats, but for short sound clips, .caf and .aiff formats are preferred. Test the AVAudioPlayer class with a short grunt sound file you can download from the book website at http://troybrant. net/iphonebook/chapter17/grunt.aiff.

After adding the grunt.aiff file to your project, you can use the NSBundle object to help construct a path to the sound file. The URL of this path will then be used to initialize the audio player. To know when the audio file stops, AVAudioPlayer uses delegation to notify an interested object. You need to implement the AVAudioPlayerDelegate protocol to become the delegate, as well as implement the following two methods:

```
// Called when the audio file finishes playing
- (void)audioPlayerDidFinishPlaying:(AVAudioPlayer *)player
    successfully:(BOOL)flag;

// Called if an error occurred decoding the audio file
- (void)audioPlayerDecodeErrorDidOccur:(AVAudioPlayer *)player
    error:(NSError *)error;
```

As the AVAudioPlayer's delegates, these methods are called when the sound file finishes playing or if there is an error playing the file.

CRASH AND LEARN

You must add the AVFoundation framework to your project for the code in this section to work. .

To see exactly how it works, the following code loads the grunt.aiff file, plays it, and invokes the delegate methods when the file is finished playing:

```
#import <AVFoundation/AVFoundation.h>

// Use NSBundle to get the file path
NSString *soundFilePath =
  [[NSBundle mainBundle]
      pathForResource:@"grunt"
      ofType:@"aiff"];

// Build a URL object
NSURL *fileURL = [NSURL URLWithString:soundFilePath];

// Initialize the player with the file URL
NSError *error;
```

```
audioPlayer =
  [[AVAudioPlayer alloc]
      initWithContentsOfURL:fileURL
      error:&error];

if (!error)
{
  // Set delegate so you can know when sound clip is done
  audioPlayer.delegate = self;

  // Play the grunt sound
  [audioPlayer play];
}
else
{
  NSLog(@"Error loading audio clip: %@",
      [error localizedDescription]);
}
...

#pragma mark -
#pragma mark AVAudioPlayerDelegate methods

// Called when the audio file finishes playing
- (void)audioPlayerDidFinishPlaying:(AVAudioPlayer *)player
  successfully:(BOOL)flag
{
  // Simple way to convert BOOL to string
  NSString *successString = flag ? @"YES" : @"NO";

  NSLog(@"Done playing audio. Successful? %@",
      successString);

  // Clean up so you can reuse audioPlayer
  [audioPlayer release];
}

// Called if an error occurred decoding the audio file
- (void)audioPlayerDecodeErrorDidOccur:(AVAudioPlayer *)player
  error:(NSError *)error
{
  NSLog(@"Error decoding audio: %@",
            [error localizedDescription]);

  // Clean up so you can reuse audioPlayer
  [audioPlayer release];
}
```

If the AVAudioPlayer can't load the audio file for any reason—for instance, the file doesn't exist or the file format is unsupported—then initWithContentsOfURL:error: returns nil. In this case, the error object is populated, so you can use it to find out exactly what the problem was.

As a reminder, a BOOL is just a C int value, which means printing a BOOL will either print 0 or 1. As shown in the audioPlayerDidFinishPlaying: method, you can use a simple ternary operation to create a much nicer YES or NO string from the BOOL value.

ONE MORE THING

If you are interested in recording audio, use the AVAudioRecorder class that became available in iPhone OS 3.0.

Media App

If you would rather play with code than just read about it, you can download the Media example app online at http://troybrant.net/iphonebook/chapter17/Media-done.zip.

Media app demonstrates how to implement everything covered in this chapter, from recording videos and taking pictures to playing audio and saving media to the shared Camera Roll. You can try it out and examine the code in-depth to help build your own media-rich application.

Wrapping Up

You found out in this chapter how you can record photos or video using UIImagePickerController, save the resulting media, and even play back video using MPMoviePlayerController. You learned how NSNotificationCenter is used to broadcast a notification to several objects at once. Finally, you learned about audio and how to use AVAudioPlayer to play audio clips.

The next chapter covers one of my favorite APIs: Core Location. Using the Core Location framework, you can find your user's latitude and longitude coordinates. In addition to learning about Core Location, you build a distance-tracking sample application.

The Least You Need to Know

- Use the `UIImagePickerController` to allow your users to take pictures and video inside your application.
- To save an image to a device's Camera Roll, use `UIImageWriteToSavedPhotosAlbum`.
- To save a video to a device's Camera Roll, use `UISaveVideoAtPathToSavedPhotosAlbum`.
- Play a video using the `MPMoviePlayerController` class.
- Although there are many options for playing audio, the easiest to use is the `AVAudioPlayer` class.

GPS and Location Management

In This Chapter

- The Core Location framework
- Using CLLocationManager to get location updates
- CLLocation properties for accessing location data
- Detecting inaccurate location data
- Distance app

"Where are you?" One of the frequently asked questions of all time is now becoming much easier to answer with the ubiquity of location-enabled devices. You take it for granted now, but how impressive is it that you can open the Maps application and instantly—and visually—know your location?

In this chapter, you see just how simple it is to use this powerful feature. You use the Core Location framework to allow your users to figure out exactly where they are. The CLLocation object reported by the phone will tell your app the latitude, longitude, and even the elevation of your user. Although the location reported by the phone is usually quite accurate, it can also sometimes report wildly inaccurate values. You learn how to make sure location data is safe to use. Finally, you get some practice using Core Location by building a simple distance-tracking application.

Using Core Location

Core Location is the framework that provides access to the phone's location data. iPhone OS devices use a combination of techniques to identify your location. In addition to GPS, your device can triangulate your position based on nearby WiFi networks or cell towers. Both WiFi and cell tower triangulation can be used to provide your location quickly, but they are not as accurate as a GPS unit. Combined, these techniques provide fast and accurate location information to apps leveraging the Core Location framework.

ONE MORE THING

Although the iPod Touch and the WiFi iPad model don't have a GPS chip, they still approximate location based off nearby WiFi networks. This method will probably not work at all in areas where the WiFi networks are not "known" by Apple.

To use the Core Location API, you just need to know how to use two classes: `CLLocation` and `CLLocationManager`. You will learn about each of these classes here, starting with `CLLocation`.

CLLocation

CLLocation is the object that contains your user's location data. The object provides the following useful properties:

- **coordinate**: A `CLLocationCoordinate2D` struct that contains the latitude and longitude of the user's location. To access the latitude and longitude, use the following syntax: `location.coordinate.latitude` and `location.coordinate.longitude`.

- **horizontalAccuracy**: The *radius of uncertainty* around the location's position, measured in meters. This is the transparent blue circle around the tracking dot you see in the Maps application when your position is being determined. A negative value indicates an invalid coordinate value.

DEFINITION

The **radius of uncertainty** is a measure of the accuracy of a location reading. For instance, a 100-meter radius of uncertainty means the device's true position can be up to 100 meters away from the generated location.

- **altitude**: The user's distance above or below sea level, also reported in meters.

- **verticalAccuracy**: The accuracy of the altitude value, reported in meters. A negative value indicates an invalid altitude reading.

- **timestamp**: An `NSDate` object representing the time at which the location was determined.

As indicated in some of these property descriptions, the CLLocation object reports distance values in meters. Those in metrically challenged countries would likely prefer to see units in feet and miles instead of meters and kilometers. It is up to you, the developer, to make that conversion. You see how it's done in the sample application a bit later on.

In addition to providing useful properties, CLLocation can calculate the distance between two locations for you. To find the distance between two CLLocation objects, use the getDistanceFrom: method, as shown in the following:

```
CLLocation *location1 = ...;
CLLocation *location2 = ...;

// Compute the distance in meters between the two locations
double distanceInMeters = [location1 getDistanceFrom:location2];
```

These CLLocation objects sure do seem neat, but how do you get them populated with real location data? Say hello to CLLocationManager.

CLLocationManager

The CLLocationManager is the class responsible for generating CLLocations objects for your user's position. Like most APIs in the iPhone SDK, CLLocationManager reports location changes using delegation. To receive these updates, you must adopt the CLLocationManagerDelegate protocol and assign yourself as the manager's delegate.

CLLocationManagerDelegate

Let's take a look at the methods that should be implemented by an object that adopts the CLLocationManagerDelegate protocol:

```
// Called every time a new location reading is available
- (void)locationManager:(CLLocationManager *)manager
    didUpdateToLocation:(CLLocation *)newLocation
    fromLocation:(CLLocation *)oldLocation;

// Called when there was an error determining the location
- (void)locationManager:(CLLocationManager *)manager
    didFailWithError:(NSError *)error;
```

When the manager reports a new location to the delegate, it graciously includes the previous location reading as well. The primary purpose of including the `oldLocation` in the first delegate method is so you can compute the distance between the two locations, which is exactly what you do in the sample application.

THERE'S A TIP FOR THAT

The very first time `locationManager:didUpdateToLocation:fromLocation:` is called, the `oldLocation` parameter will be set to `nil`.

CLLocationManager Initialization

Before the delegate methods can be called, you must first initialize the `CLLocationManager` and start the location-finding process. Typically, you assign the `CLLocationManager` as an instance variable in your view controller or perhaps your application delegate. In the following example, assume a `locationManager` instance variable has been declared for the imaginary `MyViewController` class:

```
// MyViewController.m

// Initialize the location manager
locationManager = [[CLLocationManager alloc] init];

// Assign yourself as the delegate
locationManager.delegate = self;

// Start receiving location updates
[locationManager startUpdatingLocation];
```

After the preceding code, `locationManager` will call the delegate methods `MyViewController` any time a new location update comes in.

ONE MORE THING

If your user enters a part of your app where location data is not needed, you should stop receiving location updates to preserve battery life. Call [locationManager stopUpdatingLocation] to halt location updates.

CLLocationManager Properties

You can also control the frequency of updates from CLLocationManager by using the distanceFilter and desiredAccuracy properties. A description of each follows:

- **distanceFilter:** Measured in meters, this value indicates how far the device must move before the delegate is messaged with a new location. The default value is kCLDistanceFilterNone, which means all movements are reported by the manager. In practice, this setting seems to generate locations every five seconds or so. If you do not need every single movement, you can conserve battery life by setting this property to a higher value.

- **desiredAccuracy:** You can set the desired accuracy from a 3-kilometer radius to the best accuracy possible. By default, the accuracy is set to kCLLocationAccuracyBest. However, the higher the desired accuracy, the harder the device has to work to achieve that accuracy, which means that more battery life is used. For a tracking application, you need the best accuracy possible, so the default value is the right value.

If your application just needs periodic location updates, setting these properties to more relaxed values will help your phone save battery.

CRASH AND LEARN

Using location services can be one of the single biggest battery-draining activities on an iPhone OS device. On a full charge, an iPhone 3GS will die after roughly two to three hours if your application runs the location manager at full blast the entire time. For distance-tracking applications, you must run the manager at maximum settings to get an accurate distance measurement. However, if you do not need to run the location manager continuously at the maximum settings, don't.

Distance App

Let's take Core Location for a spin by building a distance-tracking sample application: Distance. By the time you are done, you will have the following app.

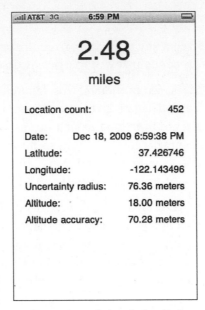

Distance app reports your distance traveled and also displays all the latest location data.

As part of building this app, you will see how to identify and filter out locations that can ruin your data.

Take the following steps to build the Distance app:

- Lay out the interface in Interface Builder

- Hook up the controller to the interface

- Add the User model object

- Add a CLLocationManager and receive location updates

- Filter out bad location data

Let's get started building the app.

CRASH AND LEARN

You need to test Distance on a physical device to get real location data. See Chapter 21 details on putting the app on a real device. The iPhone Simulator generates only a single CLLocation—Apple headquarters in Cupertino, California.

Interface Challenge

As you would expect, the Distance app displays the total distance the user has traveled. Beyond that, though, it displays all the latest location data, including timestamp, latitude, longitude, accuracy data, and elevation. With all this data to display, there are quite a few outlets to hook up, but it will all be worth it when you can see exactly what location data your phone is generating.

First Steps

Follow these steps to get started building the Distance interface:

1. Create a new View-based Application and name it "Distance."

2. Edit the DistanceViewController nib file so it matches the following image:

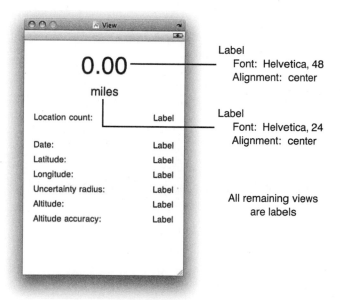

Build your DistanceViewController.xib file so it matches the interface shown.

THERE'S A TIP FOR THAT

Try to maximize the width of the labels on the right-hand side so there is enough room to display the location data for each row.

3. Add and hook up the outlets shown in the following image to your
   `DistanceViewController` class:

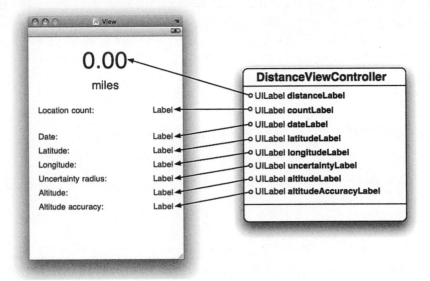

*First, add the outlets shown to your DistanceViewController code files. Then, con-
nect these outlets to the interface elements as shown here.*

Add the Model

Create a User model object that keeps track of the distance and location data. Follow
these steps to add and incorporate the model class:

1. Add an `NSObject` subclass and name it "User."

2. Add the Core Location framework to the project, and import the framework
   at the top of the User.h model file:

```
// User.h

#import <CoreLocation/CoreLocation.h>
```

ONE MORE THING

To add a framework, expand the Targets item in the Groups & Files View, and Ctrl-click **Distance**. Select **Add > Existing Frameworks ...**, then click the "+" in the bottom left corner. Select **CoreLocation.framework** from the list that slides down.

3. Add the following instance variables:

   - distance of type float
   - locationCount of type int
   - location of type CLLocation

4. Add properties for these instance variables. The distance and locationCount variables are C data types (not pointers to objects), so you will need to use the assign attribute for them instead of retain. The location variable is an object, so you need to use retain for it.

THERE'S A TIP FOR THAT

For a refresher on the difference between assign and retain, flip back to Chapter 6.

5. Add a User instance variable named "user" to your DistanceViewController class.

6. Override initWithCoder: in DistanceViewController, and alloc/init the user instance variable. Your code should match the following:

```
// DistanceViewController.m

// Override to initialize the user object
- (id)initWithCoder:(NSCoder *)decoder
{
   if (self = [super initWithCoder:decoder])
   {
        user = [[User alloc] init];
   }
   return self;
}
```

7. Manage memory properly for the user object.

Starter Code

The setup for the Distance app is now finished. Save and build your project to make sure you don't have any typos. Starter code to reach this point is available online at: http://troybrant.net/iphonebook/chapter18/Distance-starter-code.zip.

Integrating with Core Location

After a new data point comes in, you need to update the interface with the data in the User model object. Go ahead and add an updateInterface method that will take the location data in the User model object, convert the data into string values, and update the text of the UILabel outlets. Add the following code to DistanceViewController.m:

```
// DistanceViewController.m

// Convert the data in the User object to strings and
// update the labels with these strings.
- (void)updateInterface
{
    // A string like "2.48"
    distanceLabel.text =
        [NSString stringWithFormat:
            @"%.2f", user.distance];

    // A string like "452"
    countLabel.text =
        [NSString stringWithFormat:
            @"%d", user.locationCount];

    // A string like "Dec 18, 2009 6:59:38 PM"
    NSDateFormatter *dateFormatter =
        [[NSDateFormatter alloc] init];
    [dateFormatter setTimeZone:[NSTimeZone localTimeZone]];
    [dateFormatter setDateFormat:@"MMM d, yyyy h:mm:ss a"];
    NSString *dateString =
        [dateFormatter stringFromDate:
            user.location.timestamp];
    dateLabel.text = dateString;
    [dateFormatter release];

    // A string like "37.426746"
    latitudeLabel.text =
```

```
        [NSString stringWithFormat:@"%f",
                user.location.coordinate.latitude];

    // A string like "-122.143496"
    longitudeLabel.text =
        [NSString stringWithFormat:@"%f",
                user.location.coordinate.longitude];

    // A string like "76.36 meters"
    accuracyRadiusLabel.text =
        [NSString stringWithFormat:@"%.2f meters",
                user.location.horizontalAccuracy];

    // A string like "18.00 meters"
    elevationLabel.text =
        [NSString stringWithFormat:@"%.2f meters",
                user.location.altitude];

    // A string like "70.28 meters"
    verticalAccuracyLabel.text =
        [NSString stringWithFormat:@"%.2f meters",
                user.location.verticalAccuracy];
}
```

To convert the NSDate to a readable string, use the NSDateFormatter class. After defining the way you want the date to look, you use the stringFromDate: method to convert the date from an NSDate to an NSString.

You can also use NSDateFormatter to go the other way by calling dateFromString: to convert an NSString to an NSDate.

THERE'S A TIP FOR THAT

If you are wondering where the "MMM d, yyyy h:mm:ss a" string came from, these types of character sequences are defined in the official Unicode formatting guide. The table describing all the date formatting options is on the Unicode.org website, at http://unicode.org/reports/tr35/tr35-6. html#Date_Format_Patterns.

The other conversions are made using the versatile stringWithFormat: method. For a detailed look at how to use the stringWithFormat: method effectively, flip ahead to Chapter 20 on debugging techniques.

Add and Start the Location Manager

To begin adding location support to your app, add the manager and the manager start time object (used to determine valid data points) to the DistanceViewController.h file. You will also declare that your controller adopts the CLLocationManagerDelegate protocol so your class can receive location updates. Add the following code to your header file to make these changes:

```
// DistanceViewController.h

#import <CoreLocation/CoreLocation.h>
...
@interface DistanceViewController : UIViewController
  <CLLocationManagerDelegate>
{
  ...
  CLLocationManager *locationManager;
  NSDate *locationManagerStartDate;
}
...
@end
```

Follow up those changes by initializing the new variables in the initWithCoder: method. You also need to remember to release the variables in dealloc. Make sure the DistanceViewController methods that follow match your own:

```
// DistanceViewController.m

// Override to initialize the location manager
- (id)initWithCoder:(NSCoder *)decoder
{
  if (self = [super initWithCoder:decoder])
  {
      user = [[User alloc] init];

      locationManager = [[CLLocationManager alloc] init];
      locationManager.delegate = self;
      locationManager.desiredAccuracy = kCLLocationAccuracyBest;
      locationManager.distanceFilter = kCLDistanceFilterNone;
      [locationManager startUpdatingLocation];

      locationManagerStartDate = [[NSDate date] retain];
  }
```

```
    return self;
}

- (void)dealloc
{
  [distanceLabel release];
  [countLabel release];
  [dateLabel release];
  [latitudeLabel release];
  [longitudeLabel release];
  [uncertaintyLabel release];
  [altitudeLabel release];
  [altitudeAccuracyLabel release];
  [user release];
  [locationManager release];
  [locationManagerStartDate release];
  [super dealloc];
}
```

Note that it is not strictly necessary to set the `desiredAccuracy` and `distanceFilter` properties because you set them to their default values, but having them there makes it easier to experiment with different settings by making small changes to the existing code.

By keeping track of the start date of the `locationManager`, you can ensure that stale locations don't ruin your data. The next section explains how you can use this start date to keep your location data accurate.

Detecting Inaccurate Location Data

Having never used the Core Location API, you might expect that it gives you great data all the time. Unfortunately, there are situations when the data reported by Core Location can be wildly inaccurate. This is especially a problem in distance-tracking applications where a single bad data point can make your distance reading jump miles at a time.

There are four situations to check for when a new location point comes in:

- The location itself can be nil.
- The `horizontalAccuracy` property can be < 0, indicating an invalid location.
- Locations can be reported out of order. This means that the new location is really an old location and should be discarded.

● Locations that were initialized before your app was even initialized can be reported. The Core Location framework seems to cache and report points from the last time the location services were used. For instance, if you last ran your app in Montana and then launch it in Georgia, your reported point could be from Montana. If you don't check for this case, then your distance-tracking application would merrily add the thousands of miles between Montana and Georgia to your total distance.

The following helper method checks for these four cases to determine whether the newly reported location is valid or not. Add the following method so you can call it when locationManager delivers location updates:

```
// DistanceViewController.m

- (BOOL)isValidLocation:(CLLocation*)newLocation
  withOldLocation:(CLLocation*)oldLocation
{
    // Filter out nil locations
    if (!newLocation)
    {
        return NO;
    }

    // Filter out points by invalid accuracy
    if (newLocation.horizontalAccuracy < 0)
    {
        return NO;
    }

    // Seconds = newLocation.timestamp - oldLocation.timestamp
    NSTimeInterval secondsSinceLastPoint =
        [newLocation.timestamp timeIntervalSinceDate:
            oldLocation.timestamp];

    // Filter out points that are out of order
    if (secondsSinceLastPoint < 0)
    {
        return NO;
    }

    // Seconds = newLocation.timestamp - locationManagerStartDate
    NSTimeInterval secondsSinceManagerStarted =
```

```
    [newLocation.timestamp timeIntervalSinceDate:
            locationManagerStartDate];

    // Filter out points created before the manager
    // was initialized
    if (secondsSinceManagerStarted < 0)
    {
        return NO;
    }

    // The newLocation is okay to use
    return YES;
}
```

As you can see, this method checks for each case described in the previous bulleted list. The `timeIntervalSinceDate:` method subtracts the input date from the receiver date and returns the number of seconds between them. The value can be positive or negative:

- A *negative* value means the input date comes *before* the receiver

- A *positive* value means the input date comes *after* the receiver

This works just fine for checking if `newLocation` or `oldLocation` came first, but how do you know if `newLocation` was created before `locationManager` itself? You will add and initialize the `locationManagerStartDate` `NSDate` instance variable when you add `locationManager` in just a bit.

If you try to build the code above, it will fail because the `locationManagerStartDate` date object isn't defined, yet. Before you add the instance variable, however, add the `CLLocationManagerDelegate` methods so you can finally receive the new locations.

Distance Conversion Methods

True to its name, one of the major tasks of the Distance app is to report distance traveled. When using the built-in `CLLocation` `getDistanceFrom:` method, the distance is reported in meters. You will shun the metric system, however, and convert meters into kilometers and kilometers into miles. Go ahead and add the following helper methods so you can convert your distance values as new locations come in:

```
// DistanceViewController.m

// Convert miles to kilometers
- (double)milesToKilometers:(double)miles
{
    return miles * 1.609344;
}

// Convert kilometers to miles
- (double)kilometersToMiles:(double)kilometers
{
    return kilometers * 0.621371192;
}
```

The only conversion method you really need is `kilometersToMiles:`. The `milesToKilometers:` method is displayed for educational purposes only.

CLLocationManagerDelegate Methods

Add the following two delegate methods to handle updates from `locationManager`:

```
// DistanceViewController.m

#pragma mark -
#pragma mark CLLocationManagerDelegate methods

// Called when a new location is ready
- (void)locationManager:(CLLocationManager *)manager
  didUpdateToLocation:(CLLocation *)newLocation
  fromLocation:(CLLocation *)oldLocation
{
    // Update the location counter
    user.locationCount++;

    // Set the model location
    user.location = newLocation;

    // Use a helper method to determine if the
    // new point is valid
    BOOL newLocationIsValid =
        [self isValidLocation:newLocation
              withOldLocation:oldLocation];
```

```objc
    // Make sure new location is valid and old location exists
    if (newLocationIsValid && oldLocation)
    {
        // Get the distance traveled in meters
        CLLocationDistance distanceInMeters =
            [newLocation getDistanceFrom:oldLocation];

        // Convert meters to kilometers
        double distanceInKilometers = distanceInMeters / 1000;

        // Convert kilometers to miles
        double distanceInMiles =
            [self kilometersToMiles:distanceInKilometers];

        // Update the model
        model.distance += distanceInMiles;
    }
    else
    {
        if (!newLocationIsValid)
        {
            NSLog(@"Location not valid %@",
                [newLocation description]);
        }
    }

    // Display the new location data
    [self updateInterface];
}


// Called when a location cannot be acquired
- (void)locationManager:(CLLocationManager *)manager
    didFailWithError:(NSError *)error
{
    NSLog(@"Error acquiring location: %@",
        [error localizedDescription]);
}
```

Note the flow of code in locationManager:didUpdateToLocation:fromLocation:. The model is updated with every single point that comes in, though you only calculate distance for valid points using your handy helper method defined earlier. When the new location does come in, you use CLLocation's getDistanceFrom: method to get the distance, and do some simple math to make the conversion from meters to miles.

If an error occurs, simply print it to the console, though you may want to bring the error to your user's attention using a `UIAlertView`.

One Last Thing

There is one final bit of code you need to add to `DistanceViewController` to complete the application:

```
// DistanceViewController.m

// Display real data when the view appears
- (void)viewWillAppear:(BOOL)animated
{
    [super viewWillAppear:animated];
    [self updateInterface];
}
```

Since many labels in your interface initially display the string "Label," calling updateInterface will initialize these labels with real data before the view appears. Otherwise, the user would see the "Label" string for every `UILabel` on the right-hand side of the interface until the location manager sends its first update to the delegate.

Testing the App

Now, save the project, build it, hope you didn't make any typos, and let it fly in the iPhone Simulator. When the view comes up, it should sit with no data for a couple seconds, and then display all the information for a single data point. You will see the following values:

- 0.00 miles

- Location count: 1

- Date: (The current date)

- Latitude: 37.331689

- Longitude: -122.030731

- Uncertainty radius: 100.00 meters

- Altitude: 0.00 meters

- Altitude accuracy: -1.00 meters

If you do see these values, then congrats! You have written your first location-enabled application. If you had problems or just can't get the application to work, full source code for the finished Distance application is available online at http://troybrant.net/iphonebook/chapter18/Distance-done.zip.

To truly test the application, you need to put it on a real device. In Chapter 21, you learn step-by-step how to install your own apps on your phone, so you may want to jump ahead. After Distance is on your phone, you can see the live stream of updates you get from the phone, and your distance won't just sit at "0.00" forever.

Wrapping Up

Location-based applications will undoubtedly become more and more a part of your daily life. And using the Core Location framework, you can easily ride the wave and add location support to your own applications. Using the API only requires that you use two classes: CLLocation and CLLocationManager. Using the CLLocation object, you can get the user's latitude, longitude, and even their current altitude. Since there is always some degree of inaccuracy, you can access the horizontalAccuracy and verticalAccuracy CLLocation properties to see how sure the phone is of the position data. By building the Distance app, you found out how to filter out bad location data, convert meters to miles, and start getting updates from the CLLocationManager.

Next chapter, learn how to integrate with two exciting new APIs in iPhone OS 4.0: iAd and multitasking.

The Least You Need to Know

- The Core Location framework contains just two classes you need to know about to make a location-enabled app: CLLocation and CLLocationManager.
- The radius of uncertainty, displayed as a blue transparent disk in the Maps app, is a measure of the accuracy of a location reading.
- To receive location updates, your controller must conform to the CLLocationManagerDelegate protocol and define the locationManager: didUpdateToLocation:fromLocation: method.
- Core Location can report inaccurate location data, so you should verify that the reported location is valid before using it.

iAd and Multitasking

In This Chapter

- iPhone OS 4.0
- How multitasking works on the iPhone
- Running your app in the background
- Make money displaying ads in your app
- Using the iAd framework

Complaining about the iPhone's missing features is a favorite pastime of bloggers and tech journalists. They write things like, "How can you call the iPhone a real phone without third-party app support?" and "Where is copy and paste?" and "Why no multitasking?"

Apple could have chosen to include half-baked versions of these features in the first iPhone released in 2007. However, Apple would rather build a simple device with fewer features of outstanding quality instead of a complex device with a deluge of mediocre features. What's the result of this policy? Apple has the most successful App Store, the best copy and paste, and now the most battery-efficient multitasking system of any phone on the market.

In this chapter, you learn how to run your app in the background using the 4.0 multitasking API. You also explore the iAd framework so that you can see how easy it is to generate ad revenue in your apps.

iPhone OS 4.0

iPhone OS 4.0 is a big upgrade to the iPhone OS. Here are some of the 4.0 APIs you can now use in your application:

- **Multitasking**—You can now run multiple third-party applications at once.

- **iAd**—By taking advantage of the new iAd framework, you can make money by serving Apple-approved ads to your users.

- **Game Center**—Do you want to build a multiplayer game? With Game Center, you can easily add matchmaking and leader boards to your game.

- **Local notifications**—Local notifications give you the ability to display an alert to the user even when your app is running in the background. For instance, alert your the user when a message arrives in your chat application.

- **Event Kit**—Access the user's calendar data.

- **Quick Look**—Use the quick look view controller to preview for images, documents, and PDFs.

- **Encryption**—Store and read sensitive user data safely.

- **Core Telephony**—Access your user's cellular service provider.

ONE MORE THING

For the full list of iPhone OS 4.0 features, head over to http://developer.apple.com/iphone and search for the document titled "What's New in iPhone OS 4."

The biggest change in the new API, however, is the addition of multitasking. The following section details how multitasking works on the iPhone OS and what you must do as a developer to support it in your app.

Multitasking

So what exactly is multitasking? *Multitasking* gives you the ability to run multiple applications at once. Contrary to popular belief, the iPhone OS has always had multitasking. For instance, the Mail app downloads new mail messages even when the app isn't open. Safari can stream audio from a website even after you close the app. However, for various reasons, Apple didn't provide a way for third-party developers to use multitasking. Until now.

DEFINITION

Multitasking is the ability to run two or more applications at once.

With multitasking, you can write a chat application that alerts the user when a new message arrives. You can track your user's location while the user checks e-mail. You can play music for your user while she checks Facebook. Entirely new classes of applications are now possible due to multitasking in iPhone OS 4.0.

Okay, so it's a big deal. How do you use it?

Getting Started with Multitasking

Not all iPhone devices can run apps in the background. In fact, not even all iPhone OS 4.0 devices can run in the background. 3G iPhones running iPhone OS 4.0 in particular do not support multitasking.

Due to this fact, you should check to make sure multitasking is supported before using multitasking features. You can safely check for multitasking using this snippet of code:

```
// Checks to see if the app can run in the background
- (BOOL)canRunInTheBackground
{
   UIDevice *device = [UIDevice currentDevice];
   BOOL backgroundSupported = NO;
   if ([device respondsToSelector:@selector(isMultitaskingSupported)])
   {
       backgroundSupported = device.multitaskingSupported;
   }
   return backgroundSupported;
}
```

The code above handles both iPhone OS 4.0 devices—devices that have the isMultitaskingSupported method defied—and pre-iPhone OS 4.0 devices—devices that don't have isMultitaskingSupported defined.

You should be able to do most of your background processing without even checking if multitasking is enabled. However, in the case that you do need to know, the previous method provides an easy way to check.

Background Tasks

Most mobile devices that support multitasking don't require any additional code on the part of the programmer. On these devices, apps that run in the background are no different than the app you are viewing at the time. However, battery life on these devices is generally poor since the OS has to work really hard to keep all these applications running at once.

To address this battery issue, Apple has implemented multitasking very differently. When the user switches from your app to another, your app by default is *suspended*. Suspended applications do not execute a single line of code. They are kept in memory so they can be launched quickly when the user switches back to your app.

DEFINITION

A **suspended** application is an app that is halted but not completely removed from memory. This allows the app to be restarted promptly by the user. The suspended state is new to iPhone OS 4.0.

If you want to run code while in the background, you must tell the iPhone OS. Even then, there are only a few types of interactions the OS allows while your app is in the background. Currently, the iPhone OS supports only three types of background tasks:

- Playing audio
- Tracking the user's location using Core Location
- Continuing VOIP phones calls uninterrupted

To support one or more of these tasks in your apps, you must include the `UIBackgroundModes` key in your project's `Info.plist` file. The value for this key is an array, and the possible values for the array are `audio`, `location`, and `voip`. Without setting the `UIBackgroundModes` key, your app does not run in the background. Don't forget to set it!

ONE MORE THING

Setting the `location` key in the `Info.plist` file enables you to track the user's location using maximum precision. However, this drains the device's battery really quickly. If your app does not require precise location information, you should instead register to receive only big changes in position by calling `startMonitoringSignificantLocationChanges` on `CLLocationManager`. This drastically saves battery usage. Note that calling this method delivers location updates to your app without having to set the `location` key in your `Info.plist` file.

In addition, two other ways to perform background processing include:

- **Request more time to complete a single task**—To request more time for a task, call UIApplication's beginBackgroundTaskWithExpirationHandler: method when the app enters the background. When the task is completed, notify the system by calling endBackgroundTask:.

- **Schedule a local notification**—To schedule a *local notification*, create a UILocalNotification object and set its fireDate property to the time the alarm should go off. You can customize the text of the alarm by setting the alertBody property, and you can even play a custom sound by setting the soundName property on the local notification object.

DEFINITION

A **local notification** is a new feature in iPhone OS 4.0 that enables you to display an alert message to the user. A local notification is styled exactly like an SMS message alert, but you can customize the text and sound made when it displays.

After indicating that your app is background ready, you need to know when the application enters and exits the background. This process is explained in the next section.

Application Life Cycle for Background Processing

Before multitasking, your *application life cycle* was simple. Your app was either on or off. If the user was looking at your app, it was on. When they clicked the home button, the app was off.

DEFINITION

The **application life cycle** describes the different states your application can be in from the time it is created to the time it exits.

Two methods are called on your application to reflect these two states. When the app is created, the application:didFinishLaunchingWithOptions: method is called on the UIApplicationDelegate. When the app is about to exit, applicationWillTerminate: is called on the app delegate.

Now that multitasking is available on iPhone OS, your app can run in both the *foreground* and the *background*. Two new methods are invoked on the application delegate in iPhone OS 4.0 to notify you when the app enters and exits these states:

- `applicationDidEnterBackground:`
- `applicationWillEnterForeground:`

DEFINITION

A single application is displayed to the user at a time, and this application is said to be running in the **foreground**. Apps that run even when they are not visible to the user are said to be running in the **background**.

These methods notify you when your app enters and exits background execution. When entering the background, you should save your application state because your app can be terminated when running in the background. When the user switches back to your app, the `applicationWillEnterForeground:` method is called. This is a great place to redraw your interface and re-enable any settings you turned off when entering the background.

CRASH AND LEARN

Be aware that the user can manually quit your app when it is running in the background. When this happens, `applicationWillTerminate:` is invoked immediately.

THERE'S A TIP FOR THAT

Apple provides a really great explanation of the application life cycle in their documentation. Head over to http://developer.apple.com/iphone, and search for the page titled "The Core Application Design" in the "iPhone Application Programming Guide" document to locate this excellent resource.

Sample Code

To see how multitasking works in practice, several sample projects are available online:

- **Local Notifications app**—The first example sets an alarm that goes off 5 seconds after the app enters the background. The Xcode project is available here: http://troybrant.net/iphonebook/chapter19/LocalNotifications.zip.

- **Background Audio app**—The second app shows how to play audio in the background. The Xcode project is available here: http://troybrant.net/iphonebook/chapter19/BackgroundAudio.zip.

- **Significant Change Location Tracking app**—The third app tracks significant changes in the user's location. The Xcode project is available here: http://troybrant.net/iphonebook/chapter19/SignificantChangeLocationTracking.zip.

- **Precise Location Tracking app**—The fourth app shows how to get precise location data while the app is running in the background. The Xcode project is available here: http://troybrant.net/iphonebook/chapter19/PreciseLocationTracking.zip.

Be sure to check the `Info.plist` file in the sample projects to see when you need to set the `UIBackgroundModes` key and when you don't.

Be a Good Multitasking Citizen

When your app enters background execution, there are some rules you need to follow to be considered a well-behaved background application. These rules include:

- **Do not make any OpenGL ES calls**—If you issue any OpenGL ES calls while running in the background, the iPhone OS immediately terminates your application. Although most of these rules are recommendations, this rule is a requirement.

- **Avoid updating your windows and views**—When your app is running in the background, the user won't see the interface until she activates the application again. Save battery and processing power by queuing all your redrawing for when the app is brought to the foreground.

- **Save your application data before moving to the background**—Your application might terminate while in the background, so be prepared to restore the state in the event of early termination.

A full list of best practices can be found on http://developer.apple.com/iphone on the page titled "Executing Code in the Background" in the "iPhone Application Programming Guide" document.

iAd

In addition to multitasking, iPhone OS 4.0 introduces the iAd framework for delivering ads in your application. The following section details how you can generate additional revenue in your apps by displaying ads.

You might be wondering, "Why on earth would I want to annoy my users with ads?" The answer: Using ads, you can release your app for free while still generating revenue.

You might also be thinking, "Mobile ads are awful." Apple agrees with you. In fact, Steve Jobs noted the poor state of mobile ads during his keynote introducing iPhone OS 4.0. Just as the iPhone was a reimagining of the mobile phone, iAd is an attempt to revolutionize mobile ads by providing nothing but beautiful, high-quality ads to users.

How It Works

The process for delivering ads is quite simple. Display an ad, and make money. Display more ads, and make more money. You should exercise restraint, however, and ensure that you aren't impacting the user experience of the app too much.

At the time of this writing, there are two standard sizes for ads: 320×50 for portrait ads and 460×32 for landscape.

To display an advertisement on your app, you insert a *banner ad* in your interface. The iAd framework provides the `ADBannerView` class for displaying a banner ad. The `ADBannerView` class displays a series of ads and handles user interaction. When you create the banner view, the view automatically downloads ads from Apple in the background. When the ad is visible, the view cycles through a series of ads.

DEFINITION

A **banner ad** is a rectangular advertisement used extensively on the web. On mobile devices, a banner ad can usually be found at the very top or very bottom of an app's interface.

When the banner view is tapped by the user, any number of events can happen. The ad can launch a movie, display an interactive modal view, or even launch Safari to show a web page. Note that in the case Safari is launched, your app will exit. In iPhone OS 4.0, however, this means your app either will be suspended or will begin to run in the background if you support it.

To find out when ads are loaded, when the user taps them, and when the user exits the ad, you must be set as the banner view's delegate. The `ADBannerViewDelegate` protocol provides callbacks for each of these events.

That's all there is to iAd. The framework consists of two files: the banner view and its delegate. The next section provides some sample code for adding and displaying a banner view in your app.

Sample Code

Imagine you want to have a view controller—let's call it `AdTestViewController`—that displays a table view with an ad at the top. The interface for `AdTestViewController` is as follows:

```
#import <UIKit/UIKit.h>
#import <iAd/iAd.h>

@interface AdTestViewController : UIViewController
  <ADBannerViewDelegate>
{
  UITableView *tableView;
  ADBannerView *bannerView;
}

@property (nonatomic, retain) IBOutlet UITableView *tableView;

@end
```

Assume that the `tableView` property is properly hooked up to the view in Interface Builder. In the preceding code, notice the view controller conforms to the `ABBannerViewDelegate` protocol and that a reference to the `ADBannerView` is stored as an instance variable.

The implementation file for `AdTestViewController` follows:

```
#import "AdTestViewController.h"

@implementation AdTestViewController
```

continues

```
@synthesize tableView;

- (void)viewDidLoad
{
    if (!bannerView)
    {
        // Create the banner view programmatically
        bannerView = [[ADBannerView alloc] init];

        // Set the size of the banner view to 320x50
        bannerView.currentContentSizeIdentifier =
                ADBannerContentSizeIdentifier320x50;

        // Become the delegate
        bannerView.delegate = self;

        // Display the banner view in the table's header section
        tableView.tableHeaderView = bannerView;
    }
}

@end
```

A few comments on the preceding code:

- Note how the size of the banner view is set. Instead of setting the banner's `frame` as you have seen with sizing most views, you must set the `currentContentSizeIdentifier` property. Currently, there are only two options: `ADBannerContentSizeIdentifier320x50`, used while in portrait mode, and `ADBannerContentSizeIdentifier480x35`, used while in landscape mode.

ONE MORE THING

You can see all the content sizes supported by an `ADBannerView` by checking its `requiredContentSizeIdentifiers` property.

- You can add arbitrary views to the top and bottom of a table view by setting its `tableHeaderView` and `tableFooterView` properties, respectively. Note that if you use these properties to place an ad, the ad scrolls with the table.

When run in the simulator, the completed application looks as follows:

An ADBannerView set as a table's header view is on the left, and the result of tapping the ad is on the right.

You can be notified when the ad is tapped and what it does by becoming the delegate of the ADBannerView. The ad delegate is explained in the next section.

ADBannerViewDelegate

Using the previous code, you have an ad in your app in no time. If you want to be notified of key changes in the app caused by the ad, you need to implement the methods defined in ADBannerViewDelegate, shown in the following:

```
#pragma mark -
#pragma mark ADBannerViewDelegate methods

- (void)bannerViewDidLoadAd:(ADBannerView *)banner
{
    // The banner view has finished downloading the ads and is ready
    // to show them to the user.
}

- (BOOL)bannerViewActionShouldBegin:(ADBannerView *)banner
```

continues

```
                    willLeaveApplication:(BOOL)willLeave
{
  // You should save your application data at this point. Also,
  // you can control whether or not an ad displays. You should
  // return YES here as much as possible.
  return YES;
}

- (void)bannerViewActionDidFinish:(ADBannerView *)banner
{
  // The user exited the ad view and is now returning to your app.
}

- (void)bannerView:(ADBannerView *)banner
  didFailToReceiveAdWithError:(NSError *)error
{
  // A flaky network connection is one reason when an ad can fail
  // to display. You may want to report this error to the user.
}
```

Every application that uses ads should have at least two of these methods defined—
bannerViewActionShouldBegin:willLeaveApplication: and
bannerViewActionDidFinish:. You should minimize the amount of work your app
is doing when the user touches an ad and restore the app back to a fully active state
when the user comes back to your app.

The full sample code for displaying an ad using iAd is available online at http://
troybrant.net/iphonebook/chapter19/AdTest.zip

That's all there is to iAd. It's a simple framework, and if you want to release your
app for free, using iAd can be a good way to generate some revenue and recover your
development costs.

Onward and Upward

That's a wrap for Part 4. You have covered a sampling of some of the most exciting
APIs in the iPhone SDK: multi-touch, location services, media, and maps. There are
many more APIs out there that you can use in your app, and the Xcode API documentation is your greatest asset for figuring out how to use them.

The next part is quite possibly the most important sequence of chapters in this
book. You see how to fix broken code, how to test your apps on your phone, tools

for optimizing your code, and finally how to submit your app to the App Store. You kick off Part 5 by going over debugging techniques no iPhone programmer should be without.

The Least You Need to Know

- To support background processing, set the `UIBackgroundModes` key in your project's `Info.plist` file to an array with possible values `audio`, `location`, or `voip`.

- `UILocalNotification` enables you to set an alarm that can go off when your app is in the background.

- When displaying ads using iAd, you earn 60% of ad revenue, and Apple gets the remaining 40%.

- To display banner ads in your app, simply add a `ADBannerView` to your interface.

Make Your Millions

Okay, so you have finally made it to the finish line. Before you take the plunge and submit your app to the App Store, there are some steps you can take to ensure it is the highest possible quality. Learn how to test your app on a physical device. Learn the debugging techniques the pros use. Use the Clang, Instruments, and Shark to identify memory leaks and areas where you can improve performance. After making these optimizations, you can finally submit your app to the App Store and reap the rewards.

Debugging in Detail

In This Chapter

- Debugging with GDB
- Breakpoints
- Using GDB in Xcode
- Debugging with NSLog

You know the feeling. You have just put the finishing touches on what has to be the most elegant, succinct, beautiful piece of code you (or the world?) have ever seen. Running the code is just a formality—completely unnecessary—because you accounted for every branch, every input, every conceivable value that could find its way into your system. Obviously, no one who knew the extent of your efforts could possibly doubt the brilliant masterpiece you just produced.

But then you compile. Looks like there are errors and warnings in several places. After an hour, you finally get a clean build. Then you run the app, and it crashes on launch. You fix that bug, but then it crashes in another place. This continues for hours, as you fix one problem, and another, and another. You could have sworn your code was perfect, but there were bugs to fix anyway.

This is why learning how to effectively debug iPhone and iPad apps is so important. All code has kinks that need to be worked out, and the better you are at finding and fixing those problems, the faster you'll ship your app. This chapter covers techniques you can use to debug iPhone and iPad apps and additionally shows you how to use the GDB debugger. There are also several debugging exercises you can try to help practice your debugging skills.

Debugging on iPhone OS Devices

There are two primary debugging techniques at your disposal on iPhone OS devices:

1. **GDB:** Add breakpoints. Step through code line by line. See the values of your instance variables. Knowing how to use GDB in Xcode is absolutely essential for all iPhone programmers.

2. **NSLog:** This is by far the most popular technique. Use NSLog to print out values to the console or just to see how far your code gets before the app crashes.

On iPhone OS devices, each of these techniques has their place. GDB should be the tool you use for most of your debugging, but there are times when NSLog is the best way to get the information you need.

Let's start off by taking a look at debugging using GDB.

GDB

If you have programmed in C or C++, you likely already know GDB, one of the most widely used debuggers. You may also know how to use the GDB command-line interface inside and out, in which case this part of the chapter will be very familiar to you. However, it will be assumed you have never heard of GDB and may not know how to use a debugger. Even if you know GDB, it's worth paying attention here to see how to use the GDB interface in Xcode.

A *debugger* is a tool used to step through your code line by line and inspect values in your application at runtime. You set *breakpoints* in your source code, and when you run it in the debugger, your application stops at these points. When your app is stopped at a breakpoint, you can step over a line of code, step into a method call, or step out of the current method. You can also inspect local and instance variables to see what values they are set to. When you're done investigating, you can tell the application to *continue* running.

DEFINITION

A **debugger** is a tool used to test and examine a running application. When the debugger stops on a line of code, you can inspect the values of variables in the surrounding code. A **breakpoint** is a line marker in source code the debugger will stop at when hit.

The first step in using GDB in Xcode is to set breakpoints in your code.

Breakpoints

To set a breakpoint in code, click the line number on the line you want to set the breakpoint on. A blue marker will appear on the line number, as shown in the following:

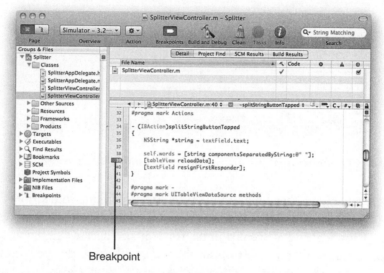

Breakpoint

Clicking the number next to a line sets a breakpoint.

THERE'S A TIP FOR THAT

Don't see line numbers? You can enable them in the Xcode preferences menu:
Xcode > Preferences... > Text Editing > Show line numbers.

When the breakpoint is hit, execution will stop *before* running the line of code highlighted in blue. This line will be highlighted in blue, as shown in the following figure.

To remove breakpoints, click and drag the blue breakpoint arrow horizontally and let go. In true Apple style, it will turn into a puff of smoke and make a "whoosh" sound when you release it. You can also click-and-drag the breakpoint vertically to move it to another line of code.

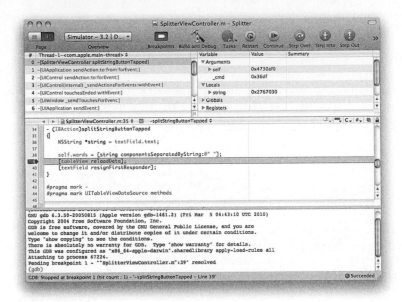

When the breakpoint is hit, the line in blue is the next line to be executed.

Sometimes, when you have breakpoints littered throughout your project, you'd like to see a single list of all the breakpoints. This list does exist, and to access it, select menu item **Run > Show > Breakpoints**. You can also access the menu using the keyboard shortcut ⌘⌥B (command-option-b). This will bring up the list of breakpoints in the detail view, shown in the following image:

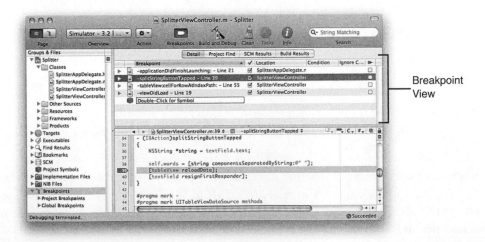

The breakpoint view displays a list of all your breakpoints.

To delete a breakpoint using the breakpoint window, just select the row the breakpoint is on and press **delete**.

CRASH AND LEARN

Is your breakpoint orange while your app is running? If so, you have encountered the Orange Breakpoint of Doom. When a breakpoint turns orange, it means the breakpoint will never be hit. One solution that may work for you: select menu item **Xcode > Preferences... > Debugging > Uncheck "Load symbols lazily"**.

Two Essential Breakpoints

There are two crucial breakpoints that are useful to set. These breakpoints are for debugging exceptions and memory issues:

- **obj_exception_throw:** Normally, when an exception is thrown, it goes all the way up the call stack before being caught. This means that you lose the exact stack frame where the exception was thrown and have no way of knowing what line in your code caused the exception. With this breakpoint set, execution is stopped *before* the exception is actually thrown, which means you can find exactly which line in your code caused the exception.

- **malloc_error_break:** If you happen to over-release an object—that is, send an object the release method after it has already been deallocated—then adding the malloc_error_break breakpoint can help you to debug the problem.

THERE'S A TIP FOR THAT

To see if your use of autorelease is to blame for problems with your app, you should try enabling NSZombie. Search for NSZombie online for more details.

To add these breakpoints, follow these steps:

1. Open the breakpoint window using menu item **Run > Show > Breakpoints**.

2. Double-click the **Double-Click for Symbol** text box, enter the text **obj_exception_throw**, and press enter.

3. Double-click the **Double-Click for Symbol** text box, enter the text **malloc_error_break**, and press enter.

Setting these breakpoints will help tremendously in your debugging efforts.

GDB Functions

After your breakpoint is hit at runtime, you need some way to advance through the code. Using the debugger, you have a few options:

- **Step over:** You can choose to step over the line of code the debugger has currently stopped on. This means you move to the line of code immediately after the line highlighted in blue.

- **Step into:** If the line you stopped on contains a method call, you will move to the first line of that method if you step into it.

- **Step out:** To execute all the remaining lines in the current method, use the step out option.

- **Continue:** Finally, to resume normal execution of your app, use the continue option.

The debugger view in Xcode is optimized for these debugging tasks and for displaying runtime information. If the debugger window does not appear automatically, you can access it by selecting **Run > Debugger** from the top menu. A breakdown of the debugger window interface is shown in the following image:

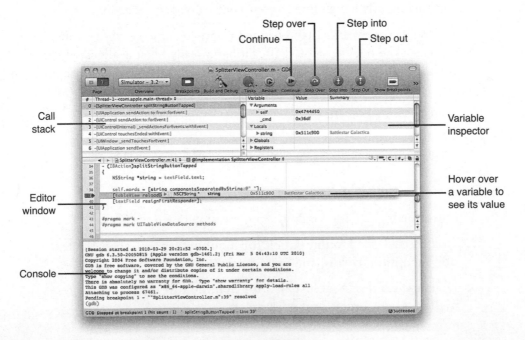

Take some to time to learn how to use the debugger view.

Using the debugger window, not only can you control the debugger, you can also see the *call stack*. The call stack is the list of methods that were called to arrive at the current line in code. At the top of the list is the method containing the line of code the debugger stopped in.

DEFINITION

The **call stack** is the list of methods called to arrive at the current line of code.

ONE MORE THING

As you might expect, Apple does not provide source code for their core libraries. So when you jump to Apple code when using the debugger, you will only see assembly code and memory addresses.

To inspect the values of your local and instance variables, you can use the value inspector at the top right of the debugger window. Another way to see variable values is to hover over the variable you want to inspect.

Limitations of GDB

GDB should be your first line of defense when debugging problems in your iPhone and iPad applications. It's fast, informative, and doesn't add a line of code to your project. In short, try to become comfortable using GDB.

That being said, the Xcode implementation of GDB does have some limitations. For instance, you can't view the contents of a dictionary without using the command line. GDB—and debuggers in general—are also inherently poor at debugging race conditions, where two threads compete for use of the same resource. Sometimes, logging to the console is a better option for debugging than GDB.

NSLog

And now it's time to discuss every programmer's favorite pastime: debugging by printing to the console. Whether it's using `printf`, `System.out.println`, `cout`, `Console.writeln`, `echo`, `print`, or `NSLog`, printing out values to debug a program is as old and sacred as programming itself. My official stance is that you should use GDB everywhere you can, but let's face it: sometimes you just feel like throwing in an `NSLog` to see what's going on. Also, as mentioned previously, there are some cases where using `NSLog` in your app is a debugging necessity.

So instead of pushing you firmly away from using NSLog to debug, I'll give you some tips on how to use it effectively.

NSLog Syntax and Formatting

To truly master NSLog, you must understand the formatting syntax. NSLog allows you to use NSString stringWithFormat: syntax without calling it directly. For example, see the following code:

```
// option 1: create a string using stringWithFormat and log it
NSString *numbers =
  [NSString stringWithFormat:@"%d, %d, %d",
      1, 2, 3];
NSLog(@"%@", numbers);

// Output:
//    1, 2, 3

// option 2: just NSLog using the stringWithFormat syntax
NSLog(@"%d, %d, %d", 1, 2, 3);

// Output:
//    1, 2, 3
```

Using the proper syntax, you can print out any value in your application. Let's go over how to log various data types:

- **C primitives:** If you are familiar with C, you use the exact same formatting rules in NSLog statements as you do for printf. If you are not familiar with C, here are some examples of using NSLog to print common primitive types:

```
int seven = 7;
double pi = 3.14159265;

NSLog(@"%d, %f, %.2f", seven, pi, pi);

// Output:
//      7, 3.141593, 3.14

BOOL valid = YES;

// BOOLs are really just integers, so if you want to see
```

```
// "YES" or "NO", you need to print the string yourself

NSLog(@"valid=%d or valid=%@", valid, valid ? @"YES" : @"NO");

// Output:
// valid=1 or valid=YES
```

THERE'S A TIP FOR THAT

In the preceding code, the ternary operator is used to select which string to print. The ternary operator is really just a shorthand if/else statement. The syntax is [boolean ? value if boolean is true : value if boolean is false].

- **Strings:** You can use NSLog to concatenate several strings into a single line of output:

```
NSString *string1 = @"Troy";
NSString *string2 = @"Macon";
NSString *string3 = @"GA";

NSLog(@"%@ was born in %@, %@", string1, string2, string3);

// Output:
//        Troy was born in Macon, GA
```

- **Arrays and dictionaries:** Use the %@ format specifier to print the contents of both types of collections, as shown in the following:

```
NSArray *letters =
  [NSArray arrayWithObjects:@"a", @"b", @"c", nil];

NSLog(@"letters=%@", letters);

// Output:
//        letters=(
//        a,
//        b,
//        c
//        )

NSDictionary *me =
  [NSDictionary dictionaryWithObjectsAndKeys:
        @"Troy", @"name",
```

continues

```
            @"Menlo Park", @"city",
            @"California", @"state",
            nil];

    NSLog(@"me=%@", me);

    // Output:
    //      me={
    //      city = "Menlo Park";
    //      name = Troy;
    //      state = California;
    //      }
```

- **Other NSObjects:** In the previous code, you can see how the %@ replacement characters is used for strings, arrays, and dictionaries. In fact, %@ works for *all* NSObjects. The description method—like toString in Java—is called on the object to retrieve its string representation. Many built-in classes—those starting with NS— implement the description method to return something useful by default. You can override the description method for your own classes so they print out meaningful information when logged.

NSLog is useful, but it should be used with some restraint. Every time you add a logging statement, that's a line of code you need to either comment out or delete later on. If you forget to remove an NSLog, your console output can get polluted to the point you can't see the output you really care about. GDB doesn't have this problem.

Done with Debugging

Using the GDB debugger in Xcode to hunt down your bugs will take a while to get used to if you haven't used it before. After you get comfortable with it, though, your productivity will skyrocket because you won't be adding and removing NSLog statements all over the place. That being said, you will find that sometimes using NSLog to debug is the most efficient option. When you do use it, remember the formatting tips and tricks you learned in this chapter to output any value in your application.

Next chapter, you will finally learn how to run Xcode apps on an iPhone or iPad.

The Least You Need to Know

- Debugging using GDB consists of setting breakpoints and stepping through code line by line.
- Get comfortable using GDB as your first line of defense for debugging and only resort to NSLog when necessary.
- Add the obj_exception_throw and malloc_error_break breakpoints to catch some otherwise difficult-to-find bugs.
- Use NSLog for debugging problems with multiple threads.
- All NSObjects can be printed using the %@ format specifier in NSLog.

Testing Apps on Your Device

In This Chapter

- iPhone Developer Program
- Provisioning
- Program portal
- Installing provisioning profile in Xcode

So you want to try out these apps you're building on a real iPhone, iPad, or iPod Touch. The iPhone Simulator is great, and you can use it to do most of your iPhone development without using a device at all. However, there comes a point where you want to test how your code interacts with the phone's camera, video, compass, GPS, accelerometer, or iPod APIs. You need to make sure your app performs well on a real device. And, perhaps most importantly, you want to show your friends what you've been working tirelessly on these past few weeks.

The process of putting your own applications on your phone is called provisioning. In this chapter, you walk through each step required to provision your phone with your app. You register for the iPhone Developer Program, create a provisioning profile using the iPhone Developer Program Portal website, install the provisioning profile in Xcode, and change the Xcode project settings to run on a device instead of the simulator. It may sound complex, but we'll take it one step at a time and have apps running on your device in no time.

Strategy

To be able to run apps on your phone, you need to take the following steps:

1. Register for the iPhone Developer Program, which costs $99.

2. After getting accepted into the program, you will use the Development Provisioning Assistant to create a developer provisioning profile.

3. After downloading your provisioning profile from the iPhone Developer Program Portal website, you will install the provisioning profile in Xcode.

4. Finally, you will plug in your iPhone or iPad, build the project using the Device SDK, and launch the application on the phone.

Without further ado, let's get started.

iPhone Developer Program

The first step in putting apps on your phone is to dish out $99 to enroll in the iPhone Developer Program. There are actually two programs: a small team/individual account for $99 and a $299 option for companies who want to release apps internally. Most people fall in the $99 category, but if you think the $299 option applies to you, be sure to read all the information about it online before making a decision. The rest of this section is written assuming you chose the $99 option.

THERE'S A TIP FOR THAT

For a full explanation of the iPhone Developer Program, refer back to Chapter 1.

Register

Since the registration process is straightforward, you can follow the instructions provided by Apple. Here's how to get started:

- Go to http://developer.apple.com/iphone/program/start/enroll/.

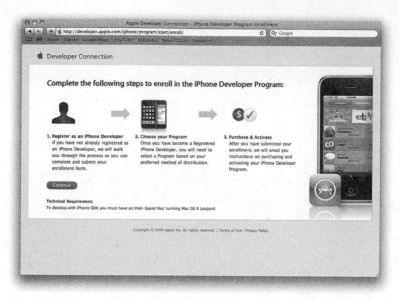

Alternately, you can get here from the iPhone developer center homepage.

- Click **Continue** and follow the instructions on the website to complete the registration process. There are roughly 10 steps for both Standard Individual and Standard Company options.

- If you choose Standard Company, you must be part of a *real* company. Apple will ask for your legal documents, so if you want to go this route, you need to become incorporated before registering for the iPhone Developer Program. If that doesn't appeal to you, you can register for a Standard Individual account instead. You won't have the team features the company account offers, but you can at least get started developing on real devices.

After you have successfully registered for your iPhone Developer Program account, your developer homepage should look similar to the following:

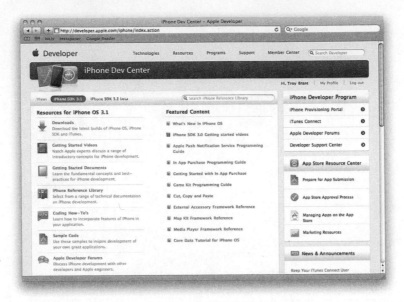

Now that you have applied for the iPhone Developer Program, your homepage on http://developer.apple.com/iphone should resemble this image.

Provisioning

Now that you're officially in the iPhone Developer Program, you can start testing your applications on a physical device! But, wait! Hold that celebratory confetti toss. There's still the whole matter of creating a *provisioning profile* so your apps can run on a physical device.

DEFINITION

A **provisioning profile** is a file that allows you to run your apps on a physical device. The profile uniquely identifies you, your app, and the devices your app can run on.

So what exactly is a provisioning profile? It's a single file that uniquely identifies you, your app, and the device (or devices) you want to run your application on. Here's a visual diagram of what a provisioning profile consists of:

Provisioning Profile

Certificate
iPhone Developer: Troy Brant

Devices
2e2ddc154bb9110c49c4ab6803bfe37b8d28776e

App ID
L4A3627.*

A provisioning profile is required to install your apps on a physical device.

Shown in the previous image, a provisioning profile consists of three parts:

- **Certificate:** Used to sign your app binary when you build it. The phone then checks to make sure the binary signature is valid at runtime. This encryption technique is used to prevent piracy and distribution of applications outside of the App Store.

- **Devices:** You must specifically identify which devices your application will run on during development. Each device contains a unique identifier, called a UDID, which you can find by accessing the **Window > Organizer** menu item in Xcode with your device plugged in.

- **App ID:** The app ID is the identifier that specifies the application the profile is associated with. Using a wildcard "*" in the name, you can have the profile work with multiple applications. For instance, the App ID in the image above—L4A3627.*—works for all apps.

ONE MORE THING

What's up with the "L4A3627" prefix in the App ID name? This is known as the "seed" for the App ID, and Apple generates the seed when you create a new App ID. The seed is useful when you build multiple apps that need to share data, but if you are creating a standalone app, you can ignore the seed.

However, there are two services you can't use if your App ID has a "*" in it: in-app purchases and push notifications. These services require that your App ID is unique—for instance, L4A3627.com.mycompany.appname.

The provisioning process used to be the single most painful part of iPhone development. If you ever went off track from the minimally documented provisioning guide, you could spend days searching for the one incorrect setting. Forums and message boards were littered with frustrated, broken developers.

Luckily, the provisioning process has improved drastically since those hard-luck early days. Apple now offers a Development Provisioning Assistant on their website that guides you through each step of the provisioning process. Creating your developer provisioning profile is now a snap.

Generate a Developer Provisioning Profile

The online Development Provisioning Assistant will walk you through the steps required to generate a provisioning profile. To get started, follow these steps:

1. Navigate to http://developer.apple.com/iphone/, and log in using your Apple ID.

2. Click the **iPhone Provisioning Portal** link on the far right side of the page.

THERE'S A TIP FOR THAT

Is your iPhone developer homepage missing a link to the iPhone Provisioning Portal? Make sure you have logged in and successfully completed the registration process for the iPhone Developer Program.

3. In the center of the screen, next to the iPhone icon, click the **Launch Assistant** button.

Navigate to the developer program portal, and launch the Development Provisioning Assistant.

4. The screen should be titled "Choose an App ID." Select **Create a new App ID,** and click **Continue**.

5. The screen should be titled "Create an App ID." In the App ID Description field, enter **All Apps**. After entering the description, click **Continue**.

6. The screen should be titled "Choose an Apple Device." Select **Assign a new Apple device**, and click **Continue**.

7. The screen should be titled "Assign Development Device." In the Device Description field, assign a name descriptive of your device. I have a 3G iPad, for instance, so I used "Troy Brant 3G iPad." Use something similarly descriptive for your device.

   The next field asks for your Device ID. Also known as your UDID, you can find this 40-character sequence in Xcode. The image and steps that follow show you precisely how to find this information:

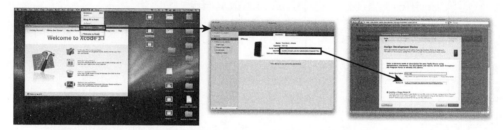

Use the organizer window in Xcode to find your device UDID.

   • Connect the device to your Mac.

   • In Xcode, select the **Window > Organizer** menu item.

   • Under Devices on the left side, select your device.

   • Double-click the 40-character string next to the Identifier field.

   • Copy and paste it into the Device ID field back in your browser.

   After you enter the **Device Description** and **Device ID**, as shown in the preceding image, click **Continue**.

8. The screen should be titled "Generate a Certificate Signing Request." For this step, you need to launch the Keychain Access application on your Mac to generate a certificate. Follow the following steps to generate the certificate.

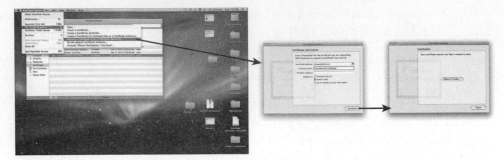

Create a certificate request.

- Launch the **Keychain Access** application on your Mac.
- Select menu item **Keychain Access > Certificate Assistant > Request a Certificate From a Certificate Authority ...**
- In the Common Name field, leave it as is, or provide a more descriptive name, as shown in the image.
- Select **Saved to disk**.
- Click **Continue**.
- Click **Save** to save the CertificateSigningRequest.certSigningRequest file.

9. After the certificate request file has been generated, click **Continue** in the browser to progress to the next screen.

10. The screen should be titled "Submit Certificate Signing Request." Click **Choose File**, select the **CertificateSigningRequest.certSigningRequest** file, and click **Continue**.

11. The screen should be titled "Name your Provisioning Profile." In the Profile Description field, name your profile something descriptive. I used "Troy 3G Development." After entering the description, click **Generate**. When the profile is generated, your screen should roughly match the one on the right that follows:

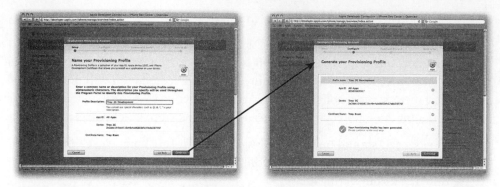

Give your profile a descriptive name, and generate the profile.

At this point, you have successfully generated your developer provisioning profile! Now it's time to install the profile in Xcode, and you will continue to use the Development Provisioning Assistant to help you through the process.

Installing in Xcode

Switch back to your browser, and pick up where you left off with the Development Provisioning Assistant:

1. Click **Continue** on the screen titled "Generate Your Provisioning Profile" if you haven't already.

2. The screen should be titled "Download & Install Your Provisioning Profile." In the Step 1 section, click the **Download Now** button to download the profile.

3. The downloaded file will have the extension .mobileprovision. Just drag and drop the file onto the Xcode icon in the Dock, as shown in the following:

Drag and drop the .mobileprovision file onto the Xcode icon in the Dock.

4. Back in the browser, click **Continue**.

5. The screen will still be titled "Download & Install Your Provisioning Profile," but the subheading will be "Step 3." The image they show is a bit misleading. If you *don't* have your device connected, you will not see the Organize screenshot they show. You will verify the profile installation yourself a bit later, so you can essentially skip this step. Click **Continue**.

6. The screen should be titled "Download & Install Your Development Certificate." In the Step 1 section, click the **Download Now** button to download the certificate.

7. The downloaded file will be named "developer_identity.cer." Double-click the file to start the install wizard.

8. When the Add Certificates window shows up, leave the Keychain set to login, and click **OK**.

9. Back in the browser, click **Continue**.

10. The screen will still be titled "Download & Install Your Development Certificate," but the subheading will be "Step 3." In the Keychain Access app, select the **Keys** category, and make sure your private key has a dropdown arrow next to it. Expand the arrow and make sure the certificate named "iPhone Developer: [Your Name]" is there. See the following image for an example.

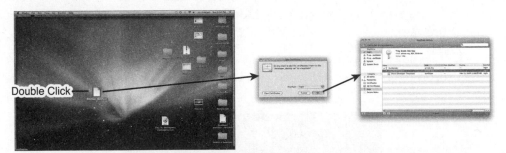

After installing the certificate, make sure the certificate shows up under your private key in Keychain Access.

11. If the certificate shows up under your private key as shown previously, then click **Continue** back in the browser. If your certificate doesn't show up, you may need to restart the Development Provisioning Assistant.

Now, you have successfully installed both your provisioning profile and your developer's certificate. The only thing left to do is configure Xcode to build your device. We're almost there!

Configure Xcode

The Development Provisioning Assistant takes you the rest of the way:

1. Your browser screen should be titled "Install your iPhone application with Xcode." Go through the three steps listed on the page.

2. First, make sure your device is connected to your Mac.

3. Open one of your Xcode projects. The screenshots that follow show the ICE app from Chapter 3, but you can choose any project.

4. Click on the **Simulator | Debug** section of the top toolbar and select **iPhone Device**. See the image that follows for an example. Note that you will likely have a later version of the SDK than the one shown.

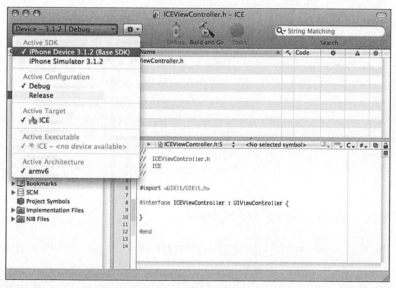

Use the Overview button in the top-left corner to change the API from Simulator to Device.

5. Click **Build and Go.**

THERE'S A TIP FOR THAT

With only one profile installed, Xcode will automatically use that profile. If you install more than one profile, refer to the iPhone Developer Program User Guide on http://developer.apple.com/iphone/ for instructions on how to switch profiles.

6. If the app launches on your device, you are finished! If it doesn't work for any reason, make sure you followed every step listed previously. If you are completely stuck, you can always start over with the Development Provisioning Assistant again.

And there you have it! From this point forward, you can run your apps on your phone during development.

Cleaning Up

If you followed all the previous steps, you'll have a few files littering your Desktop or Downloads folder. Feel free to trash the .mobileprovision, CertificateSigningRequest. certSigningRequest, and developer_identity.cer files. And with that, you are completely done creating your developer provisioning profile.

Now that you can install apps on your phone, you have taken one more step toward submitting apps to the App Store. Testing your apps on a real device is a crucial step in making sure your apps are ready for prime time. However, are you sure your app won't crash or leak memory? Next chapter, you will go over three powerful tools— Clang, Instruments, and Shark—used to identify bugs and memory problems in your app. Knowing how to use these tools is essential to releasing the highest-quality app to your users.

The Least You Need to Know

- The first step to putting apps on your phone is to pay $99 to register for the iPhone Developer Program.
- You can register for the iPhone Developer Program at http://developer.apple. com/iphone/.
- A provisioning profile consists of a developer certificate, an App ID, and a list of Device IDs.
- Use the Development Profile Assistant when you plan to test your own apps on your phone.

Tools of the Trade

In This Chapter

- Clang
- Instruments
- Shark

Imagine that you need to take your car in for a tune-up, but your favorite auto shop is closed. Instead, you decide to try out a different auto shop down the road. When you arrive, instead of a garage bustling with activity, there's a smiling mechanic standing in the middle of an open parking lot. You drive up, roll down your window, and he says, "Looks like you need a new carburetor, air filter, and your transmission needs to be replaced." You stare at the mechanic in disbelief, roll up the window, and drive off to find a real auto shop.

What was wrong with the parking lot auto shop? Why didn't you trust the mechanic's judgment? Well, he just *looked* at your car to come up with his diagnosis. He didn't use any tools to see what was really going on inside. The mechanic may very well have been right, but how could he be *sure* without running the car through a battery of tests?

The exact same situation applies to iPhone programming. The car is your application, the driver is your user, and the mechanic is you, the developer. Instead of eyeballing your code like the mechanic in the parking lot, you can use several development tools to properly assess problems. In this chapter, you will learn about three of these tools: Clang, Instruments, and Shark. By the time you're done, you won't just be a mechanic in a parking lot; you'll have your own garage full of state-of-the-art equipment.

Three Tools Every iMechanic Should Master

All apps should be run through three tools before you even think about putting them on the App Store. Using these tools could prevent many of the problems that plague applications—namely, poor performance and memory problems. So what are these tools? Here's a quick overview:

- **Clang Static Analyzer:** The Clang Static Analyzer—or just "Clang" for short—is great for identifying memory leaks. Clang is unique in that it doesn't attach to a running process. Instead, it goes through your uncompiled code to perform its analysis. Clang provides a diagnostic report about your code, which includes potential problem areas and optimizations in addition to memory leaks.

- **Instruments:** Instruments is also great for finding memory leaks. You can also use it to monitor CPU usage, memory usage, animation performance, and 3D graphics performance. It comes packaged with the iPhone SDK, so you already have it installed.

- **Shark:** Shark is used to determine where your application spends its time. If your app spends 90 percent of the time in one method, you know that rewriting or optimizing that method will give your app a huge performance boost. Shark will help direct these optimization efforts.

CRASH AND LEARN

Although Instruments and Shark can be used with the iPhone Simulator, the only way you'll get accurate information from these tools is by using them with your app running on a real device.

The purpose of this chapter is to enable you to use these tools. However, it will take more time and practice to become proficient in their use.

To demonstrate how to use each of these tools, you will apply them to a sample application: EveryDayCounts. You can download the application online at http://troybrant.net/iphonebook/chapter22/EveryDayCounts.zip.

The application is simple: it displays a table view populated with individual date strings. You will try using your new tools on this toy application to see if you can find any leaks and performance problems.

Clang

Clang works by looking at your code *before* you run it. Using Clang, you can easily identify memory leaks, uninitialized variables, and other bugs in your code.

Using Clang is really simple since it is built into Xcode. To have Clang analyze your code, just select **Build > Build and Analyze** from the top menu bar in Xcode. Click the **Build Results** tab in the Editor window to see the results. Selecting each item in the list will take you to the line of code where there is a potential bug. Pretty nice, right?

Using Clang

To see a real-world example, analyze the EveryDayCounts application by following these steps:

1. If you haven't already, download the EveryDayCounts application at http://troybrant.net/iphonebook/chapter22/EveryDayCounts.zip.

2. Run the app and play with it just to see how it works.

3. Run Clang by selecting **Build > Build and Analyze** from the top menu bar.

4. Click the **Build Results** tab in the Editor window to see the build results. You should see the following list of memory leaks:

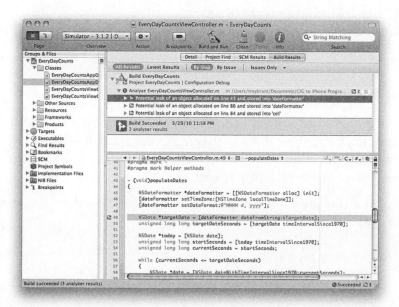

Clang identified three memory leaks.

5. Now, it's just a matter of going through the list and fixing the bugs found, one by one.

> **CRASH AND LEARN**
>
> Although Clang is great for quickly identifying bugs, it is not perfect. Clang will generate false positives, and it can miss errors as well. You should not trust Clang results unquestioningly. Instead, you should evaluate each bug Clang identifies using your own judgment.

When identifying bugs in your code, run it through Clang first, then Instruments. Clang can't give you information about the overall size of memory used or CPU performance, but it does point out memory leaks in a much nicer format than Instruments.

Instruments

Instruments is an application that comes bundled with the iPhone SDK, so you already have it installed if you have the SDK installed. As mentioned earlier, Instruments is great for seeing an overview of what your application is doing while running. You can see how much memory and CPU you're using, and it can even identify leaks for you.

Unlike Clang, Instruments works by analyzing the application while it is running. You can have Instruments analyze your app while it runs either in the iPhone Simulator or on a real device.

Launching Instruments

Instruments is launched like any other Mac application, either via Spotlight or from the application's location on disk. By default, the application is located in /Developer/ Applications. By launching Instruments manually, however, you have to attach Instruments to your app manually as well.

A better choice is to launch Instruments directly from Xcode and automatically attach it to your app, as shown in the following figure:

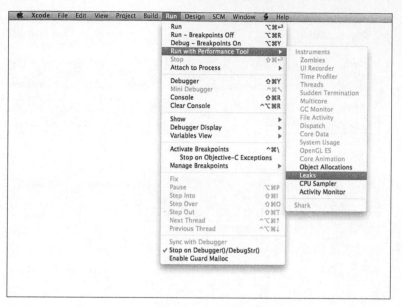

Launching your app and attaching Instruments automatically from within Xcode.

As shown in the previous image, to launch your application with Instruments attached, select Xcode menu item **Run > Start with Perfomance Tool > Leaks**. There are several other Instruments templates to choose from, but Leaks is the one to use for identifying memory-related issues. Feel free to experiment with the different templates to see what kind of information they provide.

THERE'S A TIP FOR THAT

Sometimes launching Instruments from Xcode just doesn't work. If Instruments refuses to attach to your application, try closing Instruments completely before your next launch. It's the old reboot strategy, and strangely enough, it usually works.

The Interface

Instruments is much easier to use if you take some time to understand the various parts of its interface. The following is a screenshot of its interface, using the Leaks template to analyze the EveryDayCounts application:

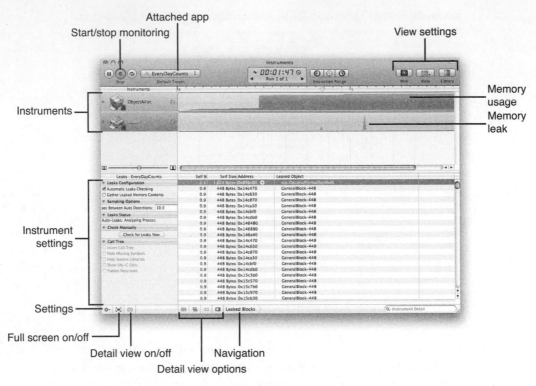

The Instruments interface using the Leaks template.

Let's take a look at each of the interface elements, from top to bottom:

- **Top toolbar:** You can use the top bar to start and stop monitoring your application with Instruments. Using the Default Target field, you can select which process to attach to. If you launch from Xcode, this box will already be set to your application. If you launch Instruments on your own, you will need to start your application and then manually select the application's process from the Default Target list.

  In the middle of the top bar, you can see the status of your currently running process. On the far right, there are a few buttons (Mini, View, and Library) you can use to customize the window. Most of the time, though, you won't need to use these buttons for debugging purposes.

- **Instruments view:** Below the top toolbar are your *instruments*, that is, individual reports about certain aspects of your application. The first instrument is the Object Allocation instrument, and it shows your memory usage over time. In the previous image, you can see that about a quarter of the way through, there was a huge spike in memory usage. This is a sign of a possible memory problem you need to investigate further.

DEFINITION

An **instrument** is used to measure a single aspect of your application. There are instruments for reporting memory leaks, CPU usage, and object allocation, to name a few.

The second instrument shown here is the Leaks instrument. Each orange cone represents one or more memory leaks. The height of the cone indicates the severity of the memory leak; you can see the second leak in the previous image is worse than the first one.

- **Detail view:** The entire bottom section of the window is known as the Detail View. Using the Detail View, you can customize each of your instruments. In the image, for instance, you can set how often the monitor checks for leaks.

The table to the right of the settings view is a core part of Instruments. The table is context-sensitive and shows you specific information about each instrument. In the previous image, the Leaks instrument is selected, and the table is showing a list of all the observed memory leaks in the application. Knowing how to navigate this table is key to hunting down leaks.

- **Bottom toolbar:** Don't let its size fool you: the bottom toolbar is one of the most important parts of Instruments. Here are the most useful buttons in the bar:

  - **Table view button:** Use the table view button to display a list of items. For instance, in the previous image, you see a flat list of leaking objects with this button toggled.

  - **Outline view button:** Use this button to trace a leak back to its source.

  - **Diagram view button:** With the Object Allocation instrument selected, use this button to see a timeline of when each object in your app was allocated.

  - **Extended view button:** Perhaps the most essential button for hunting down memory leaks, use this button to see the call stack for each memory leak.

Using Instruments

You now have a rough idea of what's in the Instruments interface. Next, you need to put it into use to track down bugs and memory leaks in your code.

Let's run the EveryDayCounts app through Instruments and find some memory leaks. Follow along using these steps:

1. If you haven't already, download the EveryDayCounts application at http://troybrant.net/iphonebook/chapter22/EveryDayCounts.zip.

2. Run the app and play with it just to see how it works.

3. In Xcode, select the **Run > Start with Performance Tool > Leaks** menu item to launch Instruments.

4. After the app finishes launching, tap the **Populate Table** button.

5. Watch the leaks instrument. See the orange spike? This is a memory leak. To identify what leaked, select the **Leaks instrument**. Then click the **extended detail** button on the bottom bar to see a stack trace of the code causing the leak. Your screen should look similar to the following:

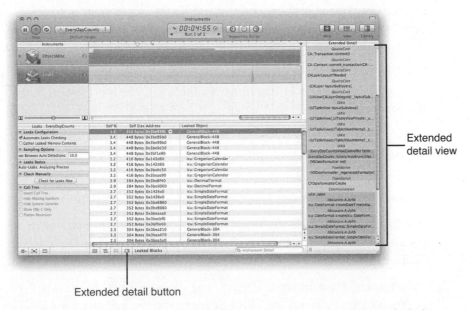

Extended detail button

Extended detail view

The extended detail view displays a stack trace you can use to track down the leak in your code.

6. The detail table will contain a list of all the leaks detected by Instruments. Press the **outline button** on the bottom bar to group repeated leaks into a single line. This is an excellent view for identifying leaks since it also shows you the methods in your code where the leaks take place. The following image shows the outline view of the EveryDayCounts app:

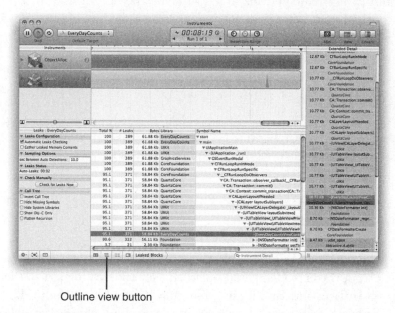

Outline view button

Outline view gives you a nice hierarchical breakdown of the leaks in your code.

7. Click to expand the method tree until you see methods from the EveryDayCounts app, as shown in the previous image. It may take a while, but you will eventually hit the `tableView:cellForRowAtIndexPath:` method in EveryDayCountsViewController.m.

Your numbers will be different, but see how there are 371 leaks (95 percent of the total) in this method? Whatever the leak is, it's happening *a lot*, so let's try to fix it.

In the previous image, you see that 322 of the 371 leaks are on `[NSDateFormatter init]`, so double-click the `[NSDateFormatter init]` row in the call tree, the one below the highlighted row in the preceding image.

8. This will switch back to Xcode and highlight the line of code. You see on this line that the code calls alloc/init on an `NSDateFormatter` object. Is there a release or autorelease to balance the alloc/init? Nope—that's the problem. Add in a release, and the leak is fixed.

At this point, you should go back to Instruments and see if there are any other leaks you can fix right now. Then save your code, and run it through Instruments again to see if there are any new leaks that pop up. Rinse and repeat until Instruments doesn't indicate any remaining leaks.

ONE MORE THING

Sometimes leaks occur in system code. Other times, Instruments erroneously identifies a leak that doesn't actually exist. Always make sure that you understand the cause of a leak before adding a release or autorelease call to your code.

Shark

And now, time for something completely different. Imagine you have already run your application through Clang and squashed the reported bugs. You then ran your app through Instruments, and it gives your app a clean bill of health. But when you run your application, you can't help but notice that it has choppy scrolling or lags when you tap a button. The performance is just awful. How do you go about making sure your app runs smooth as butter?

Introducing: Shark. Shark *profiles* your application to determine how much time is spent in various functions. Profiling is the process of sampling code at runtime. Using Shark, you can see where to get the biggest bang for your buck when optimizing your code. If 90 percent of your CPU time is spent in a single method, while 10 percent is spent in all the rest of your code combined, then it's probably a good idea to work on optimizing the 90 percent method.

In this section, you will again use the EveryDayCounts app as the guinea pig. When the EveryDayCounts app is run on a physical device—not the iPhone Simulator—you will notice that the app hangs when you tap the Populate Table button in the app. Using Shark, you can figure out what your code is doing during that long delay. Let's give it a shot.

Device vs. Simulator

Even though it is possible to use Shark to profile your code in the simulator, this is not very helpful. Where performance is concerned, CPU and RAM make all the difference. The simulator makes full use of your Mac's computing resources, so you will always see much better performance on the simulator than on a real device. This is why you should always perform extensive testing of your application on a real device before submitting it to the App Store.

So when you use Shark, you should use it to profile your code running on a real device. Here are the steps you need to take to prepare your device for Shark profiling:

1. Attach your device to your Mac.

2. In Xcode, launch the EveryDayCounts application on your device. Remember to use the Overview button in the top-left corner to easily switch between simulator and device launch.

THERE'S A TIP FOR THAT

To launch custom apps on your device, you must be enrolled in the iPhone Developer Program and have a developer provisioning profile installed. See Chapter 21 for all the details on installing custom apps on your phone.

3. You just want the app installed on your phone, so after the app has completely launched, close it.

Getting Started with Shark

Shark comes bundled with the iPhone SDK, so there's nothing extra you have to do to install it if you have the SDK installed.

You can launch Shark simply by typing "Shark" in Spotlight.

After the main screen launches, there are two steps to enable iPhone and iPad profiling:

- Select the **Control network profiling of shared computers** radio button.

- As shown in the following image, select the **Sampling > Network/iPhone Profiling...** menu item to enable iPhone compatibility:

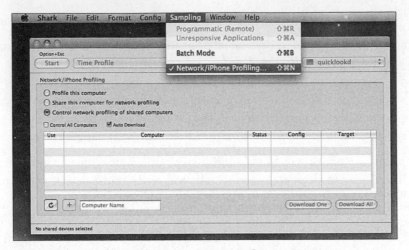

You must enable iPhone profiling before Shark can work with iPhone.

Note that the profiler works on iPad as well, even though the sampling menu item only includes "iPhone."

Now that device profiling is enabled, check out the following best practices for using Shark before profiling the EveryDayCounts app.

Using Shark

If there were only two words to describe best usage of Shark, they would be "short bursts." You control when Shark starts and stops sampling the running application. Instead of trying to sample the entire lifetime of your application, sample *just* the parts where you notice performance is poor. The problem with sampling over long periods of time is that your results get diluted. More time is spent in methods that don't have any problems.

So to best utilize Shark, you should use the following steps, which incorporate the "short bursts" idea:

1. Play with your app and identify an individual action that causes performance to lag.

2. Quit and relaunch the app to get it into a fresh state.

3. With your device connected, launch Shark, and set the target to your app.

4. Prepare to perform the action that causes poor performance.

5. In Shark, click the **Start** button to start sampling.

6. On your device, perform the action that causes poor performance.

7. As soon as the action completes, press the **Stop** button in Shark.

8. Shark will then report the results. Use these results to determine where to optimize your code.

9. After optimizing, play with the app again, and see if the performance is improved. Start over from Step 1 to tackle the next performance bug.

Testing with EveryDayCounts

Now try the "short bursts" pattern on the EveryDayCounts app. You want to figure out why it's so slow when you tap the "Populate Table" button. Follow these steps to try to identify the problematic code:

1. Make sure EveryDayCounts is on your device. If it is not, go through the steps in the "Device vs. Simulator" section to put it on your device.

2. Launch the EveryDayCounts app.

3. In Shark, check the checkbox next to your device name. It takes a moment for the click to register, and you might need to click twice.

4. In the Target column, select **EveryDayCounts**. Your Shark interface should match the following image:

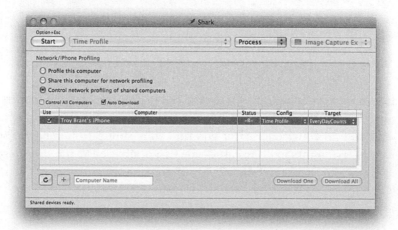

Make sure the EveryDayCounts target is selected.

5. These next few steps should be done in quick succession:

   • Click the **Start** button in the top-left corner of the Shark interface.

   • Tap the **Populate Table** button in the EveryDayCounts app.

   • As soon as the table in the app fills with data, press the **Stop** button in Shark.

6. Wait for Shark to analyze the samples. This can sometimes take a while.

7. Shark will then display the breakdown of where time was spent in the code. You will see a call tree with each line representing a method call, similar to the one in the following image:

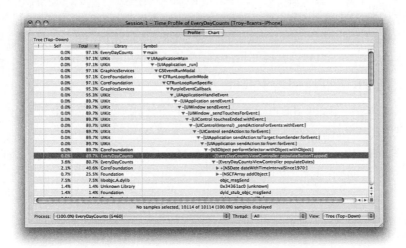

Tree view showing the percentage of time spent in a each method.

I have found the easiest way to navigate this is to press the left arrow key until the tree is collapsed. Then expand the tree, one line at a time, until you start to find your code. After you find your application code in the tree—EveryDayCounts in your case—you can double-click the line to see the code itself, as shown in the following image:

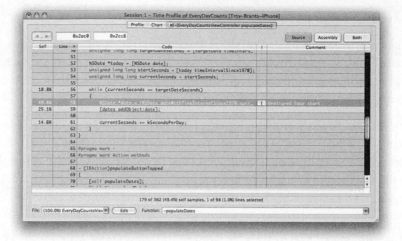

Shark displays both a tree view of activity and a code view to help you identify areas for optimization.

Interpreting the Results

You should see output similar to that shown previously. From the image, you can see that roughly 90 percent of the time is spent in populateButtonTapped. You can also see that most of the time spent in populateButtonTapped is actually spent in populateDates, a method that fills an array with all the dates between now and the target date.

At this point, you have identified exactly which methods are chewing up all those clock cycles. Now it's up to you to figure out if there's some way you can better optimize the code. For instance, in EveryDayCounts, thousands of dates are computed when the table view really needs only 10 or 15 at most to display at any given time. Instead of painstakingly precomputing all those dates up front, you could just compute the dates for the table view as it requests them in the datasource method. You can find a couple optimized versions of the EveryDayCounts app online that compute the dates only when they are needed:

- http://troybrant.net/iphonebook/chapter22/EveryDayCounts-better.zip
- http://troybrant.net/iphonebook/chapter22/EveryDayCounts-best.zip

Wrapping Up

This chapter gives you the essentials you need to start using Instruments, Clang, and Shark. I highly recommend getting some practice under your belt with these tools and learning more about them in the official Apple documentation on http://developer.apple.com/iphone.

You have almost reached the end (of this book, anyway). Only one chapter remains: submitting your app to the App Store. In addition to the technical details of putting your app on the store, the next chapter covers steps you can take to improve your chances of making it through the app approval process unscathed.

The Least You Need to Know

- Instruments is a convenient tool for monitoring your app as it runs. It can help find memory leaks as well as other performance issues.

- The Clang Static Analyzer uncovers potential problems in your code without running it. It presents memory leaks and other problem areas in a nice report.

- Shark profiles your code and is the best way to find the sections of code where your app spends most of its time.

- Always run your app through these three tools before submitting it to the App Store.

The App Store and Beyond

In This Chapter

- Learning the app submission process
- Building your app for App Store distribution
- Tips to avoid app rejections
- Farewell

Could the title of this final chapter be any more melodramatic? Perhaps if there were an echo: "The App Store … AND BEYOND! … *ond … ond … ond.*" Even though the title is as cheesy as they come, it does at least indicate that you have reached the end of the road for this book. The very last stop on your journey to developing iPhone and iPad applications is learning how to submit your apps to the App Store.

As it turns out, the App Store submission process is relatively painless. You fill out a lot of forms, but that is the worst of it. The "Beyond" part of the app submission process, however, is filled with potential pitfalls. After submitting to the App Store, your app goes through an approval process that is mysterious and not well understood. In this chapter, you learn both the technical details of submitting your app and the steps you can take to maximize the chance your app is approved.

Intro to the App Submission Process

Perhaps you are reading this chapter having completed your first app. If so, then first let me say "Congrats!" There are many who start learning iPhone programming, but very few actually have the tenacity and perseverance to completely finish an app and release it to the App Store. Hats off to you for reaching this point.

However, if you are reading this chapter before finishing—or even starting—the app you want to release, then you should still keep reading. Even without a finished product, there is much you can—and should—do before you upload your *application binary* to the App Store.

> **DEFINITION**
>
> An **application binary**—or app binary for short—is the .app file generated for your application when built successfully in Xcode. The application binary is the "app" that will be installed on your users' devices. For any Xcode project, the .app file can be found in the Products group in the Groups & Files panel.

Three Steps

From a bird's-eye view, there are three major steps required to submit your app to the App Store, summarized below:

- **Step 1: Request paid contract**—If you plan to sell your app at any point, your first step is to request a seller's contract from Apple.

- **Step 2: Add application**—Even if you haven't completely finished developing your app, you can add the app in iTunes Connect. This is especially useful for reserving an app name.

- **Step 3: Submit app binary**—Once your app binary is uploaded, your app will officially enter the App Store review queue.

Of these steps, only submitting the application binary requires that your application is actually done. In fact, you can complete steps 1 and 2 right now.

If you are considering selling your app, you should go ahead and request a paid contract now. It doesn't take long, and there is a short approval process your request must go through separate from the app approval process. So it's better to do it sooner than later.

You can also add your application right this moment even if you haven't finished the app. The App Store requires each app have a unique name, and the advantage of adding your app now is you can prevent someone else from using the name before you do.

The last step in submitting an app is building it for distribution on the App Store. Once you upload the binary, the submission process is complete. Then, it is a waiting game while your app sits in the queue waiting to be reviewed. Tips are provided at the end of the chapter for making sure you successfully navigate the app approval process.

If you want to get paid for making iPhone and iPad apps, follow along to the next section. If you have a free app and don't want to fill out payment information right now, skip ahead to "Adding Your App."

Getting Paid

If you plan to sell your application, you must first fill out a bit of online paperwork. However, there isn't really that much of it, and the process consists of only four steps:

1. Request the contract.

2. Fill out your contact information.

3. Fill out your bank information.

4. Fill out your tax information.

After you fill everything out, you will have to a wait a day or two for Apple to accept the contract. At that point, you are free to charge for your applications.

To request a contract that allows you to sell your app on the App Store, you must access iTunes Connect.

iTunes Connect

iTunes Connect is where you go to manage your content on the iTunes Store. Here, you walk through using iTunes Connect to manage your contracts and App Store apps. In addition to this, iTunes Connect also provides sales and financial reports for your apps.

To access iTunes Connect, log in at http://developer.apple.com/iphone, and select **iTunes Connect** under the iPhone Developer Program menu on the right-hand side of the screen.

THERE'S A TIP FOR THAT

Don't see the iPhone Developer Program menu when you log in? You must be registered for the iPhone Developer Program—and have paid the $99—to release apps on the App Store. Flip back to Chapter 21 for a step-by-step guide on registering for the iPhone Developer Program.

iTunes
Connect link

Click the iTunes Connect link on the right side of the page.

After you click the iTunes Connect link, you are presented with the iTunes Connect homepage, shown in the following:

From the iTunes Connect homepage, you can even generate promo codes so select users can download your app for free.

Take a moment to see what iTunes Connect has to offer.

Requesting the Contract

To request a contract to sell apps on the App Store, follow these steps:

1. Select the **Contracts, Tax, and Banking Information** link on the iTunes Connect homepage.

2. You will be presented with your contracts homepage. In the top section titled Request New Contracts, you will see a Paid Application contract ready and waiting for you. Check the **Request Contract** box on the left, and click **Submit**.

3. On the next screen, check the **"I have read and agree..."** box, and click **Submit**.

4. On the next screen, click **Done** to return back to the contracts homepage.

That's all it takes to request a paid contract.

Now, you have to supply a bit more detailed information to complete the contract. Before you get started, though, make sure you have an in-progress contract application, as shown in the following:

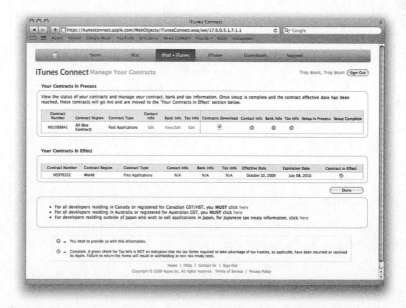

You now need to edit the Contact Info, Bank Info, and Tax Info fields.

To complete the contract information, you should have the following pieces of information close at hand before you begin:

- Bank routing number
- Bank account number

THERE'S A TIP FOR THAT

If you have a checkbook nearby, you can find your bank routing number and bank account number on any given check. Find instructions for locating these numbers with a bit of Internet searching.

Contact Info

After gathering your bank info, follow these steps to complete your contract request:

1. Under Contact Info, select **Edit**.

2. Click any one of the **Create New Person** buttons.

3. Fill out all the required fields with your information on the Create a New Contact screen.

4. If you are a single developer, set all of the Company Contact fields to the contact you just created. If you are registering on behalf of a company, create a new contact for each person requested in the Company Contact section.

5. Click **Save**.

Bank Info

After saving your contact info, you will be dumped back to the contracts screen. Now, edit the bank info:

1. Under Bank Info, select **View/Edit**.

2. If there isn't a bank account available, click **Add Bank Account**.

3. Use the website to fill out all bank information requested, including your bank routing and account numbers.

4. After entering all your information, you will see a review screen. *Double-check* that your bank account information is correct, check the **"I certify that..."** box, and click **Save**.

5. Choose the bank you just added in the Choose Bank Account: field, and click **Save**.

Tax Info

Again, you will see the contracts home screen after adding your bank info. The last step is editing your tax info:

1. Under Tax Info, select **Edit**.

2. You now need to fill out the W-9 form. Filling out the W-9 form correctly is very important, and to be 100 percent certain about how to fill out the form, you should contact a financial advisor.

3. Next to Business name, enter the name of your incorporated business or leave it empty if you are an individual developer.

4. Make the selection that applies to you for the Type of Beneficial Owner: field.

5. Make the selection that applies to you for the Exempt Payee: field.

6. Make the selection that applies to you for the Subject to Backup Witholding: field.

7. If you are an individual developer, enter your Social Security Number (SSN) next to Taxpayer Identification Number.

8. Check the **Under penalties of perjury...** box, and click **Submit**.

And with that, you have completed the contract request for paid applications. Now, you just have to wait for approval of your contract, which can take a couple of days. When you are approved, though, you can officially start making money selling your apps on the App Store. You only need to complete this process once to sell iPad, iPhone, iPod Touch apps on the App Store.

Adding Your App

One of the great parts of the app submission process is that you can register your application before you even finish developing it. When you go through the app submission process on iTunes Connect, you have the option of adding the application binary itself at a later time. The primary benefit, as mentioned earlier in this chapter, is that adding the app early reserves your application name on the App Store.

Another benefit is that you can edit your application information if you realize you made a mistake during the initial submission process. All of the app details are editable, so if you want to change the wording of the description or use different screenshots, you can make those changes before Apple reviews your application.

It is also completely safe to add the app without the binary since the app reviewers will not look at your app until it has a binary. If you haven't picked up on it yet, I highly recommend adding your app *before* submitting your binary.

Before You Begin

There are three parts of the app submission process that take a lot more time than others:

- App description
- 512×512 pixel large app icon
- Screenshots

You can likely zoom through most of the app submission forms, but these three items will take some thought and some time to generate. Feel free to jump to the subsections on these topics below to get a head start on these items.

Step-by-Step

There are quite a number of forms to fill out when submitting your app. If you aren't sure what to enter for any one field, it is perfectly fine to add some placeholder text (To-Do) or even a placeholder image. As long as you don't submit the app binary now, you can come back and change your app details later.

To add your app, follow these steps:

1. Navigate to your iTunes Connect homepage, and select the **Manage Your Applications** link.

2. Click the **Add New Application** button in the top left corner, shown in the following:

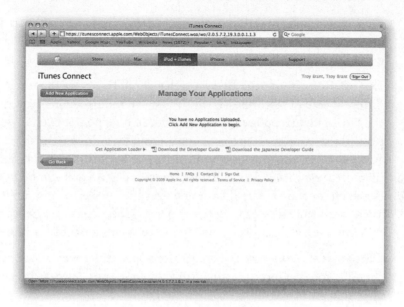

As you add applications, you can edit and view them on this page.

3. Enter your Primary Language and Company Name. If you are an individual developer, enter your name in the Company Name field. Click **Continue**.

CRASH AND LEARN

Think carefully before setting your Primary Language and Company Name. These are global settings for *all* your applications and cannot be changed later.

4. Since World War II, the U.S. government has regulated the export of cryptography for national security reasons. Even though many of the restrictions were relaxed in 1992, there is still heavy U.S. oversight over nonmilitary software that uses encryption. Because of this, Apple requires that you report if your app uses encryption of any sort. Select the appropriate option, and click **Continue**.

5. Now comes the fun part: filling out your app details. Following are some tips for filling out the requested info:

- **Name:** A good application name is short and descriptive. "Groceries" is a good name for a grocery list app. "The Gregarious Grocery List App of Awesome" is not a good name.

- **Description:** A good description gets users excited about your app, but don't exaggerate. In the end, users really just want to know what they can do with your app.

- **Device Requirements:** Be aware that iPod Touch, iPad, and iPhone have different sets of features. To specify device requirements, you must add the key `UIRequiredDeviceCapabilities` of type `Dictionary` to the Info. plist file in your app's project. Apple provides a document titled "Device Support" that explains how to identify the features your app uses. For instance, you must add the `video-camera` key if your app takes video, the `accelerometer` key if your app uses the accelerometer, and the `location-services` key if your app uses Core Location. Search online for "iPhone Device Requirements" to locate the document for more details.

- **Categories:** Make sure the categories you select are accurate. Sometimes, though, you can increase the chance of your apps' success by building apps that fit in the more obscure categories. The biggest category by far is Entertainment.

- **Copyright:** My copyright string is "2010 Troy Brant." If you are an individual developer, enter a similar string using your name.

- **Version Number:** Starting with 1.0 is always a good choice for this field.

- **SKU Number:** A SKU number is used as a product's unique identifier in businesses. You can actually make up any alphanumeric sequence for this field, although I would recommend using something predictable and descriptive. My SKU "numbers" follow the following format: "com. troybrant.[app name]".

- **Keywords:** The keywords you specify here are used by the App Store search engine when the user enters a search query.

CRASH AND LEARN

Do not use the names of your competitors' applications as keywords for your own app. This is grounds for rejection from the App Store, because your app will show up in the results when users search for your competitors' apps. You will also draw the ire and disdain of the developer community, but you can avoid this fate by simply using descriptive and legal keywords.

- **Application URL:** Although it is not required, almost all successful iPhone and iPad apps have a dedicated website.

- **Support URL:** Even if you don't have a dedicated website, you have to have at least a page somewhere users can go to if they have problems with your app.

- **Support E-mail Address:** Although you could use your personal e-mail address here, I would recommend setting up a support e-mail account specifically for your app.

- **Demo Account—Full Access:** This field, despite its name, is really for any and all additional information you need to communicate to your reviewer. You can include instructions for anything ranging from using a test account to accessing special features in your app. More than likely, you can just leave this field blank.

After entering the required information—the fields in bold—click **Continue**.

6. Select the appropriate rating for each category on the next screen. If your app has any graphic or edgy content, you need to report it here. A rating is automatically generated for your app. Although it is subjective, try to be as accurate as possible, otherwise Apple may reject your app.

After making your selections, click **Continue**.

7. You should now be on the Upload tab. The very first thing you should do is check the **Upload application binary later** box under the Application section. Even if you have your binary ready, I would still check the box and upload it later in case you need to make last-minute changes to your app details.

For the Large 512×512 Icon field, you need to provide an image for your app that has the following qualities:

- 512×512 in size

- .jpg or .tiff file type

- At least 72 dpi

This large icon is displayed on your app description page on the App Store. The 512×512 icon should look relatively similar to the smaller 57×57 icon that is displayed on the iPhone itself. The 57×57 icon is part of your app's binary bundle itself, and you'll see how to add it a bit later on.

For the Primary Screenshot field, you need to include an image that meets the following requirements:

- No status bar

- 320×480 or 480×320 (fullscreen apps)

- 320×460 or 480×300 (with the status bar removed)

The fastest way you can get your app rejected is by including screenshots that include the status bar. You must use an image editor to remove the 20-pixel status bar from any screenshot you submit.

THERE'S A TIP FOR THAT

To take a screenshot on a physical device, hold the home button and press the lock button on top of the phone. The screen will flash white, and you will hear the snap of the camera. You should use these device screenshots instead of images from the iPhone Simulator. The color balance on your phone is different from the desktop, and you get much better quality using shots from the phone.

You can optionally add up to four more screenshots. Note that after you select a file, you have to then click the **Upload File** button to complete the file upload. After you have uploaded all the screenshots you desire, click **Continue**.

8. You now need to specify both the release date of your app as well as its price. First, a word of advice on the availability date: choose a date far in the future, maybe a few months out.

Why do this? If you specify a date far in the future, you can decide when to release your app once the app is approved. Apps that don't use this technique are released to the App Store immediately once they are approved. You gain much more control over your app release cycle by using the future date.

Also on this screen, you select the price tier for your application. Price tiers are simply dollar values you can make your app available for. The lowest price for any app is $0.99 at tier 1, and the highest price is $999.99 at tier 85. If you plan to sell your application, select one of the tiers, and then follow the **Pricing Matrix** link to see what dollar value each tier corresponds to.

After making your selections, click **Continue**.

9. The next step is to provide a localized description for your app. If you choose another language, you will need to enter all the detail from Step 5 again in a different language. You can skip this step by clicking **Continue**.

10. Finally, review all the information you added, but as long as you didn't upload your application binary, the information on this screen is not set in stone. Click **Submit** to complete the process of adding your app.

When you finish, you will be taken back to the **Manage Your Applications** screen. You should see your application, and when you click on it, you should see that the status of the application is Waiting For Upload, as shown in the following:

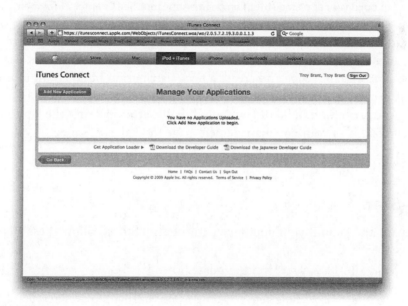

Apple will not review your app until you submit the binary, so you can freely edit the app details now.

It took a while to add all this data, but your app is now almost ready for a full submission to the App Store! The only remaining task is building the app binary for App Store distribution, and this process is described thoroughly in the next section.

Building Your App for the App Store

To complete the app submission process, you must build your app using an *App Store distribution profile*. In Chapter 25, you created a developer profile, which enables you to put apps on your own phone. App Store apps need to be built using a *distribution profile*, specially customized so the app can be installed on any iPhone—not just your own.

> **DEFINITION**
>
> A **distribution profile** is a type of provisioning profile that allows your app to be installed on your users' devices. An **App Store distribution profile** is used to build your app for distribution on the App Store. See Chapter 21 for more information on provisioning profiles.

To get started, you create an App Store distribution profile. After it is generated, you install the profile in Xcode and create a new distribution build configuration that uses this profile. You make some final adjustments to the application bundle before building a distribution build of your app. Finally, after locating the .app file, you zip it up and upload it to your app management page in iTunes Connect.

Easy, right? Let's get started.

Step-by-Step

To prepare and submit your app binary to the App Store, follow these steps:

> **CRASH AND LEARN**
>
> Be sure to follow these steps very closely. One small misstep can throw the entire process off, and leave you wading through a mess of bewildering error messages. Stay on the straight and narrow, and you will be just fine.

1. Log in to http://developer.apple.com/iphone, and select **iPhone Developer Program Portal** under the iPhone Developer Program menu on the right-hand side of the screen.

2. You need to create an App Store distribution profile, so select the **Provisioning** link on the left. Then, select the **Distribution** tab, and finally select the **New Profile** button. The New Profile button is on the far right, shown in the following:

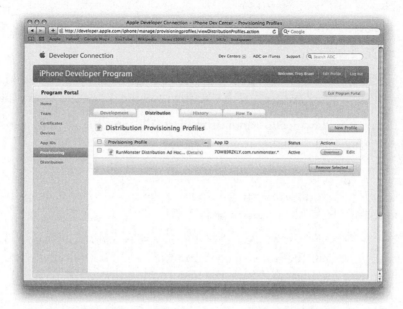

Make sure you are on the Distribution tab, not the Development tab.

3. Fill out the new distribution provisioning profile form using the following values:

   - Distribution Method: App Store

   - Profile Name: [Your App ID] Distribution App Store (For instance, if you use the generic "All Apps" App ID created in Chapter 21, then the name would be "All Apps App Store Profile")

   - App ID: [Your App ID]

ONE MORE THING

If your app uses Push Notifications or In-App Purchases, you must have a dedicated App ID—one that doesn't use wildcards. If your app doesn't use these, however, you can use an App ID with wildcards, like the "All Apps" App ID created in Chapter 21.

- Devices: (none selected)
- Click **Submit.**

4. Under the Distribution Provisioning Profiles heading, you should see the profile you just created. In the Actions column, click the **Download** button.

5. Locate the downloaded .mobileprovison file, and then install it in Xcode by dragging-and-dropping it onto the Xcode icon in the Dock.

6. Open the Xcode project you plan to submit to the App Store.

7. Right-click your project name at the top of the Groups & Files list. Select **Get Info** from the context menu.

8. In the Project Info window that pops up, select the **Configurations** tab. In that tab, select the **Release** configuration, and then select the **Duplicate** button at the bottom. Name the new configuration "Distribution," as shown in the following:

Create the Distribution configuration by duplicating the Release configuration.

9. Select the **Build** tab at the top of the Project Info window. Set the Configuration field to **Distribution**.

10. In the same tab, below the Code Signing Identity row, select the value column next to the Any iPhone OS Device setting, and choose the **App Store distribution profile** you installed in Step 5. Your window should look similar to the one that follows:

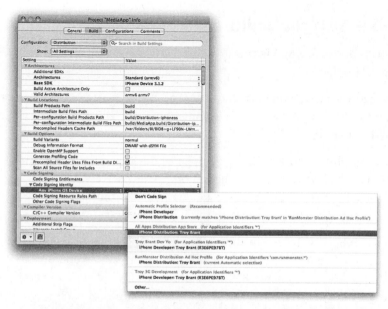

If the Code Signing Identity is set incorrectly, your app will be rejected from the App Store.

11. Close the Project Info window.

12. Expand the Targets group in the Groups & Files list, and right-click your app name. Select **Get Info** from the context menu.

13. You will see the Target Info window, which looks similar to the Project Info window but offers slightly different options. Select the **Properties** tab at the top of the Target Info window.

14. In the Properties tab, make the following changes:

   • Identifier: [unique identifier] (I recommend using an identifier of the form "com.[developer name].[app name]". For instance, for my project MediaApp, I use the identifier "com.troybrant.mediaapp".)

- Version: **1.0** (Every time you submit an update to the App Store, you should update this value.)

15. Close the Target Info window.

You are now ready to build the app for the App Store. But before you take the leap, there are a few tips to keep in mind.

Before You Finish the Build

Before you build your app for the store, here are some last-second tips and tricks you may want to implement:

- **Icon:** Every app submitted to the App Store must have an icon. For iPhone and iPod Touch apps, the icon must be 57×57 pixels in size. For iPad apps, the icon must be 72×72 pixels.

  If your app is built for a single type of device—just iPad or just iPhone— you should name the icon "icon.png." Alternatively, you can name the icon whatever you want, but add a key named "CFBundleIconFile" to your Info. plist file with the value set to the icon filename.

  However, if you are building a universal application, you will need to provide two icons: a 57×57 version for iPhone and a 72×72 version for iPad. Then you should add a key named "CFBundleIconFiles" of type Array to your Info.plist file. Add two strings to the array: the filenames of each icon. The iPhone OS will then use the pixel size of the icons to automatically select an icon for each platform.

- **Shine control:** By default, a shine overlay will be added to your icon when it is displayed. You can see the shine on built-in app icons like iTunes, App Store, and iPod. However, if you look hard enough, you notice that other apps do not have a shine, like Calculator, Notes, and Camera.

  To turn off the auto-shine for your app, select the **[app name]-info.plist** file in your Resources group. Right-click anywhere in the table and select **Add Row**. In the key column, select **Icon already includes gloss and bevel effects**, and check the box in the value column. Your icon will now be shine-free.

- **Splash image:** If you want your project to display a splash image when it first loads, simply add a 320×480 image named "Default.png" to your project. A splash image is displayed immediately on app launch, and it is replaced with your app interface as soon as your app finishes launching. Instead of displaying a company name or logo, it is recommended that the image look more or less like the first screen of your app.

- **App name control:** Sometimes, the app name below your app icon is truncated when displayed on a device. You can fix this, though, by again editing your [app name]-info.plist file in your Resources group. This time, you simply need to set the Bundle display name key to a shortened version of your app name that fits in the space allotted by the device.

If you make any of the changes suggested, you should definitely test the changes before building for the App Store.

ONE MORE THING

Before you build your app for the App Store, you should read through the Getting Approved section at the end of this chapter.

When you are completely certain your app is ready for prime time, move on the next section.

Finish the Fight

The goal of this entire process is to produce a single .app file, zip it, and upload it to iTunes Connect. Here are the final few steps to accomplish this goal and completely finish submitting your app:

1. Back in your primary project window in Xcode, click the **Overview** button, and select the **Distribution** configuration. Also, if not selected already, make sure **Device** is the Active SDK.

2. Build (but don't run) the project. The shortcut key for build-only is ⌘**B**.

3. After the build completes successfully, expand the Products group in the Groups & Files pane. Right-click the **.app file** in the group, and select **Reveal in Finder** from the context menu.

4. In Finder, Right-click the **.app file**, and select **Compress "[app name].app"**. After the .zip file is generated, drag it to your desktop for easy access.

> **THERE'S A TIP FOR THAT**
>
> You should keep a backup of the exact .app *and* .dsym files generated during the build process. Store the files somewhere safe. They will come in handy down the road if your app ever crashes on your users. They can send you the application's *crash log,* which contains a stack trace you can use to debug the crash. However, the unmodified crash log contains a mess of indecipherable hexadecimal memory addresses. To convert the log into plain English for debugging, you must *symbolicate* the file using the .app and .dsym files for the version of the app the user was using. Do an Internet search for "iphone symbolicate crash" to learn how to symbolicate crash logs.

5. Navigate to your app page on iTunes Connect, and click the **Upload Binary** link.

6. Upload the application .zip file you copied to the desktop, and click **Save Changes**.

7. Toss confetti. Dance a jig. Commence celebrating because you are D-O-N-E, done!

Your app is now added to the official app queue. Historically, the wait time has taken up to two weeks, though Apple is constantly improving the speed of the approval process.

If you decide that you have made a terrible mistake and want to take your app down before it can be reviewed, select the **Reject Binary** option on the iTunes Connect page for your app. You will lose your place in the review queue if you reject the binary, but you can always submit the app again once you fix whatever problem it had.

Tips for Getting Approved

After your app is in the official submission queue, it can take up to two weeks to get approved. If your app is rejected, you have to fix the problems, resubmit your app, and wait *another* two weeks for Apple to review the new version. So you could be looking at sitting on your hands and waiting an entire *month* if you don't submit the app up to Apple's standards the first time around.

So what can you do to improve your chances of getting approved the first time? Follow the steps below to have a better chance:

- **Do not crash:** According to Apple, this is the single biggest cause for app rejections. If you specify your app should be released on both iPhone and iPod Touch, for instance, you need to test to make sure it actually works on both of these platforms. Your reviewer will test the applications every way possible, and if the app crashes, they will send you the crash log along with your rejection letter.

- **Do not include copyrighted Apple images:** This may seem strange, but you can't include an image of an iPhone in your iPhone app. Further, you can't display Apple-owned icons, Mac desktop images, or even the Apple logo. These are all creative works owned by Apple, and although they let you use their API, they do not let you use their content.

- **Do not exaggerate in your app description:** Another leading cause for rejections is embellishing your app description. If the testers cannot test and try all the features you list in your app description, then your app will be rejected.

- **Do not include status bars in screen shots:** You are responsible for making sure your screenshots do not include the status bar. You will need to use an application like Photoshop or iPhoto to crop out the 20-pixel bar at the top of the screenshot.

- **Make sure your bundle identifier is unique:** Every single one of your applications must have a unique bundle identifier. This identifier is set on the Target Info window described earlier in the chapter. If you are releasing both free and paid versions of the same application, they must each have unique ids.

These are just a few of the reasons an app can be rejected. You can find more information regarding what Apple will and will not accept on the following websites:

- http://developer.apple.com/iphone/news/appstoretips/
- http://iphoneincubator.com/blog/app-store/rejections

Stay Classy, iPhone Developers

And that, my friends, does it for *The Complete Idiot's Guide to Developing iPad and iPhone Apps*. If you have made it this far, I thank you and commend you on coming along for the ride. It takes an enormous amount of effort and resilience to learn a new programming language, a new IDE, *and* a new operating system, and to reach this point is an extraordinary accomplishment. You should be proud, and—if I have done my job right—you should also be inspired and confident moving forward building your own iPhone and iPad apps.

Muscle Memory

When I set out to write this book, I was looking for a single word, a single idea that could be the driving force behind every topic. After observing how Stanford students best learned iPhone programming, the phrase I latched onto was *muscle memory*. The core idea behind muscle memory is that if you do the same task repeatedly, the task becomes effortless.

Muscle memory is why you built 19 sample apps over the course of this book. Muscle memory is why most of the chapters had an Interface Challenge section where you were tasked with building parts of the application with minimal instruction. If someone were to ask you to build an iPad app or an iPhone app with X interface and Y features, you now know exactly how to start.

Next Steps

Moving forward, there is still a lot of territory for you to explore as an iPhone developer. There are many great topics out there still to learn, including:

- Push notifications
- In-app purchases
- iPod and music integration
- Peer-to-peer Bluetooth networking using GameKit
- Compass (3GS and above)
- Contacts using AddressBook
- Accelerometer
- 3D graphics using OpenGL

- In-app Mail integration
- Battery status

As new iPad, iPhone, and iPod Touch models are released, there will undoubtedly be even more APIs to play with. Your greatest weapon in learning these APIs is Apple's own API documentation. For the most part, they are clearly written and helpful in explaining how to use the APIs.

Sure, I may be a little biased, but you should also check out the CS193P Stanford iPhone programming resources, taught by Apple engineers. You can access the course website at http://cs193p.stanford.edu, and you can watch all the course videos for an entire quarter (roughly 18 videos) for free on iTunes. Just search for "cs193p" in iTunes. You should definitely check out the class resources if you are interested in pursuing further iPhone study.

Final Goodbye

I would like to make a final request before we part: please, please, *please* let me know when you build your app. I can't tell you how excited I am to find out what you are building. Shoot me an email at troy@troybrant.net when your app is in the App Store.

Farewell, and good luck!

The Least You Need to Know

- There are three steps to the app submission process: requesting a paid contract, adding the app to iTunes Connect, and submitting the application binary.
- You can—and should!—add your app before you finish so you can reserve your application name.
- Every app needs to have a supporting website.
- Crashing is the most common cause of app rejections.
- If you release an app after completing this book, please let me know at troy@ troybrant.net.

Resources for Further Learning

There are a host of resources available online if you are interested in learning more about iPhone programming. The sheer number of sites can be overwhelming, so here is a condensed list of the resources you will find useful in pursuing further study.

Class-Related Websites

Several schools offer iPhone programming courses now, and the course materials for many of them are available online. Following are some of them:

- **Stanford CS193P iPhone Development class:** All the lectures and assignments from the course are available on the course website. The course was taught by Apple engineers and goes into more detail than this book did. Some of the advanced topics covered in the class but not in this book include threads, scroll views, and advanced table view usage. http://cs193p.stanford.edu

- **Google group for CS193P auditors:** After the lectures for CS193P were put on iTunes U, a community of developers who were all working on course assignments sprouted up on Google Groups. There are hundreds of posts from developers just getting their feet wet with iPhone programming, and it is a fantastic resource, especially if you are planning to work through the CS193P assignments. http://groups.google.com/group/iphone-appdev-auditors

- **BYU CocoaHeads group:** The Brigham Young University (BYU) CocoaHeads group is a community centered around the Cocoa framework. If you are looking for a hub of great tutorials and guides and want to get in touch with other iPhone developers, this is a great site to check out. http://cocoaheads.byu.edu/resources

Developer Blogs

Several notable and well-respected Mac and iPhone developers often reveal the cutting edge in iPhone development on their blogs. Here are a few of the best, along with their Twitter handles.

- **Cocoa With Love:** A treasure trove of useful iPhone development information provided by Matthew Gallagher. The subject matter is usually a bit advanced, but it's definitely worth a look if you are looking for some excellent iPhone programming techniques. http://cocoawithlove.com/

- **Furbo.org:** This blog by Craig Hockenberry, developer of Twitterfic and RampChamp, is a must-read for aspiring iPhone developers. When developers were trying to figure out how to make sense of crash reports on the iPhone, furbo.org was the first place to post a tutorial on how to symbolicate the logs into readable English. It is definitely worth a look. http://furbo.org/ (@chockenberry on Twitter)

- **Atebits blog:** Loren Brichter, developer of Tweetie and Tweetie 2, often posts on a mix of design and technical topics on his Atebits blog. An excellent resource if you are interested in learning best practices for designing your iPhone apps. http://news.atebits.com/ (@atebits on Twitter)

- **Theocacao:** Theocacao is a blog about Cocoa development, which often applies to both Mac and iPhone. It is maintained by Scott Stevenson and contains some of the best Cocoa development posts around. http://theocacao. com/ (@scottstevenson on Twitter)

Forums

If you have an iPhone development question or just want to see if the same question has been asked before, there are several great iPhone development forums to check out.

- **Apple iPhone Developer Forums:** These are the official forums provided by Apple. Somewhat sparse on content, it is the only official site where you can discuss topics related to SDK updates that are still under a Non-Disclosure Agreement (NDA). http://devforums.apple.com/

- **iPhone Dev SDK forum:** This forum has been around since the iPhone SDK first went public. Bursting with content, it's a great place to hunt for answers to your problems. http://www.iphonedevsdk.com/

- **iPhone Dev Forums:** This is similar to the last forum and similarly useful. If you hit a snag developing your app and are looking for answers, you are likely to find an answer on the iPhone Dev Forums. http://www.iphonedevforums.com/forum/

Videos

A video explanation of a complex topic is often much easier to understand than trying to figure it out on your own. There are several video resources on the web that can crystallize your understanding of iPhone development. Following are three of the best resources:

- **Stanford CS193P videos on iTunes U:** All the lectures from Stanford's CS193P class are available for free on iTunes U. You must have iTunes to access the video, and once installed, simply search for "CS193P" in the iTunes Store.

- **Pragmatic Bookshelf videos:** The Pragmatic Bookshelf offers several excellent walkthroughs on different aspects of iPhone development. The videos are not free, however. http://www.pragmaticbookshelf.com

- **Apple iPhone Development Videos:** Apple provides free videos on the official iPhone Developer site that go over introductory iPhone development topics. You can find the videos on the trusty iPhone Developer homepage. http://developer.apple.com/iphone

Index

J-K